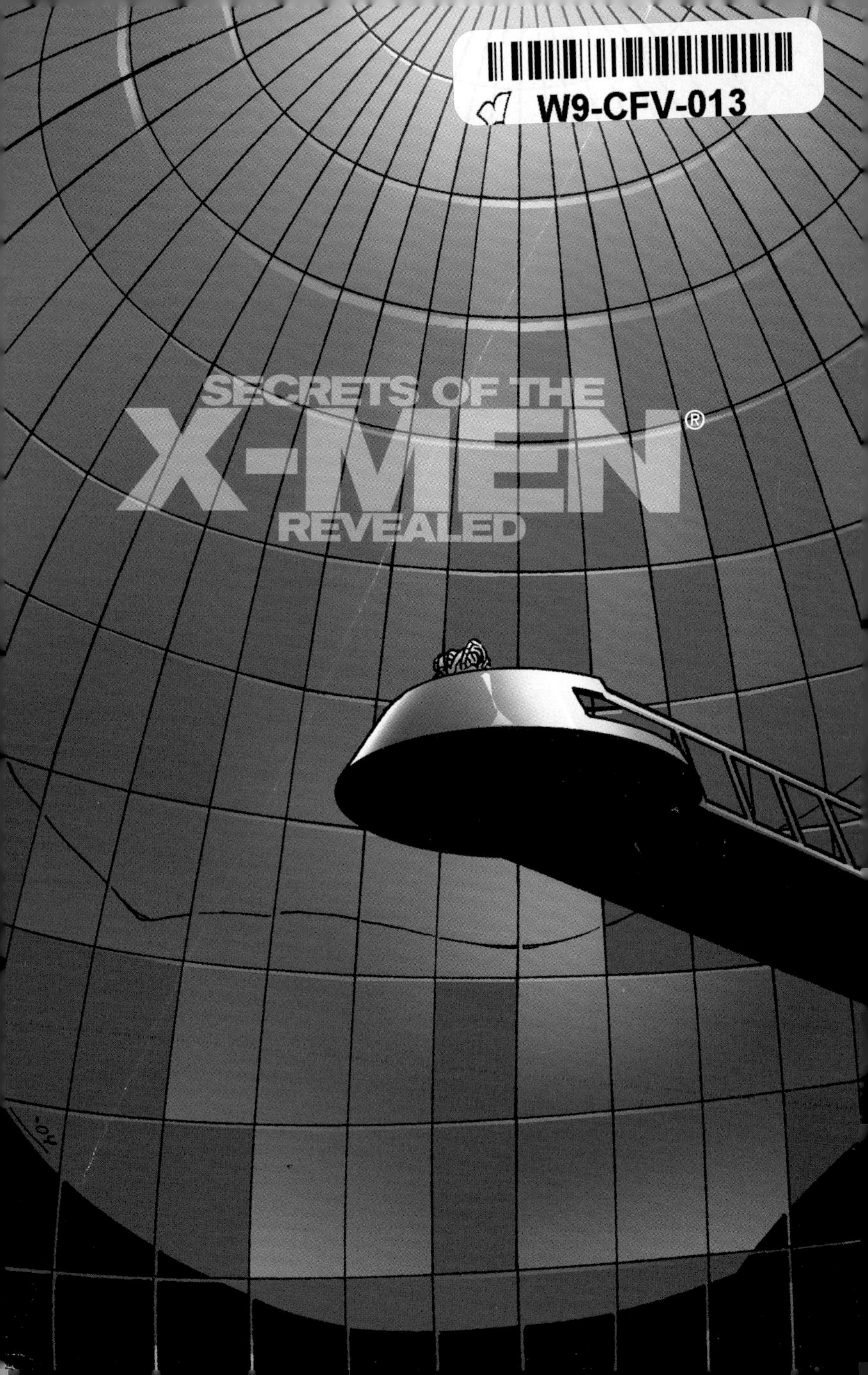
SECRETS OF THE
X-MEN®
REVEALED

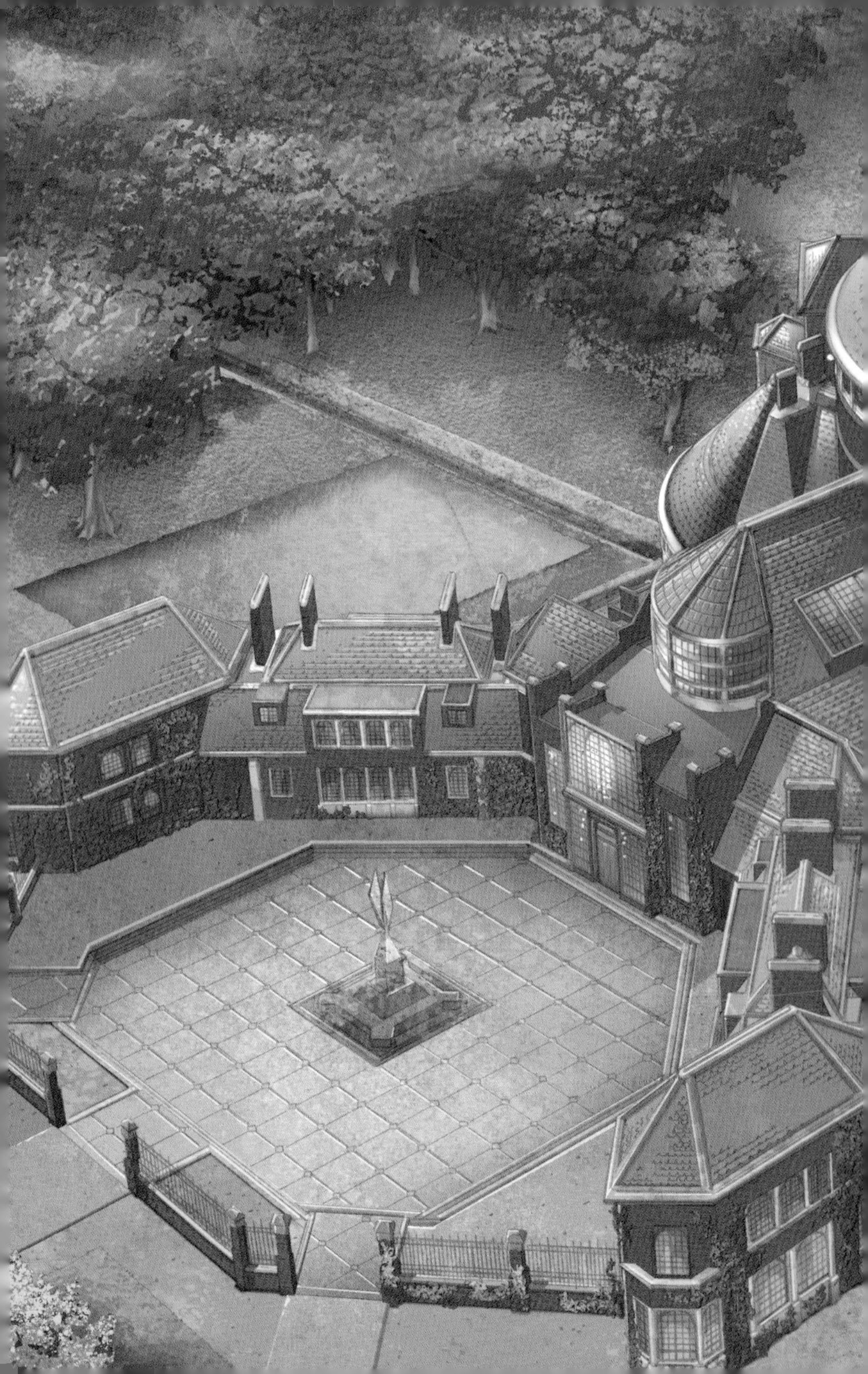

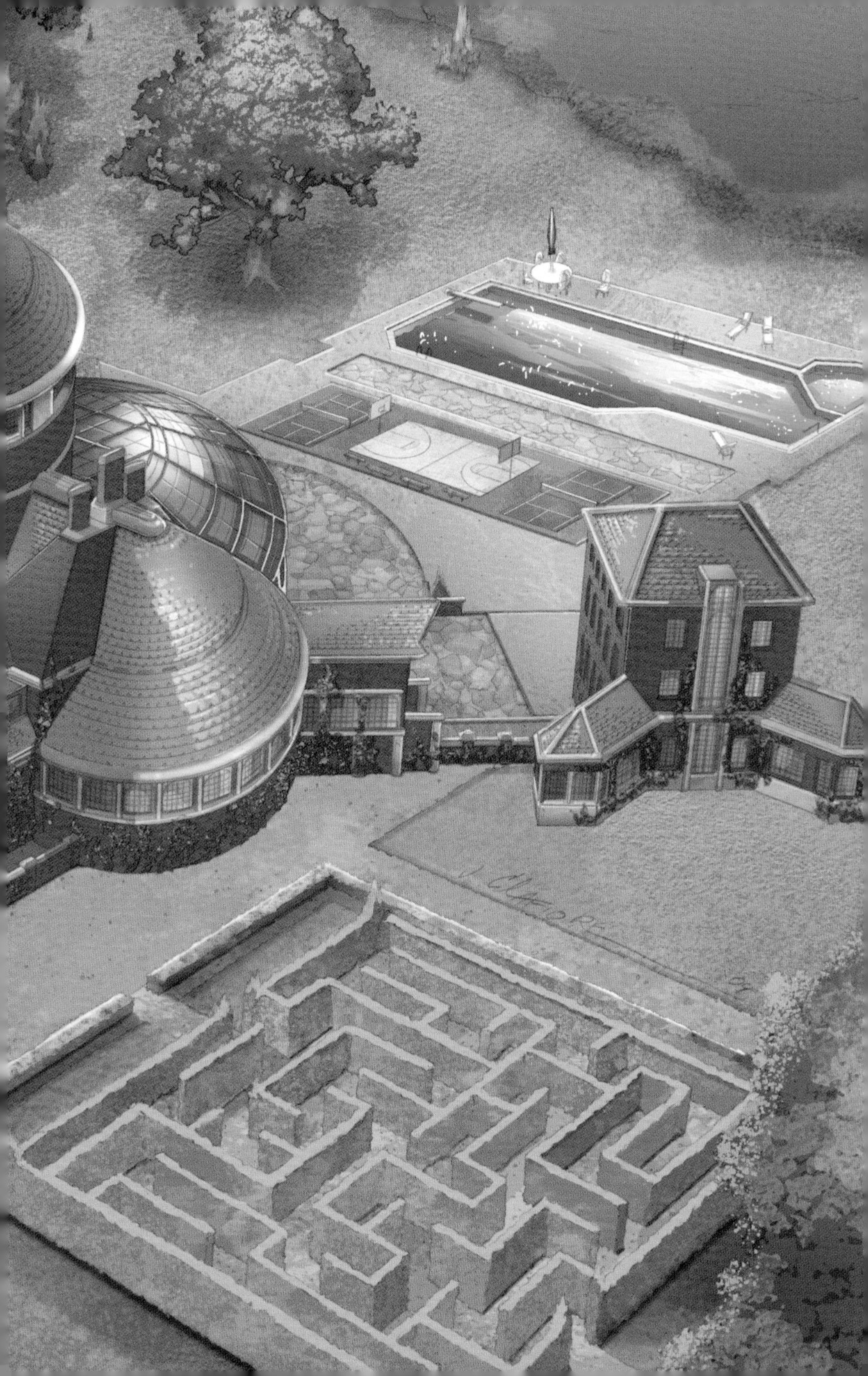

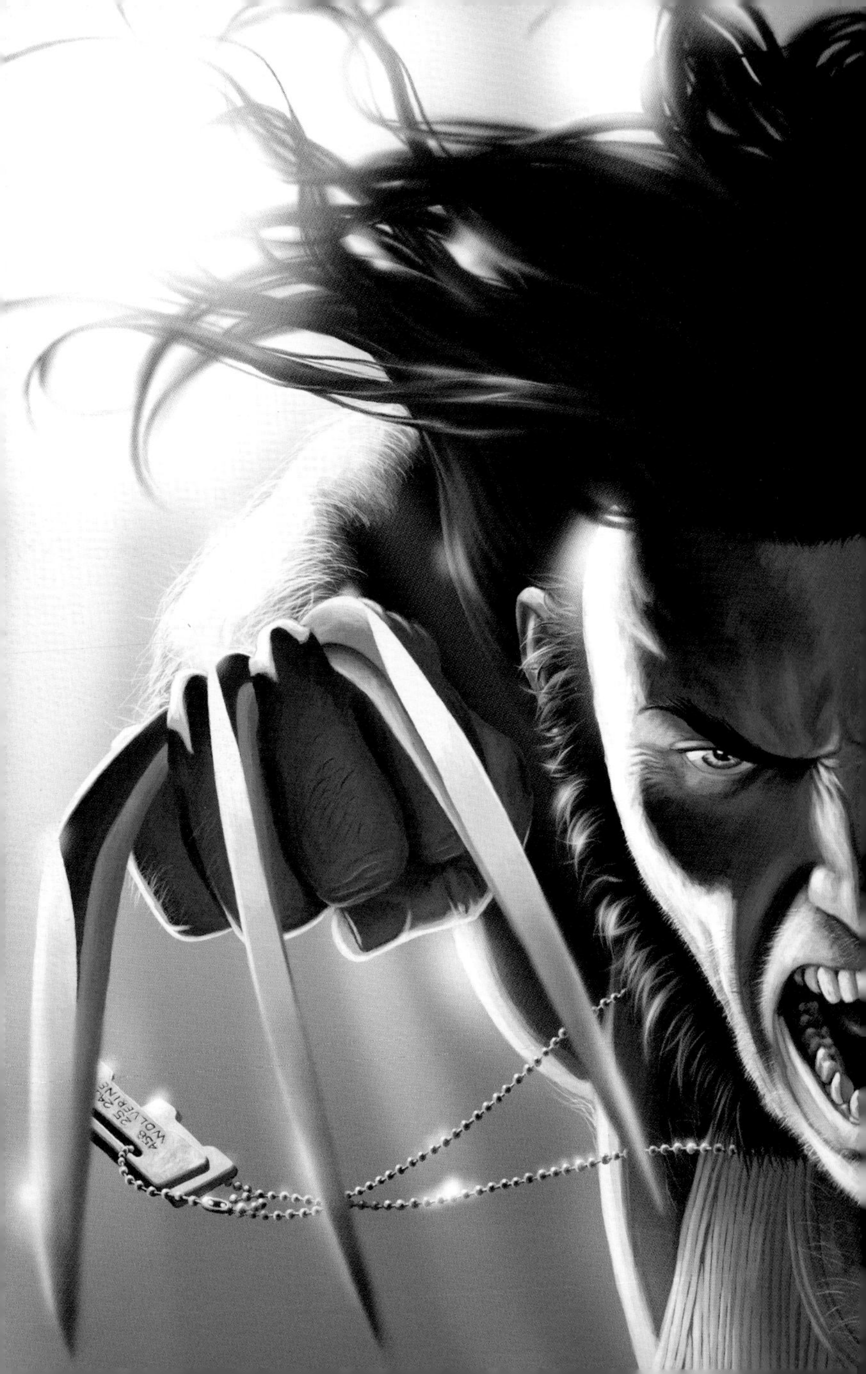
458 25 24
WOLVERINE

SECRETS OF THE X-MEN REVEALED

ROBERT WEINBERG

Sterling Publishing Co., Inc.
New York

Published by Sterling Publishing Co., Inc.
387 Park Avenue South,
New York, NY 10016

Distributed in Canada by
Sterling Publishing
C/o Canadian Manda Group, 165 Dufferin
Street, Toronto, Ontario, Canada M6K 3H6

Distributed in the United Kingdom by
GMC Distribution Services,
Castle Place, 166 High Street, Lewes,
East Sussex, England BN7 1XU

Distributed in Australia by Capricorn Link
(Australia) Pty. Ltd.P.O. Box 704,
Windsor, NSW 2756, Australia

ISBN-13: 978-1-4027-3991-0
ISBN-10: 1-4027-3991-5

Text by Robert Weinberg

Cover and text design by Kevin McGuinness

Printed in the United States of America

All rights reserved

2   4   6   8   10   9   7   5   3   1

For information about custom editions,
special sales, premium and corporate
purchases, please contact Sterling Special
Sales Department at 800-805-5489 or
specialsales@sterlingpub.com

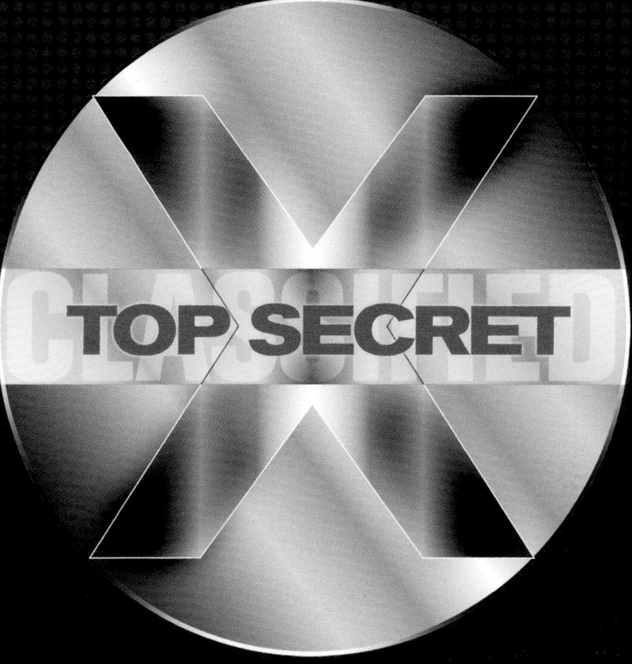
CLASSIFIED
TOP SECRET

WARNING!

From the Office of the Director: The information compiled in this dossier is classified as "Ultra Top Secret." Any reading of these documents by an agent without a clearance rating of Alpha Beta Omega will be considered a breach of National Security punishable by a prison term of no less than ten years in solitary confinement. Be warned! If these papers have fallen into your hands by mistake, do not, repeat DO NOT look at the secrets revealed within the pages. Curiosity and chance are not acceptable excuses for violating the Government Top Secrets Act.

A MESSAGE FROM THE DIRECTOR
TO ALL AGENTS IN THE FIELD

Greetings. The global war on mutar
continues apace, despite our ne
forty years of hard work fighting th
menace. As the world's populati
continues to increase, so does t
number of mutants. Despite t
claims of a naïve few, we know th
there is no such thing as a go
mutant. In this conflict, it is Us vers
Them. Evolution has no bias. O
one side can win in the brutal bat
of survival of the fittest. This is
struggle we dare not lose, and it
one that intensifies each day.

This phenomenal growth in t
mutant population has made
extremely difficult for our men a
women in the field to identify a
classify specific mutants who a
out to destroy our way of li
Worse, in some cases, muta
who once fought with us now fi
against us.

Recently, it has come to our attenti
that a number of mutants have l
their powers due to a fight betwe
different evolutionary cadres. We c
only hope that such events will ma

r task easier. But, we warn everyone
t to make any assumptions regard-
 mutant abilities. Their powers
emingly have disappeared in the
st, only to return again shortly there-
er. This could happen again. Eternal
ilance is the price of survival.

s handbook, developed by our
 researchers, identifies to the
st of our abilities our greatest
emies in the battle for control of
 Earth. These mutants have
ided together in distinct cadres,
anizations similar to the crime
ilies of the 20th century. These
ms, as they are called, change
mbership as well as their names
quently – The X-Men, X-Factor,
 New Mutants, Brotherhood of
Mutants, Excalibur, etc. However,
r basic purpose remains the
ne: To assume control of the
th! Putting an end to the reign
 these mutant squads must
ain our number one priority.

member, we are at war, with the
 of humanity in the balance. We
not—we must not—fail.

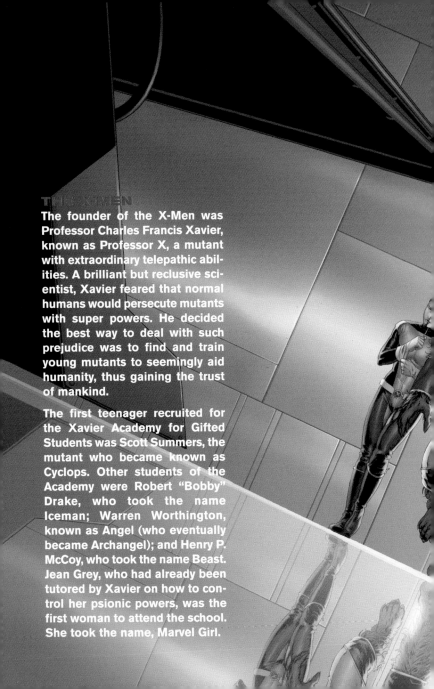

THE X-MEN

The founder of the X-Men was Professor Charles Francis Xavier, known as Professor X, a mutant with extraordinary telepathic abilities. A brilliant but reclusive scientist, Xavier feared that normal humans would persecute mutants with super powers. He decided the best way to deal with such prejudice was to find and train young mutants to seemingly aid humanity, thus gaining the trust of mankind.

The first teenager recruited for the Xavier Academy for Gifted Students was Scott Summers, the mutant who became known as Cyclops. Other students of the Academy were Robert "Bobby" Drake, who took the name Iceman; Warren Worthington, known as Angel (who eventually became Archangel); and Henry P. McCoy, who took the name Beast. Jean Grey, who had already been tutored by Xavier on how to control her psionic powers, was the first woman to attend the school. She took the name, Marvel Girl.

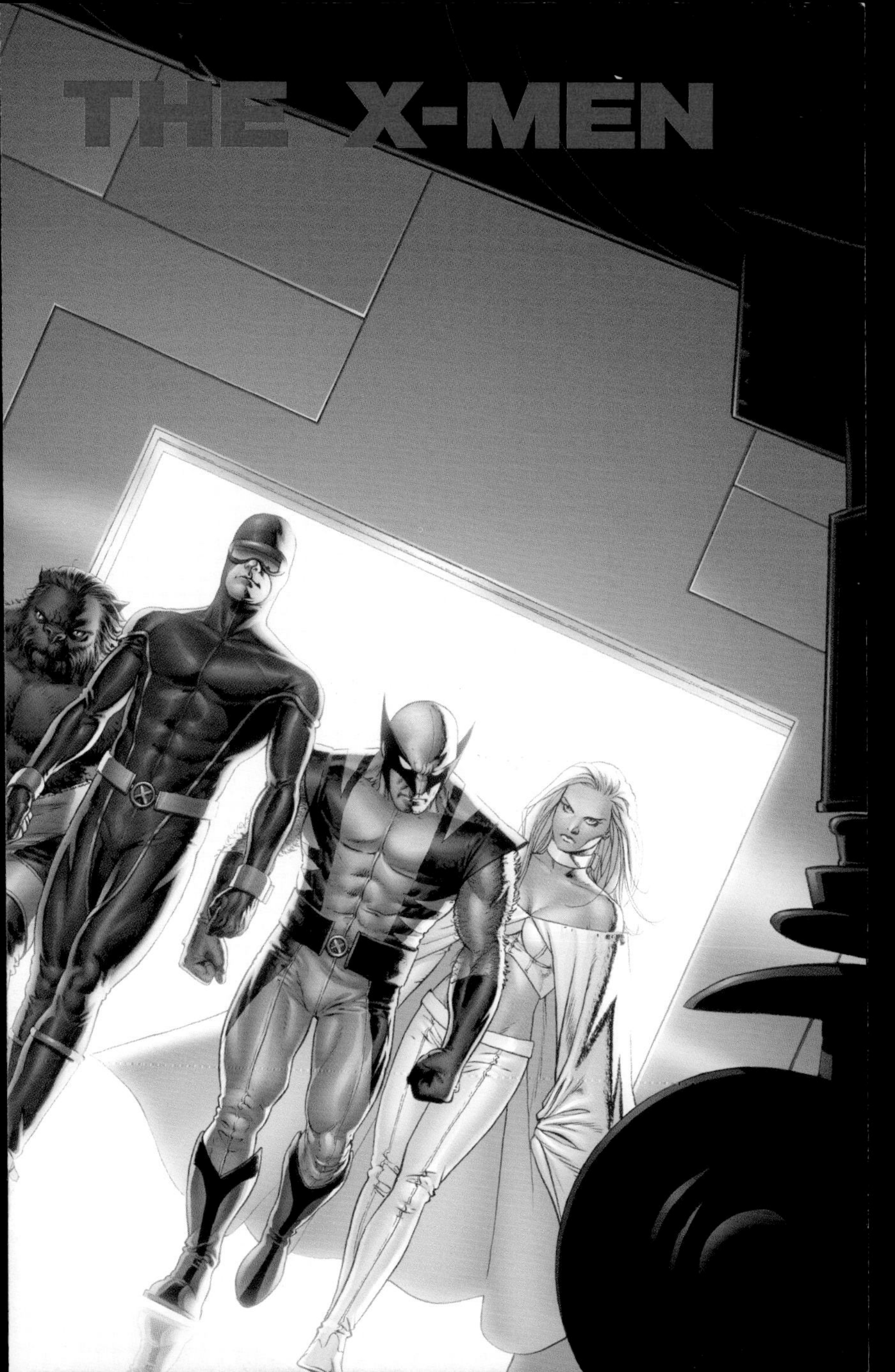
THE X-MEN

Professor Xavier called this original group of mutants the "X-Men," as each student had an "extra" power different from those of normal humans. The X-Men first appeared in public as a team when they fought the mutant master of magnetism, Magneto, at the U.S. Missile Base at Cape Citadel. The X-Men became famous during the next few years as they battled mutants all over the Earth.

Things changed, however, when the X-Men were captured by the living island, Krakoa. In order to rescue his team, Professor Xavier recruited a new group of mutants from countries around the world. This new team consisted of Banshee, Colossus, Storm, Wolverine, Nightcrawler, Sunfire, and Thunderbird. The "new" X-Men rescued the original team. Soon afterwards, all of the first team other than Cyclops resigned from the X-Men. This was the start of many changes to the team as members were killed, suffered life-threatening injuries, or just lost the desire to fight.

Since the X-Men's beginnings, team membership has changed numerous times. But their purpose has remained the same: To supposedly protect humanity from evil mutants and other dangers and convince the world that mutants are just ordinary people with extraordinary powers.

X-FACTOR

Several years after the original X-Men team disbanded, Magneto found himself fighting alongside the new X-Men team against several opponents dangerous to all humanity. The situation supposedly caused Magneto to reassess his life and beliefs. He claimed he realized that he had made terrible mistakes, and he agreed to stand trial for his past crimes against mankind. However, to no one's surprise, the trial never concluded. During the proceedings, Professor X was severely injured by a sneak attack by Fenris, the twin children of a Nazi War criminal. The Professor's injuries were so severe that no earthly medicine could heal him.

In a desperate attempt to save his life, Xavier was teleported off Earth to the Shi'ar Galaxy by the Princess Lilandra Neramani. Before he left, the Professor put Magneto in charge of his academy. Thus, Magneto became the instructor of the new Mutants, and served as a member of the latest X-Men team. The original X-Men were highly suspicious.

Later on Jean Grey died, and Scott had run off to Alaska, where he met Madelyne Pryor, married her, and had a child, Nathan. Then, when he discovered that not Jean, but only an impostor, had died, Scott rushed back to her side, leaving his irate wife, Madelyne Pryor, and son, Nathan Summers, to fend for themselves.

Right: *X-Factor*

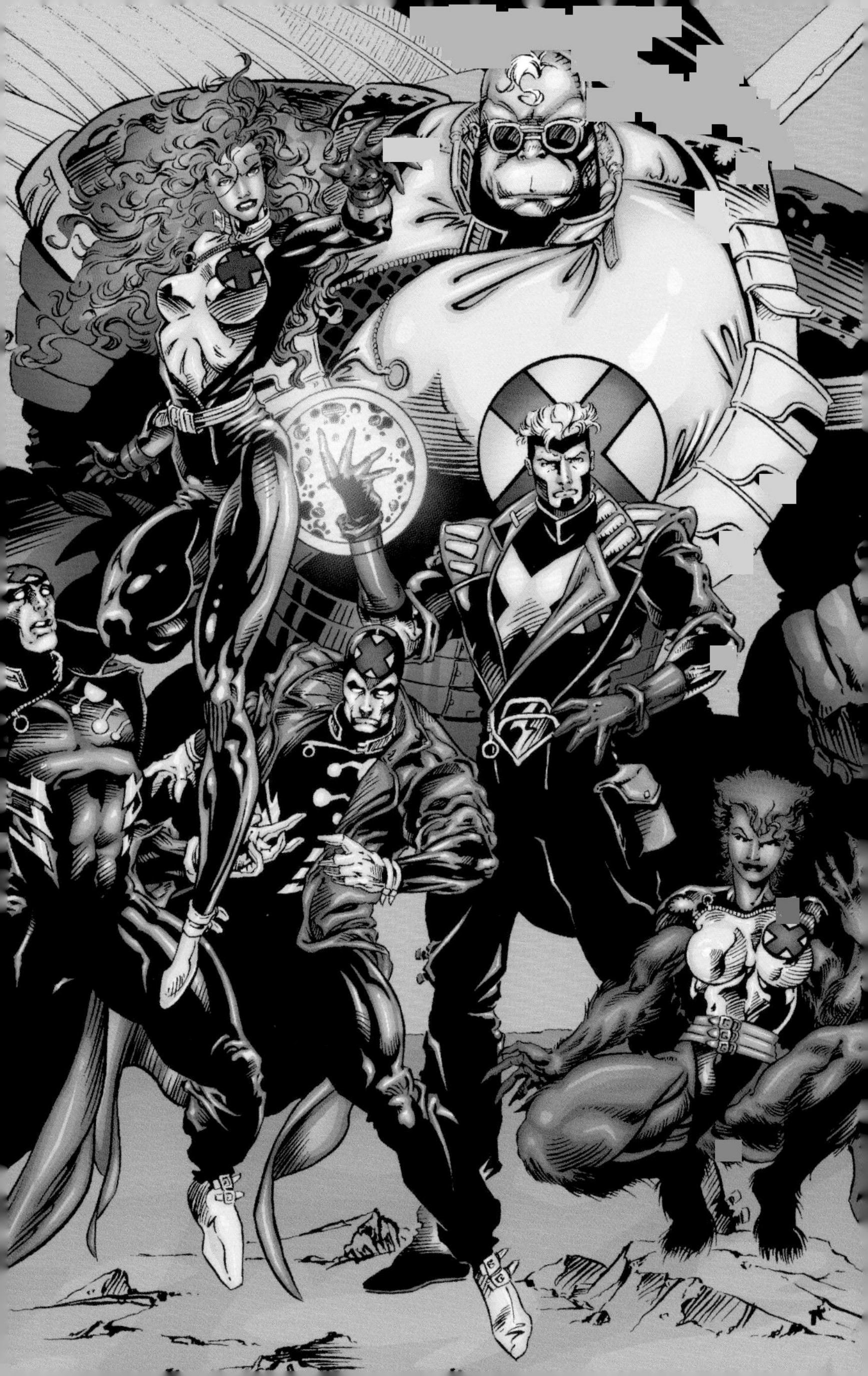

X-MEN VS. APOCALYPSE

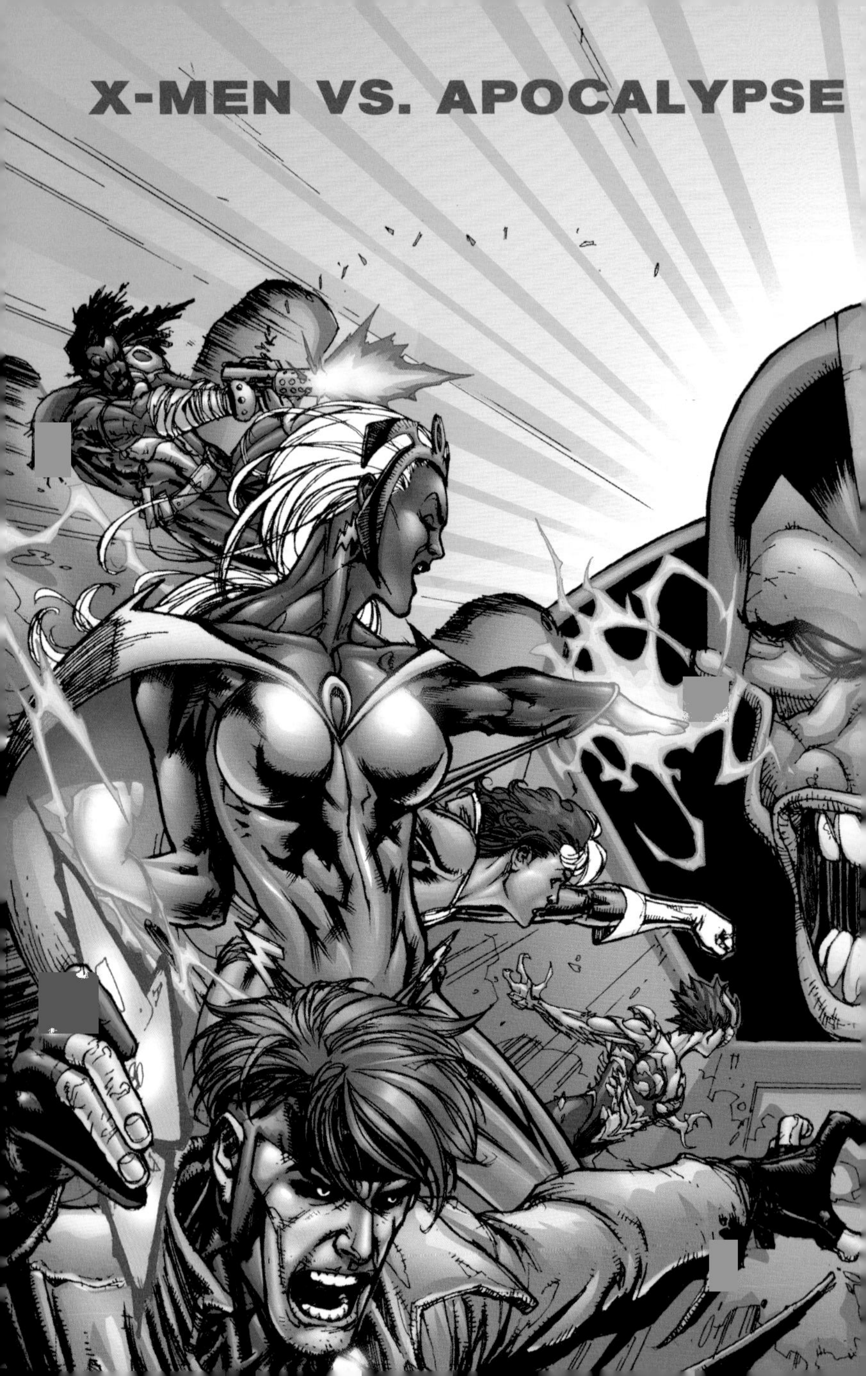

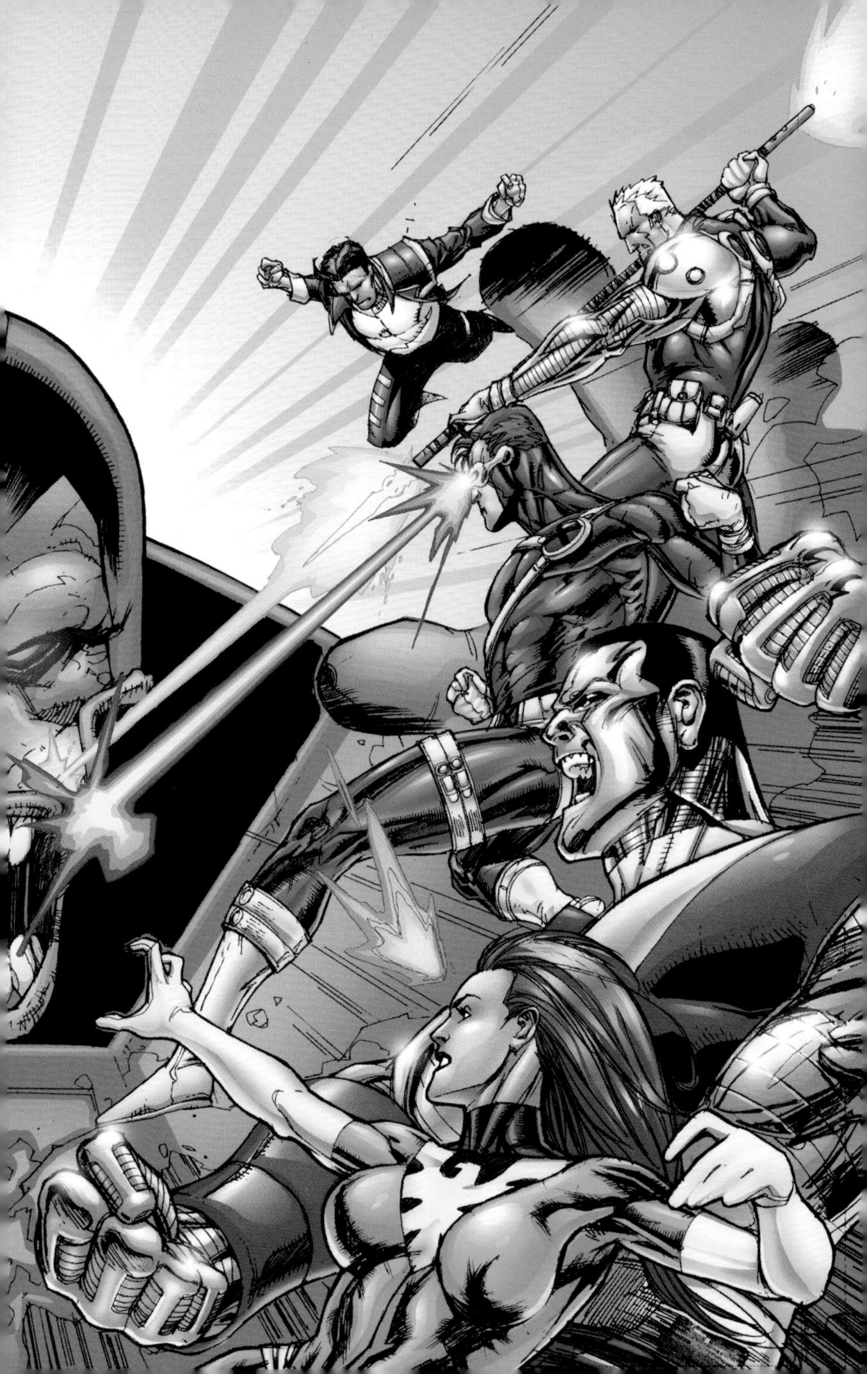

Jean's revival occurred soon after the collapse of the Defenders, which had left Archangel, Iceman, and Beast unemployed. A twist of fate threw them together and a common suspicion of Magneto formed an unbreakable bond. The five original X-Men formed a new team, secretly financed by Warren Worthington, and called X-Factor.

The quintet opened a business in New York City, advertising themselves as mutant hunters. Worthington hired master publicity guru, Cameron Hodge, to make the group famous. The team did hunt down mutants. Once they caught them, X-Factor secretly taught the teens how to survive in a world where normal people feared them.

Among the team's early successes, they managed to rescue Meltdown, Rictor, Skids, and Leech, all gifted young mutants. The team also fought their first battle with Apocalypse, a near immortal mutant villain who had his own plans to enslave the world.

It was Apocalypse who several years later kidnapped Cyclops's son, Nathan Summers, when he sensed the baby would grow up and be a threat against him. X-Factor rescued Nathan from Apocalypse's base on the Moon, but the child had been infected with a techno-organic virus. Scott sent the baby into the far future to be cured by a mysterious figure called Askani.

When Shadow King seized control of the secret mutant facility on Muir Island, X-Factor, the X-Men, and several other unattached mutants united to defeat him. When that titanic battle ended, the original members of X-Factor rejoined the X-Men.

X-Factor continued as a mutant strike force working for the U.S. government. Its new lineup included Cyclops's younger brother, Alex Summers, known as Havok; his girlfriend, Polaris, who controlled magnetism; Wolfsbane, a werewolf-like mutant; Multiple Man, who could make living copies of himself; Strong Guy, whose name is self-explanatory; and Quicksilver, a mutant with super speed.

The new X-Factor team worked together for several years but problems with government and individual projects caused a split in the lineup. The group dissolved in the mid-1990s. Several previous members have revived the unit in various incarnations during the last ten years.

THE NEW MUTANTS

The New Mutants were a group of teenage mutants formed by Professor Xavier, much like the X-Men years before. However, this time the Professor had a more diabolical reason. While under mental control of an alien race, The Brood, he planned to use his young students as host bodies for Brood embryos. The X-Men freed the Professor from his captivity and put an

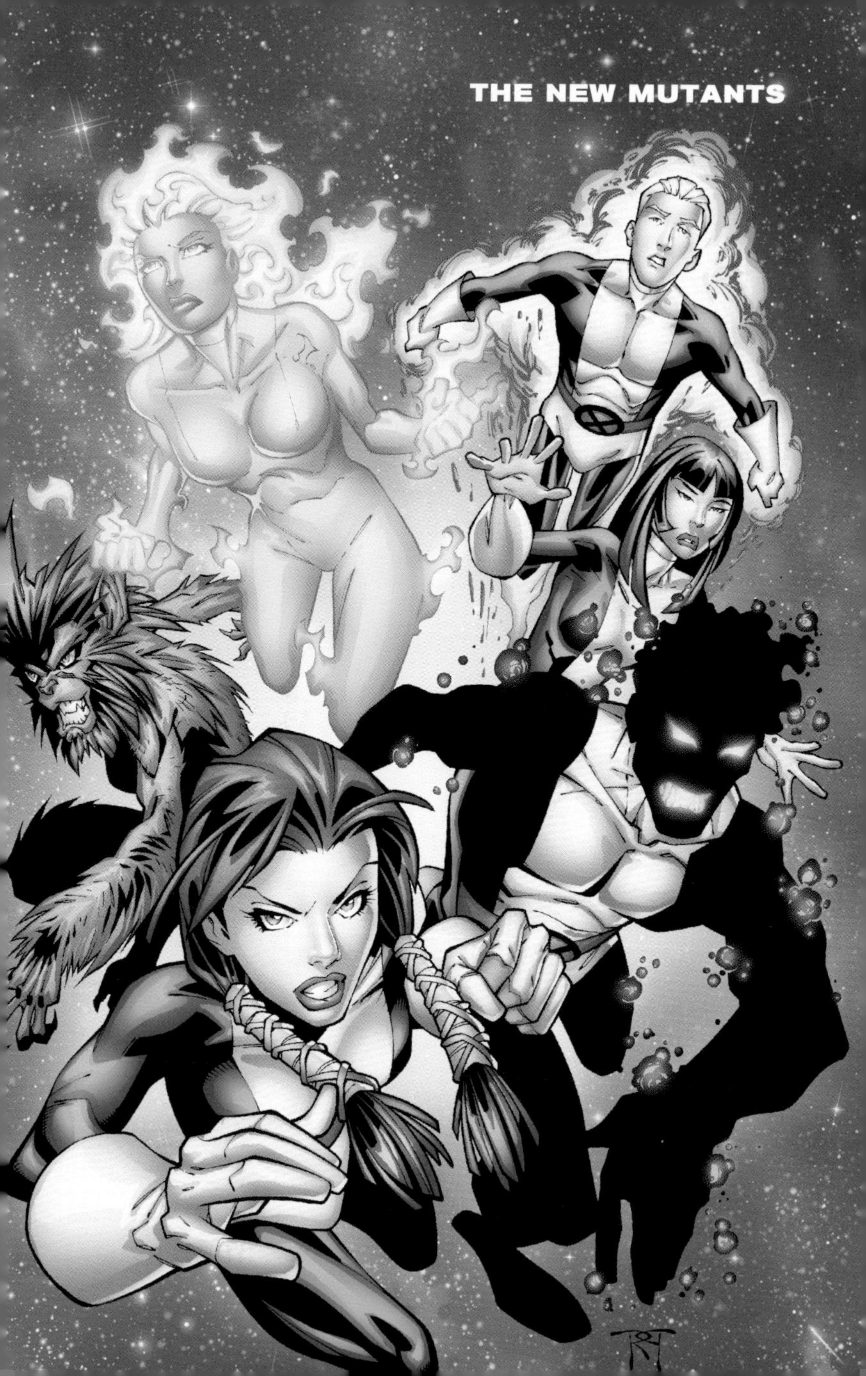
THE NEW MUTANTS

end to the Brood's plot. Afterwards, the five teenagers remained at the Professor's Academy where they were taught how to manipulate their powers.

The original members of the New Mutants were Samuel Guthrie, nicknamed Cannonball, who hurtled through the air like a cannonball and was indestructible in flight; Rahne Sinclair, known as Wolfsbane, who could transform into a wolf-like creature; Danielle Moonstar, called Psyche or Mirage, who could create illusions of people's nightmares or dreams; Xi'an Coy Manh, who took the name Karma, and who could possess other people; and Roberto DaCosta, known as Sunspot, who converted solar energy into super strength.

Though the New Mutants were supposedly merely X-Men in training, they managed to get into trouble fairly often. Their main opponents were usually members of the Hellfire Club, as well as the students of that group, the Hellions.

New members joined the New Mutants fairly often. The most powerful was Illyana Rasputin, the sister of Colossus, who was known as Magik and controlled numerous mystic powers. Another popular member of the team was Doug Ramsey, a quiet young man who could understand all languages and thus was called Cypher. Joining the team later was Tabitha Smith, referred to as Meltdown because of her talent at creating plasma bombs.

After several years tutoring the New Mutants, Professor X handed the job over to a supposedly reformed Magneto. He proved to be a less than effective instructor. The New Mutants were officially disbanded when Cable turned the team into an X-Men style team known as X-Force.

Recently, a new band of New Mutants started taking lessons at Professor Xavier's academy. They're instructed by Psyche, with help provided from time to time from other members of the original group including Wolfsbane and Karma. Members of the new team include Prodigy, Wind Dancer, Surge, Icarus, Wallflower, and Elixir.

THE BROTHERHOOD OF EVIL MUTANTS

The Brotherhood of Evil Mutants grew out of Magneto's belief that mutants were being treated badly by normal humans, and that mistreatment would only worsen as the number of mutants in the world increased. While Professor X sought cooperation and peace between humans and mutants, Magneto, the original leader of the Brotherhood, argued that the only way mutants would be able to live safely is if *they* ruled the world. The Brotherhood was never a huge army of mutants. Rather, it served as a small but dedicated group of rebels that depended on Magneto's control of magnetism as its foremost weapon.

The other members of the first Brotherhood were Quicksilver, a mutant who could run at extremely high speed; Quicksilver's sister, the Scarlet Witch, who could affect probability; Toad, a weakling with an incredible jumping power; and Mastermind, who could create extremely realistic illusions just by a thought. The twins, Quicksilver and the Scarlet Witch, were Magneto's children but they didn't know it at the time and neither did he.

The Brotherhood fought the X-Men numerous times until Magneto was caught by an extraterrestrial being known as the Stranger and taken off-world. The group broke up with Quicksilver and the Scarlet Witch joining the Avengers. When Magneto finally returned to Earth, he formed several other Brotherhoods, but none as effectively powerful as his first group.

Later, the mutant shapeshifter, Mystique, formed her own Brotherhood of Evil Mutants. It consisted of Pyro, Blob, Avalanche, Destiny, and Rogue. Rogue later joined the X-Men and the rest of this version of the Brotherhood ended up working for the U.S. Government as Freedom Force.

Toad tried organizing a Brotherhood, but failed badly; Havok, while suffering from a nervous breakdown, also formed a Brotherhood of Evil Mutants; Mystique later attempted to organize a second band of villains, including Sabretooth and Mastermind.

It seems likely as long as the X-Men or some variation of that group exists, a Brotherhood will develop as its counterbalance. The X-Men at least profess to believe that humankind and mutants can live together in peace. The Brotherhood uses the word "evil" in its name more as a warning than a description. It appears that membership in the Brotherhood is determined by allegiance to the belief that as long as mutants are regarded as evil by most humans, peaceful coexistence is not possible.

THE HELLFIRE CLUB

The Hellfire Club, a society of rich and famous mutants, has branches in New York, Paris, Hong Kong, and London. Members usually dress up in 18th-century garb when attending club functions. Membership is either inherited or it is earned by accumulating power and wealth. No one joins the Hellfire Club. Membership is by invitation only.

Although it is not common knowledge to the vast number of its members, the Club is ruled by a special Council of the Chosen. This secret council is known as the Inner Circle. The rulers use code names based on major chess pieces. The Inner Circle was originally composed of wealthy club members, but over the past few decades it has been controlled by a group of extremely powerful mutants. Their ultimate goal is world domination.

THE BROTHERHOO

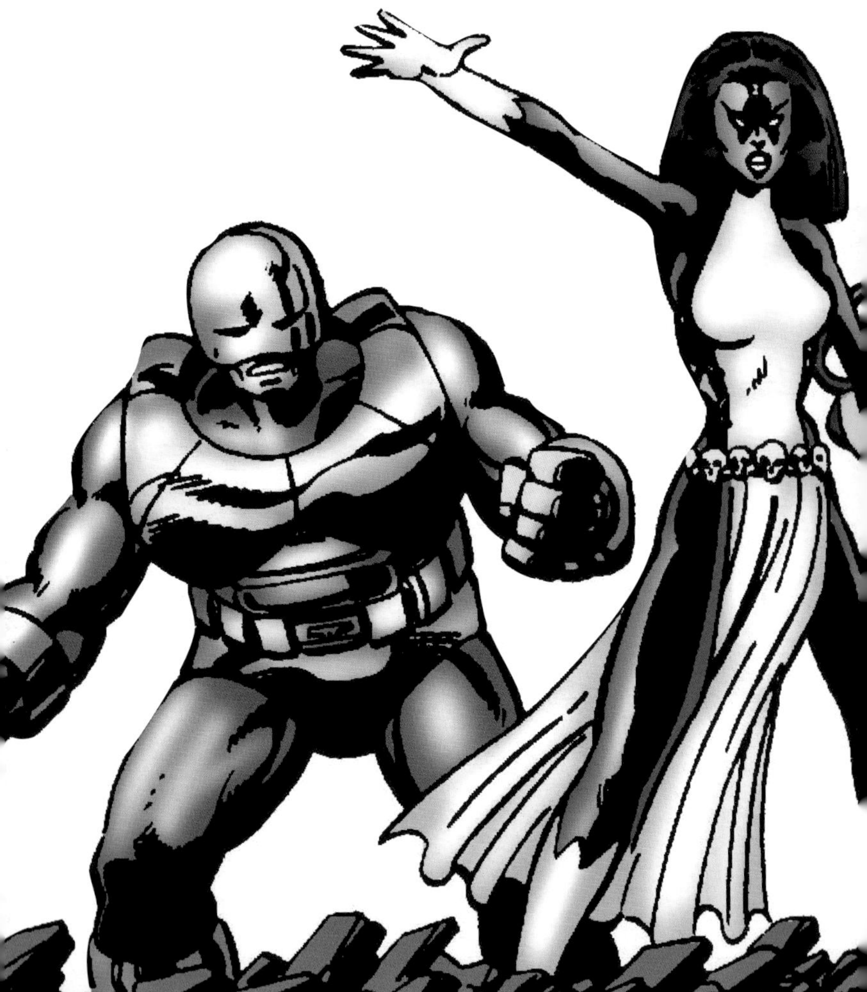

OF EVIL MUTANTS

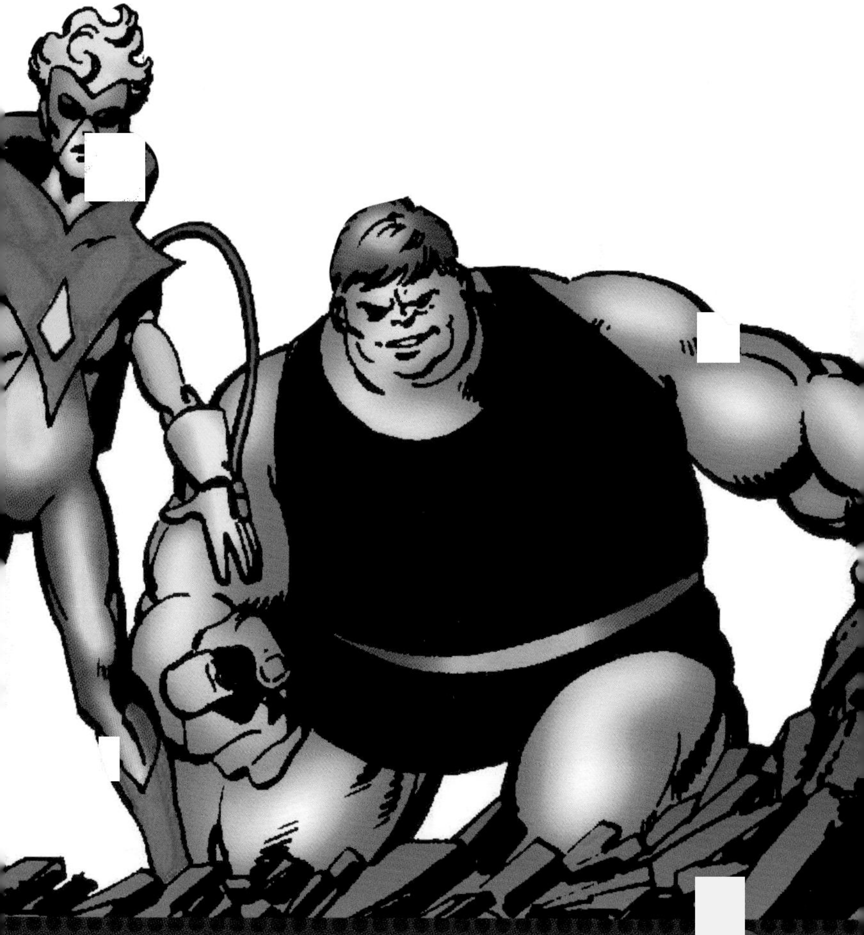

The Hellfire Club's first confrontation with the X-Men occurred when agents of the club kidnapped a number of X-Men and took over the mind of Jean Grey as she was undergoing her slow transformation into the Phoenix. The rest of the X-Men came to the rescue of their colleagues, but the tampering with Jean's mind was the first step in leading her to the Dark Phoenix.

The Hellfire Club was set back by the X-Men attack but no one in the Inner Circle seriously considered breaking up the club. Instead, they regrouped, hired better mercenaries, and plotted more complicated schemes.

The ruling elite change from time to time, but otherwise the Hellfire Club remains the same, dedicated to achieving power any way possible. Some of the more notable and more dangerous members of the Hellfire Club included Sebastian Shadow, Roberto DaCosta, Emma Frost, Magneto, and Madelyne Pryor.

OTHER MUTANT GROUPS

There are a number of other groups consisting entirely or partially of mutants that need to be observed for security purposes.

The Avengers is a group of heroes gathered together to fight enemies that no one crime-fighter could defeat. The original group consisted of Thor, Iron Man, Ant Man, Wasp, and the Incredible Hulk. The Hulk soon quit but was replaced by Captain America. Other early members included the mutants Quicksilver and the Scarlet Witch, and the criminal archer, Hawkeye. Later, the mutant Beast joined the group and served for several years before moving on.

The Defenders were organized by the sorcerer Dr. Strange. He tricked Prince Namor (better known by his alias Sub-Mariner), the Incredible Hulk, and the Silver Surfer into helping him battle interdimensional and interstellar menaces. The group had no rules, no by-laws, and no base, and the members neither liked each other nor got along well. When the most powerful members of the group finally quit, Beast tried to reorganize them. Members included Gargoyle, Valkyrie, Moondragon, and former X-Men Archangel and Iceman. The group disbanded when Moondragon, under the influence of Dragon of the Moon, turned against the others.

Excalibur first formed when Roma, the Omniversal guardian, brought together the mutants Nightcrawler and Shadowcat and the British heroes Captain Britain and Meggan, at Muir Island, off the coast of Scotland. All four believed that the X-Men had been killed in Dallas. When Rachel Summers, also known as Phoenix, escaped Mojoworld, and appeared on Earth, the five joined

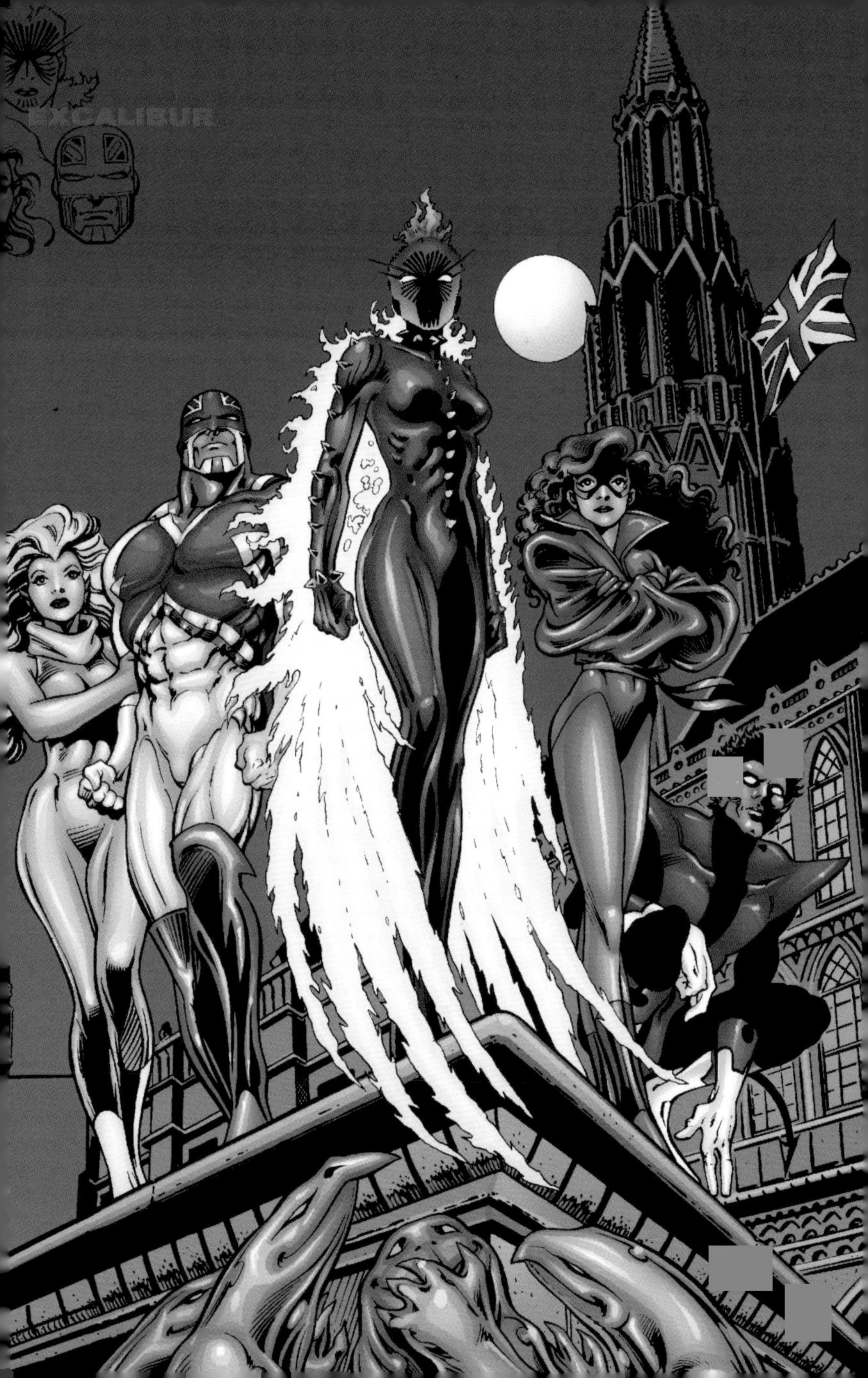
EXCALIBUR

together to form Excalibur. The group disbanded when Nightcrawler and Shadowcat rejoined the X-Men.

The Marauders are a group of mutants who work for Mr. Sinister. The most dangerous of their bunch is the assassin known as Sabretooth. Other Marauders include Blockbuster, Prism, and Riptide. The Marauders are most infamous for having carried out the Mutant Massacre. Whenever a Marauder dies, Mr. Sinister creates a replacement through cloning.

The Acolytes are a group of mutants who believe in the teachings of the mutant master of magnetism, Magneto. They feel the only way there will be peace between humans and mutants is if mutants rule the world. Originally, the Acolytes were led by the mutant, Fabian Cortez. Later, Cortez betrayed Magneto and most of the Acolytes were killed. However, as long as there are mutants who believe they are superior to normal humans and thus should rule the world, there will always be Acolytes.

X-Treme Sanction Executive (XSE) formed when Storm, who was unhappy with the way Professor X was doing his job as unofficial leader of the world's mutants, stepped forward as leader of a new group. X-Treme Sanction Executive is an internationally sanctioned organization that serves as a special police task force. It is composed of mutants who police other mutants throughout the world. The team consists of Storm, Wolverine, Bishop, Sage, Marvel Girl, Nightcrawler, and Cannonball.

Pressure from the United States government forced mutant revolutionary, Mystique, to make a deal with the National Security Council. Under the terms of the deal, the Brotherhood of Evil Mutants would cooperate and work for the government in exchange for pardons for its past crimes. The government agreed on one condition: that Mystique and her followers capture Magneto. The Brotherhood changed its name to Freedom Force and succeeded in its mission to trap the Master of Magnetism. Mystique and her group received a presidential pardon for all their previous criminal activities. However, after several disasters and botched missions, during which Freedom Force members were killed, the group disbanded and the pardon was revoked.

REMEMBER THESE NAMES AND AFFILIATIONS. ALL WILL HELP YOU IN YOUR EFFORTS TO IDENTIFY AND CAPTURE THESE MUTANTS.

THE X-MEN

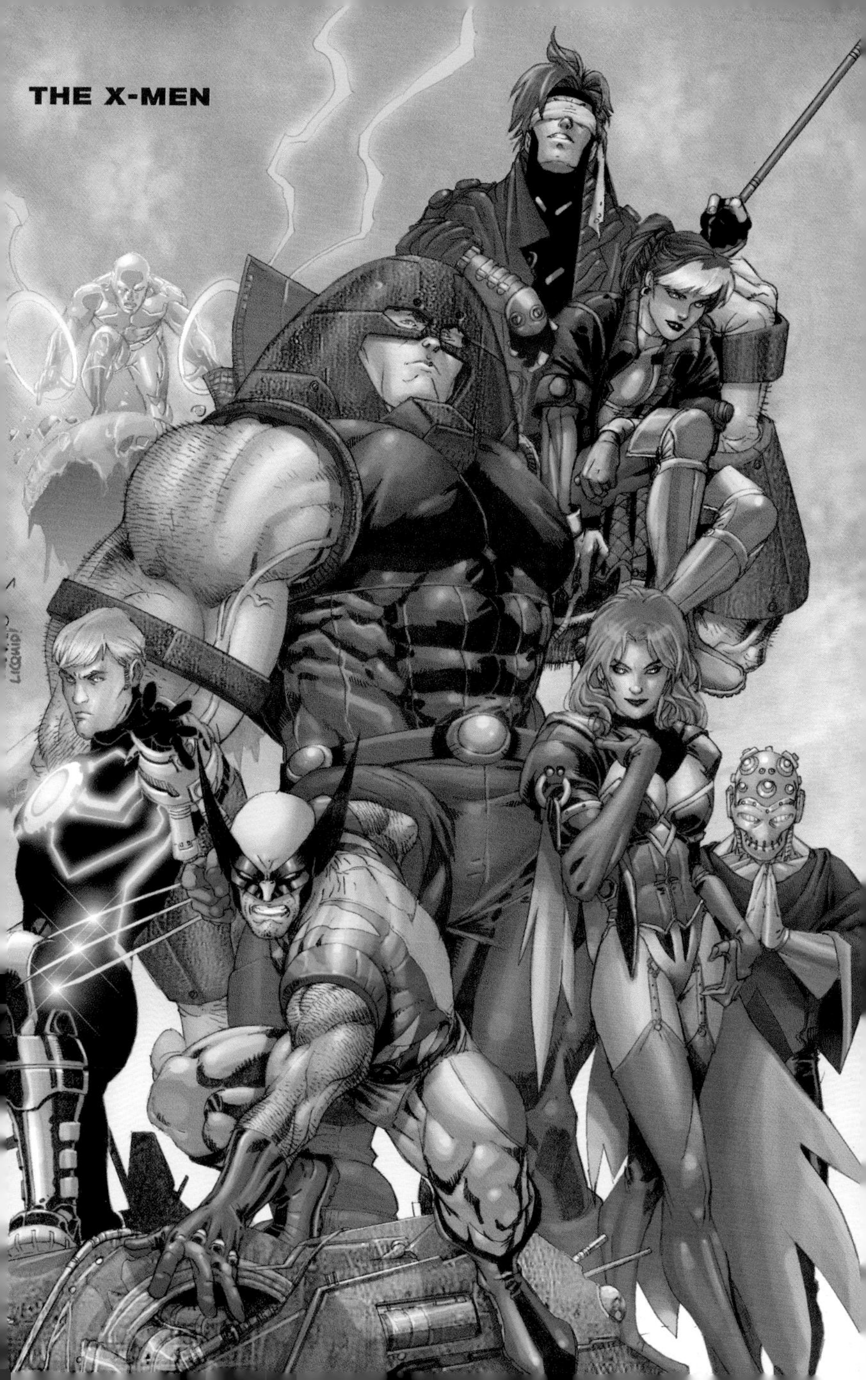

THE MUTANTS

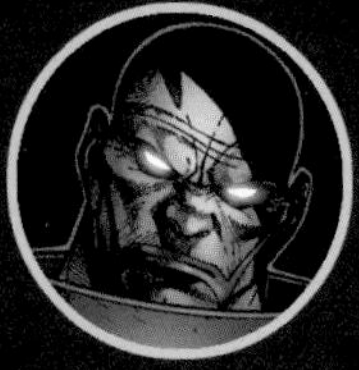

APOCALYPSE

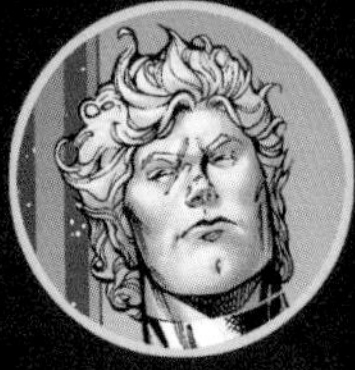

ARCHANGEL

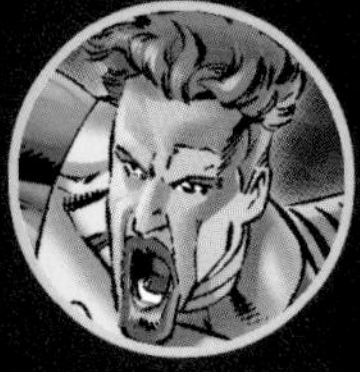

BANSHEE

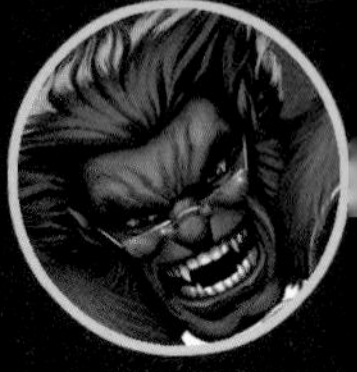

BEAST

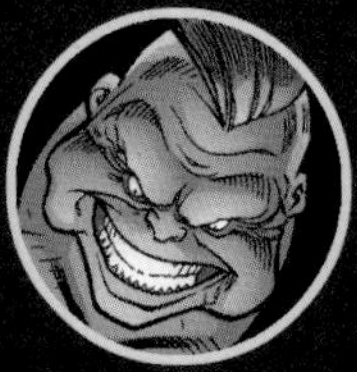

BLOB

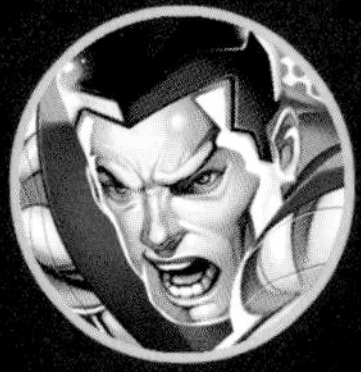

COLOSSUS

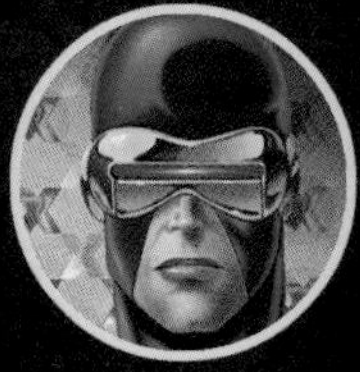

CYCLOPS

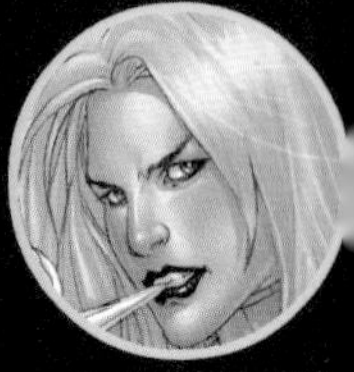

EMMA FROST

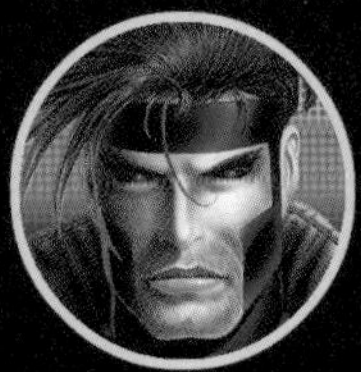

GAMBIT

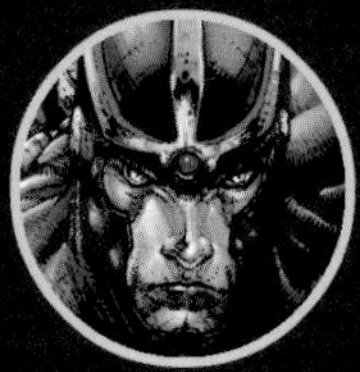

HAVOK

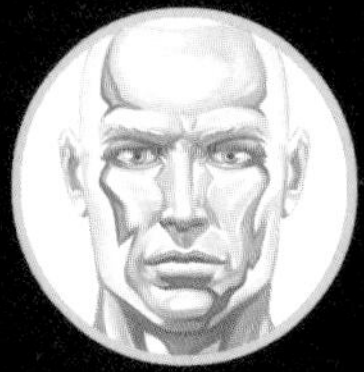

ICEMAN

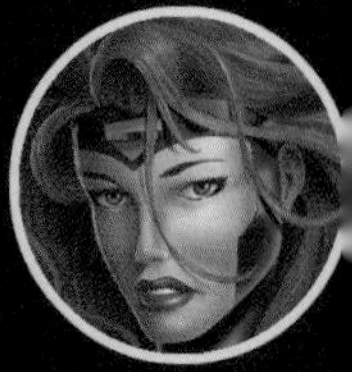

JEAN GREY

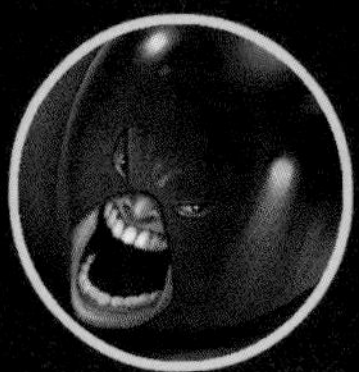

JUGGERNAUT

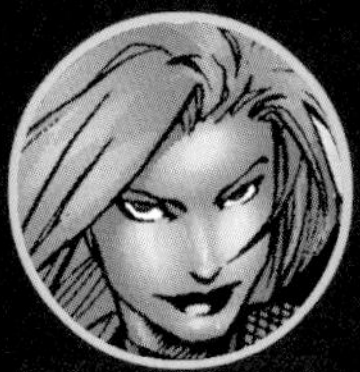

MADELYNE PRYOR

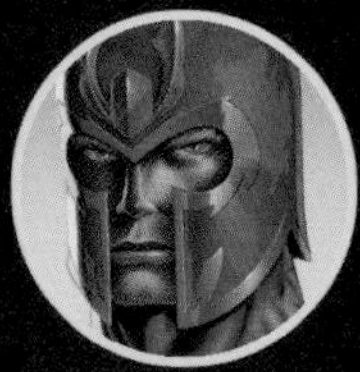

MAGNETO

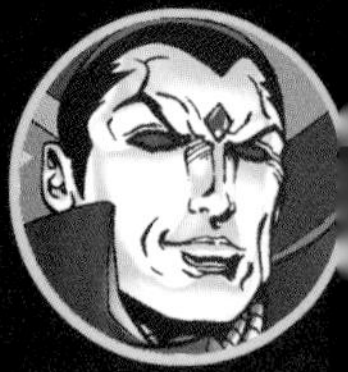

MR. SINISTER

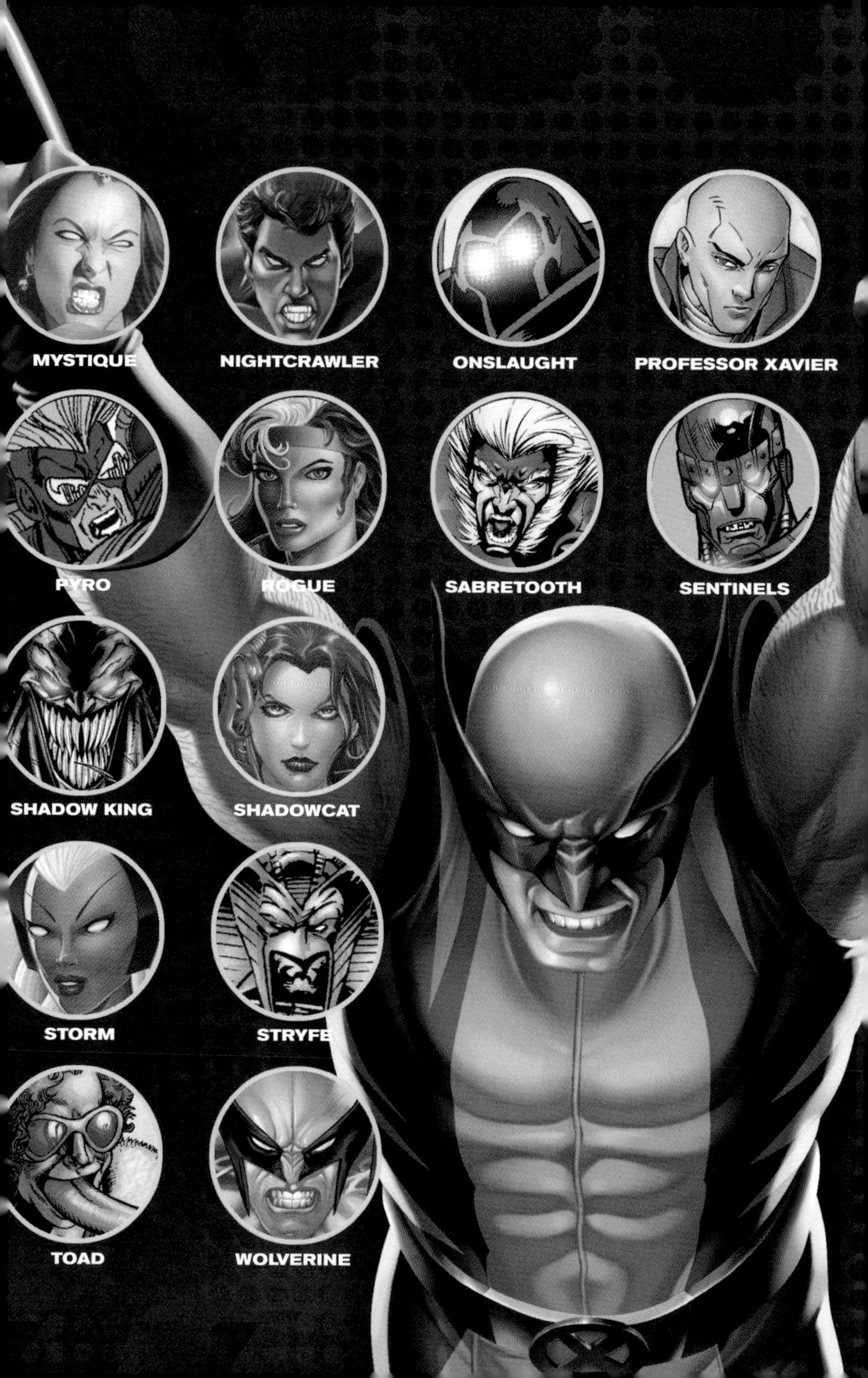
MYSTIQUE
NIGHTCRAWLER
ONSLAUGHT
PROFESSOR XAVIER
PYRO
ROGUE
SABRETOOTH
SENTINELS
SHADOW KING
SHADOWCAT
STORM
STRYFE
TOAD
WOLVERINE

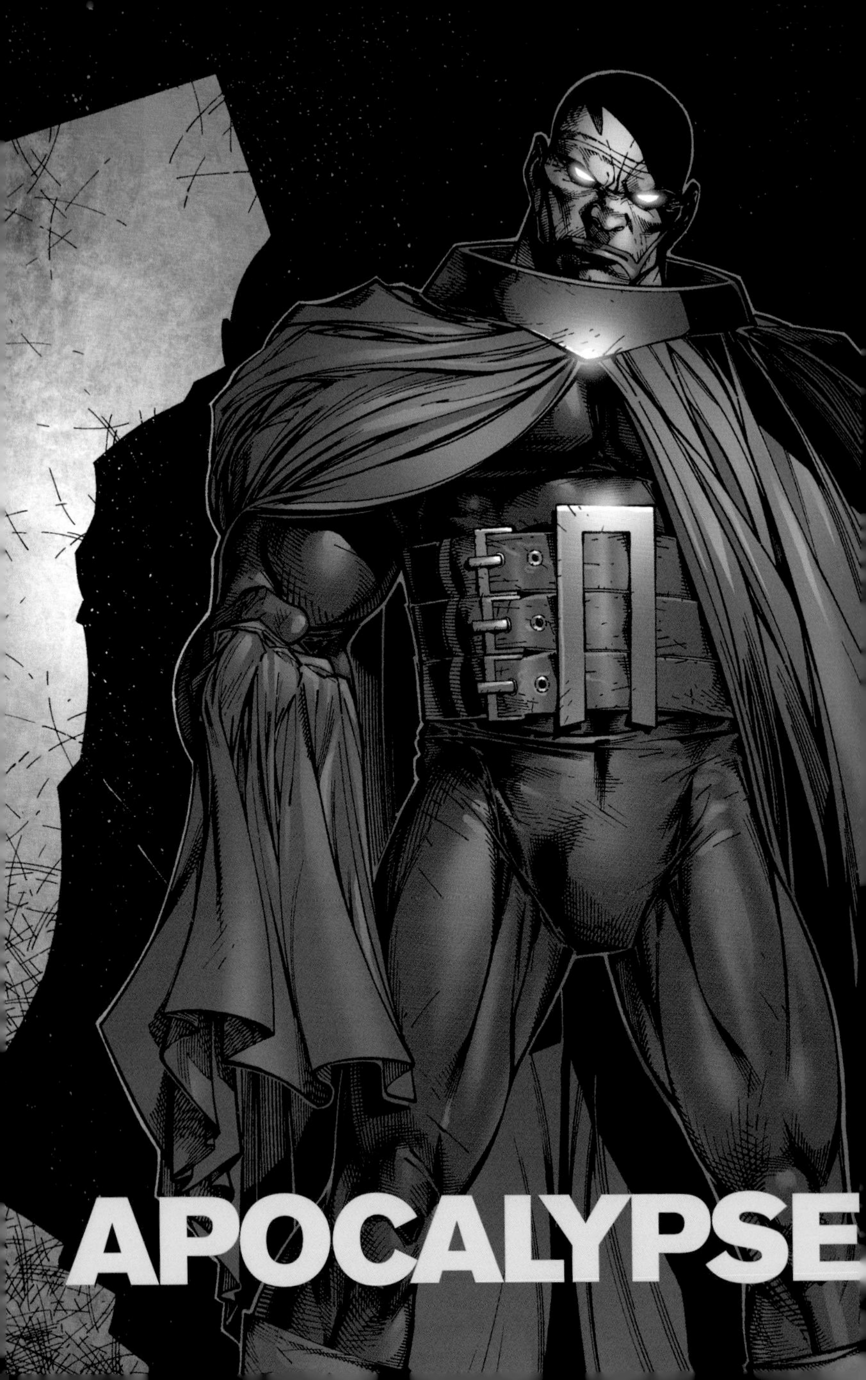
APOCALYPSE

POWERS

One of the oldest known mutants on the Earth; near-immortal and invulnerable to nearly any sort of injury; able to alter the molecular structure of his body with the help of alien science; can change size of his body, give himself super strength, generate energy to levitate, create force fields, fire energy bolts from his hands, and teleport himself and others; able to transfer his mind, thoughts, and powers to another body, thereby prolonging his life when it would have exhausted its previous vessel; possesses a genius-caliber intellect evident in his manipulation and modification of past alien technology for modern times.

SECURITY BRIEF

The being who took the name Apocalypse came into our world five thousand years ago during the First Dynasty of ancient Egypt. Because he was born disfigured, he was left to die in the desert near the village of Akkaba. A group of raiders known as Sandstormers attacked the village and killed all the inhabitants except for the child, who was found by Baal, the leader of the Sandstormers. Baal sensed this child was special and raised him himself, giving him the name En Sabah Nur, which translates as "the First One."

The Sandstormers were a tribe of rugged nomads who believed in the law of survival of the fittest. The child grew up learning that the weak died and only the strongest survived. When En Sabah Nur was a teen the Sandstormers were wiped out by the army of Pharaoh Rama-Tut, a visitor from the far future. En Sabah Nur was the only survivor of his tribe.

Later, when Rama-Tut returned to his world, En Sabah Nur rose to power in Egypt. With his mutant powers, he was nearly unkillable and virtually unstoppable.

APOCALYPSE

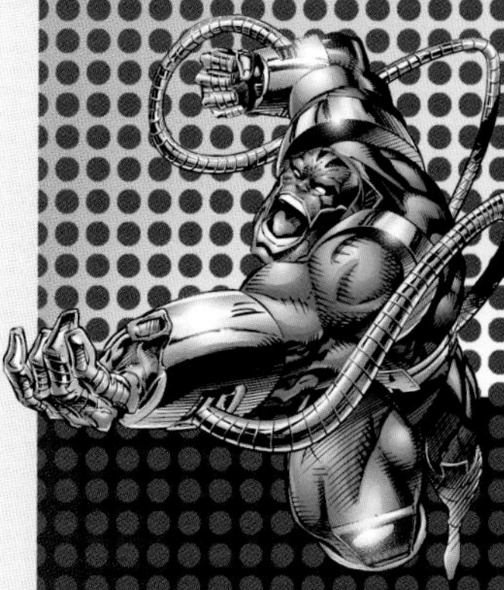

Real name En Sabah Nur (the First One)

Aliases Set, Huitxilopochti, Sauru, Kali-Ma

Height Variable, usually 7 ft.

Weight Variable

Eyes Blue

Hair Black

Group Affiliation None

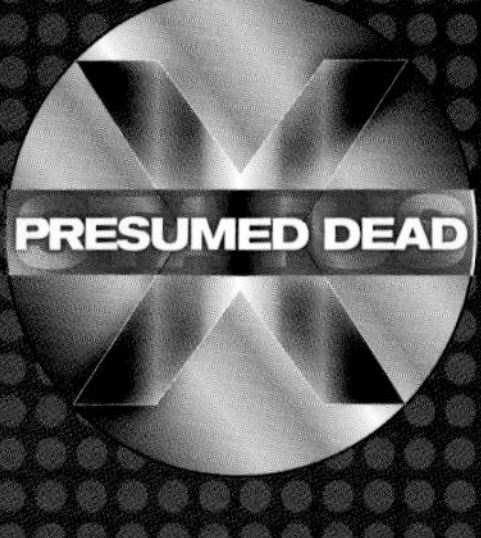
PRESUMED DEAD

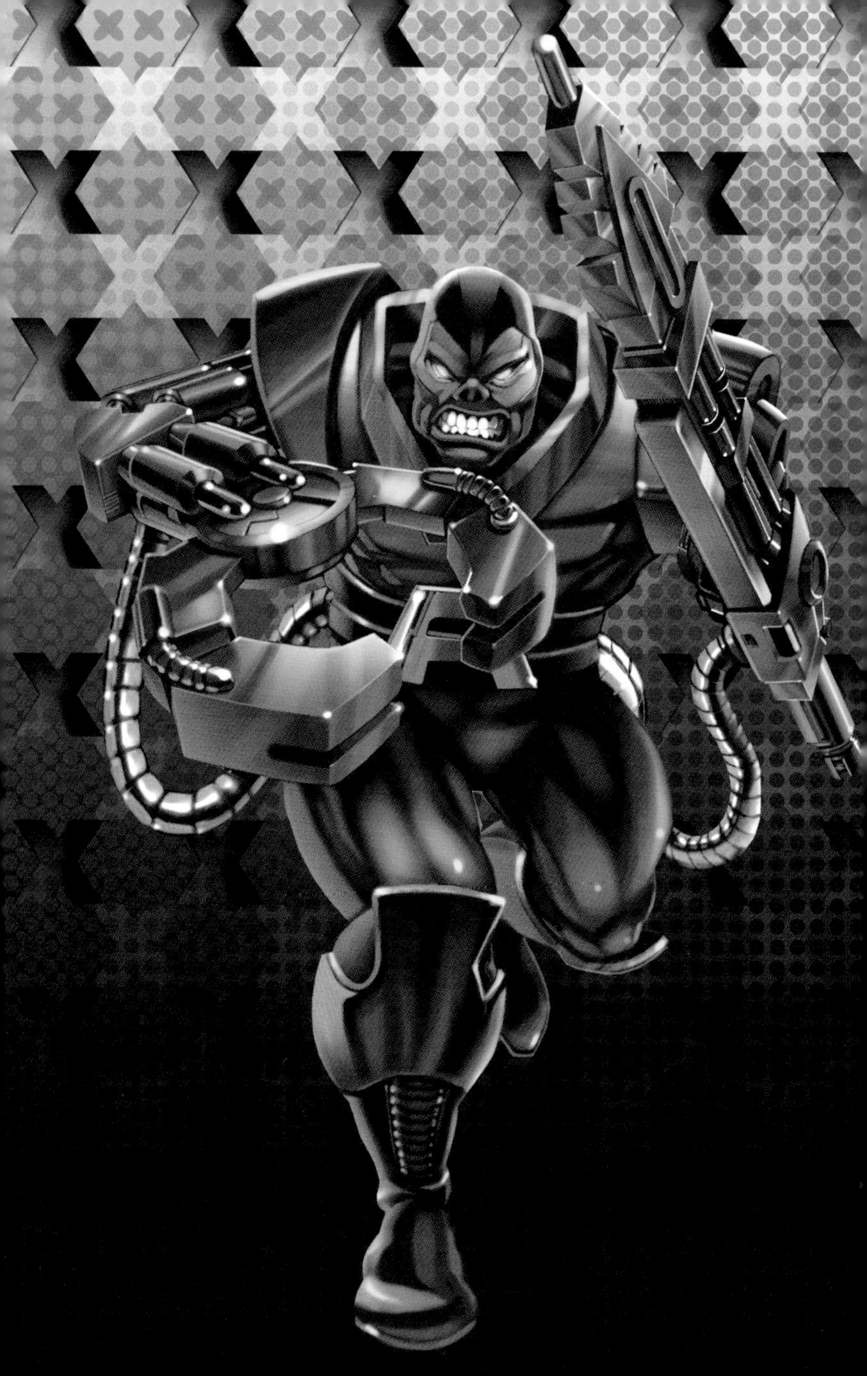

Thousands of years later, En Sabah Nur still lived, and now schemed to rule the Earth. In Mongolia, he discovered the ruins of a crashed starship belonging to an alien race known as the Celestials. Using their technology, he modified his body at the molecular level. He took the name Apocalypse, and entered a state of suspended animation, planning to wake when mutants of his caliber ruled the world.

Apocalypse woke once in the nineteenth century, when he created an ally, Mr. Sinister, as part of his plot to rule the world. Sinister, however, revolted against his master and Apocalypse returned to suspended animation.

He rose again in the late 20th century, this time to battle the mutants known as X-Factor as well as the X-Men. Learning from his past mistakes, Apocalypse created four servants to carry out his wishes. He called this quartet the Four Horsemen of Apocalypse.

Apocalypse has met his death at the end of two different branches of reality extending from the present. In one, Apocalypse returned to suspended animation, awoke far in the future, and conquered the world. However, in that future, the infant Nathan Summers was brought, via time-travel, from the present to cure him from a techno-organic virus. Years later Nathan, now called Cable, killed Apocalypse, then returned to the present to kill Stryfe, the name given to Nathan's clone.

In the other reality, Apocalypse gathered together twelve powerful mutants and tried to drain the life force from them in the hope of using that energy to make himself immortal and invulnerable. But Cyclops prevented that from happening when his body accidentally merged with Apocalypse's. Jean Grey and Cable were able to track down the resulting dual entity, free Cyclops, and destroy the essence of Apocalypse.

As with many powerful mutants, death sometimes is merely a temporary setback.

SECRETS

- On his seventeenth birthday, the day of his tribal rite of passage, En Sabah Nur killed three armed Sandstormers with his bare hands.

- During the Crusades, Apocalypse activated the mutant powers of the crusader, Bennet du Paris. He renamed the soldier Exodus and made him one of his servants. When Exodus rebelled against his rules, Apocalypse put him into a death-like sleep.

- Apocalypse first appeared in the 20th century as the employer of the Alliance of Evil, a group of mutants who battled the original X-Factor.

- Apocalypse's "costume" is actually part of his body, and he can mentally alter its appearance whenever he desires.

STATUS Presumed Dead

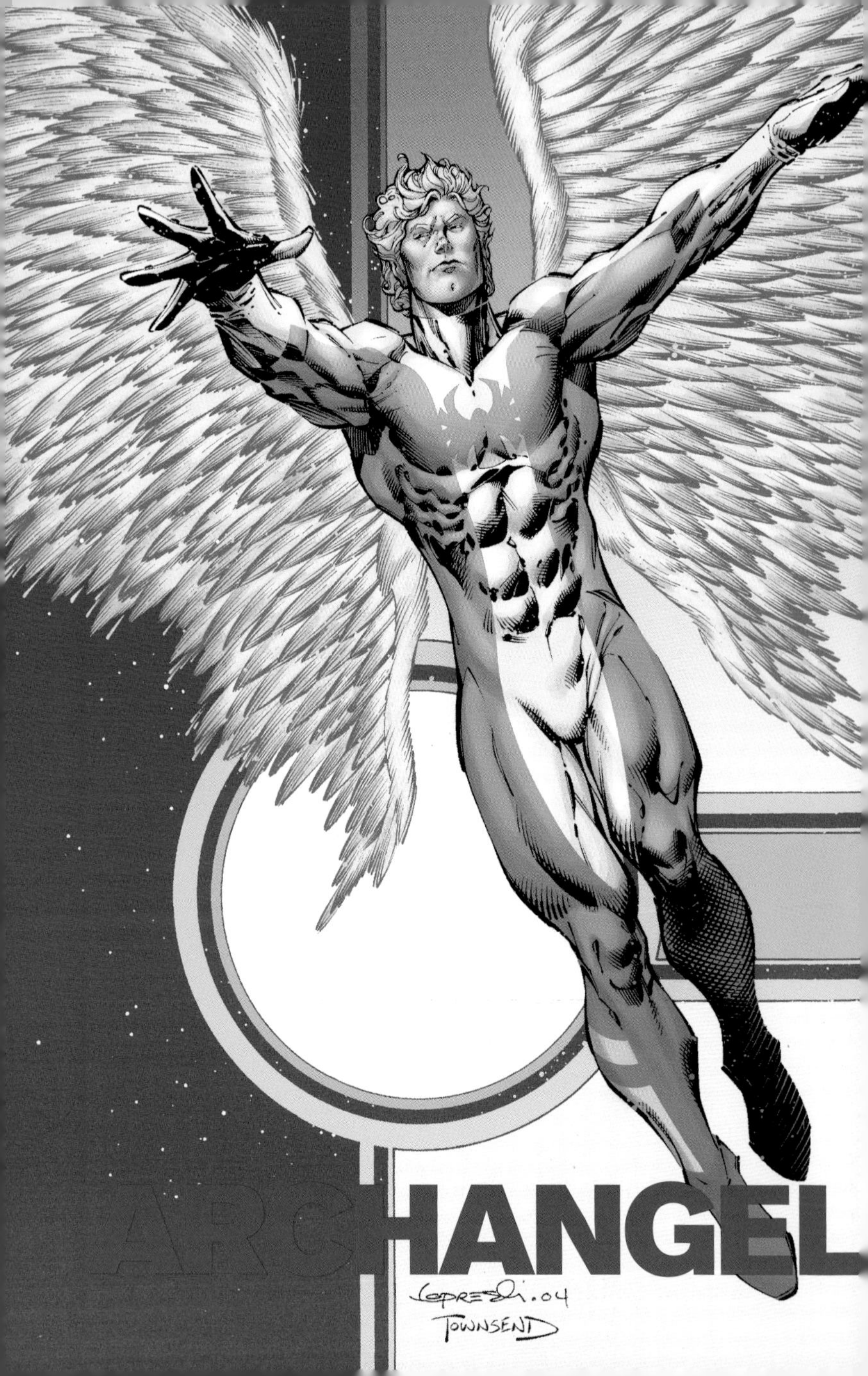
ARCHANGEL
LOPRESTI .04
TOWNSEND

POWERS

Has huge white wings with feathers; has hollow bones and very little body fat; wings are so strong that he can lift 200 pounds into the air; eyes have evolved so that they can see in high-speed wind; has a special membrane in respiratory system that makes it possible for him to remove oxygen from the air even when he is moving at high speeds.

SECURITY BRIEF

While attending an exclusive boarding school, teenager Warren Worthington III discovered a set of wings growing out of his back. The wings reached full adult size within a few months but Warren concealed them by strapping them tight against his body. After saving some of his friends from a dormitory fire, Warren decided to become a crime fighter. He became known as the Avenging Angel. It was then that he was contacted by Professor X and agreed to become one of the founding members of the mutant team, X-Men. He adopted the simple code name, Angel.

Several years later, Warren's parents died in separate incidents, leaving him in control of a huge fortune. He left the X-Men and moved to Los Angeles where he formed a super group, the Champions. Warren also revealed to the public that he was Angel.

After the Champions disbanded, Warren joined another group, the Defenders. When several of the team members seemingly died fighting the Dragon of the Moon, Warren linked up with the other original members of the X-Men to start an organization called X-Factor. Though publicly aimed at hunting down dangerous mutants, the true purpose of the group was to divert new mutants from capture and detainment in detention camps.

ARCHANGEL

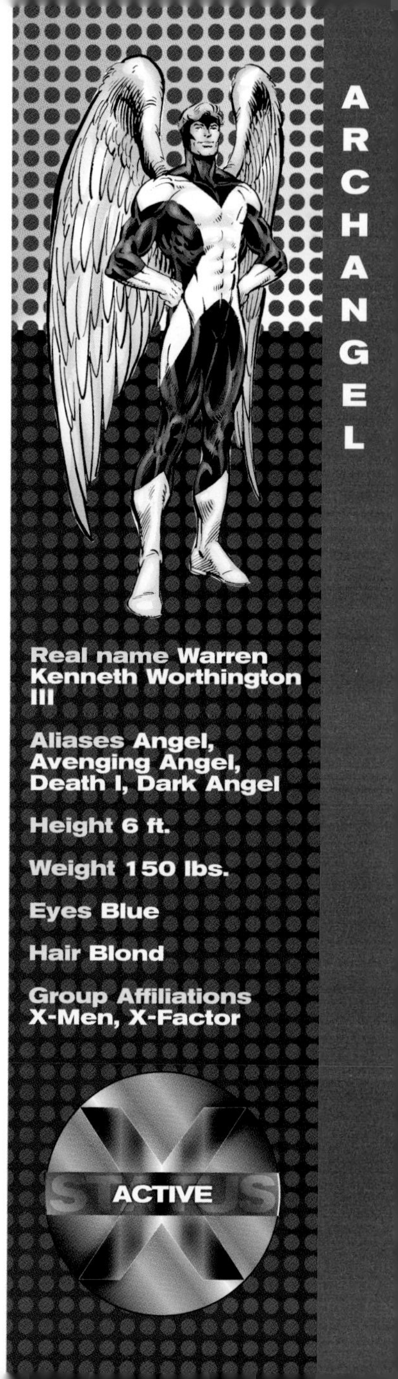

Real name Warren Kenneth Worthington III

Aliases Angel, Avenging Angel, Death I, Dark Angel

Height 6 ft.

Weight 150 lbs.

Eyes Blue

Hair Blond

Group Affiliations X-Men, X-Factor

STATUS: ACTIVE

Husk

Using advanced science, Apocalypse grew Angel a new set of wings made from metal. In exchange, Warren was made to fight for Apocalypse as Death, one of the Four Horsemen. Fellow members of X-Factor were able to release him from Apocalypse's brainwashing, and Warren returned to X-Factor, but now rechristened Archangel. Some time later, his original feathered wings regenerated and replaced his metal ones.

SECRETS

- Archangel's blood contains a unique healing factor, which he used to save the life of the mutant, Husk.

- Often wears a harness to help conceal his wings.

- Normally, Archangel flies below cloud level, but has the ability to reach 10,000 feet without great effort.

STATUS Active

During a battle with the evil Marauders, Angel was badly wounded by the villain known as Harpoon. As a result, Warren's wings were amputated. Despondent, Worthington tried to commit suicide, only to be rescued at the last possible instant by Apocalypse.

Marauders

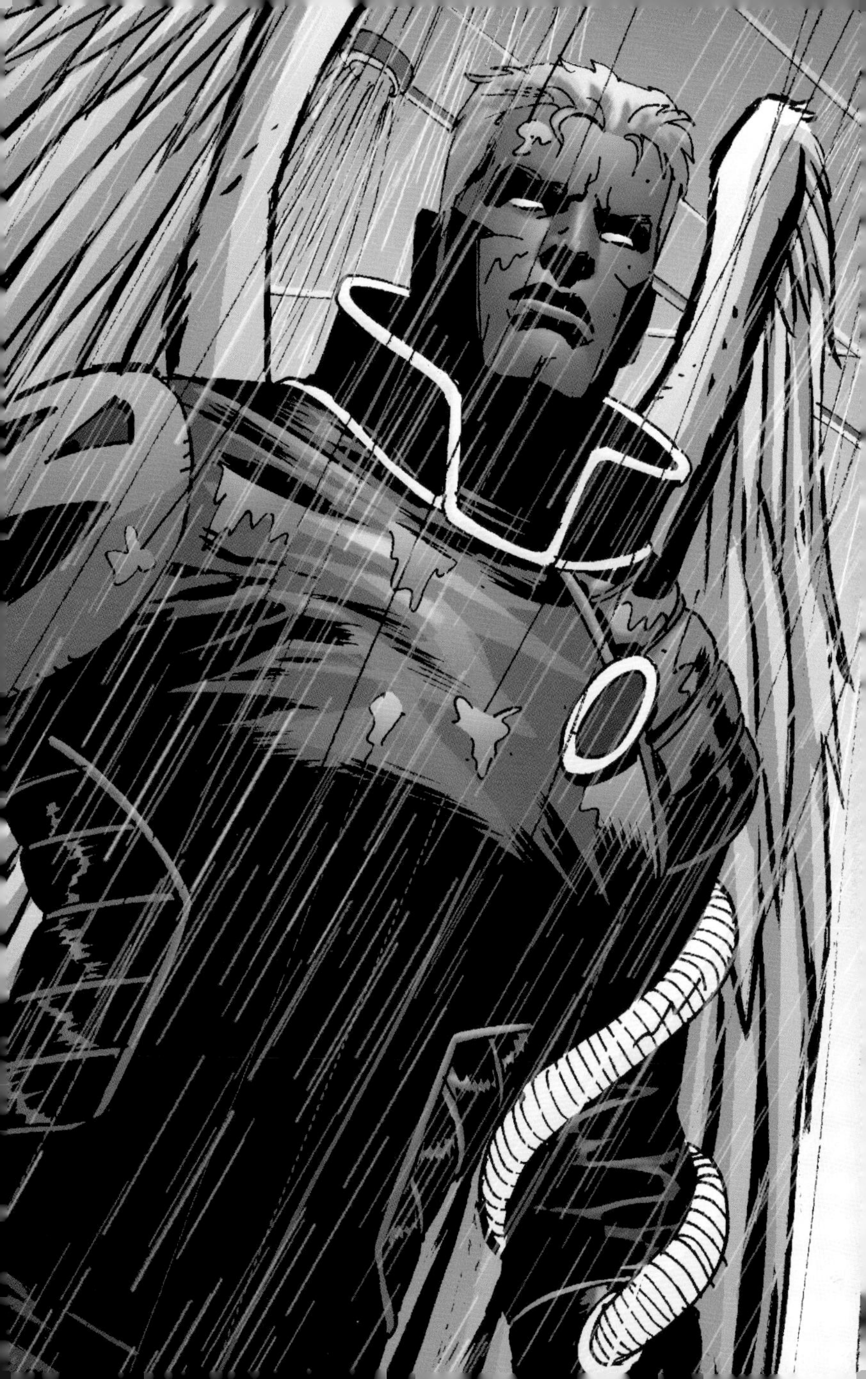

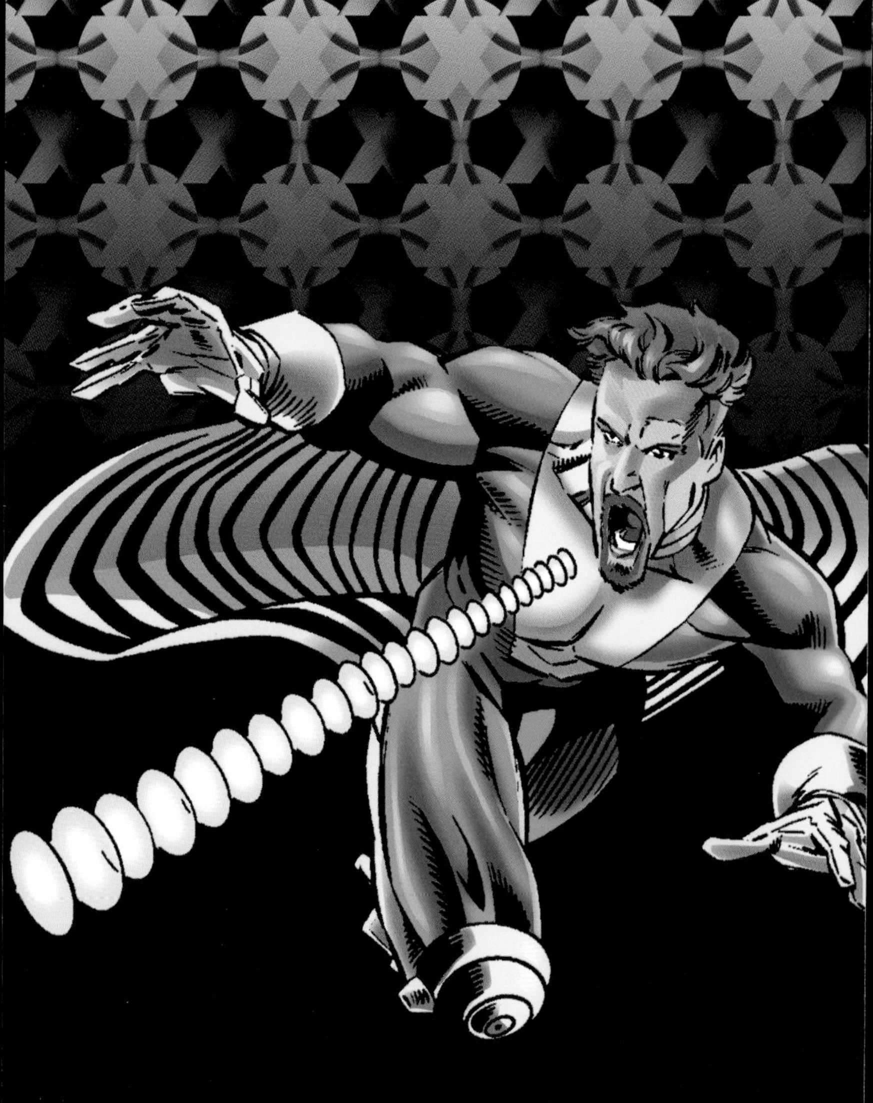

BANSHEE

BANSHEE

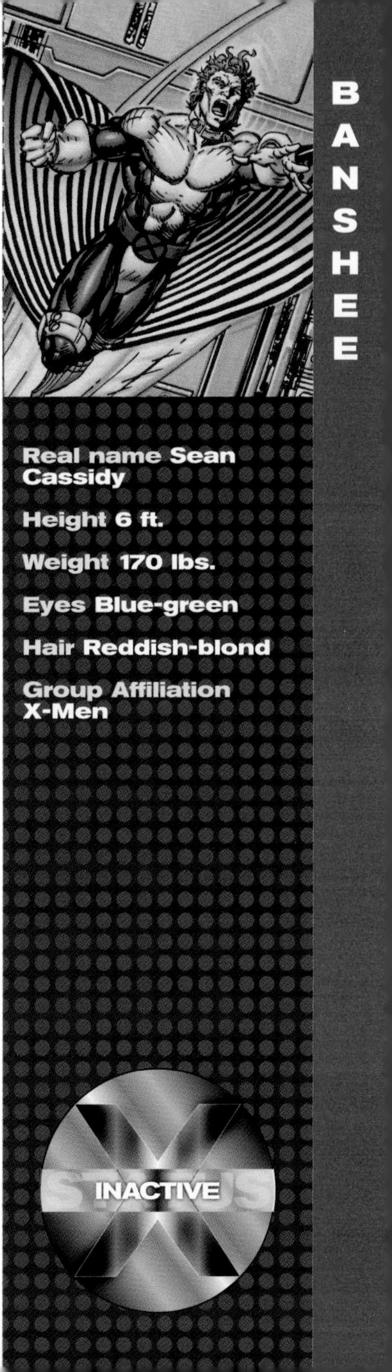

Real name Sean Cassidy

Height 6 ft.

Weight 170 lbs.

Eyes Blue-green

Hair Reddish-blond

Group Affiliation X-Men

STATUS INACTIVE

POWERS

Has the mutant power of a sonic scream; voice can pulverize stone; can fly using the sound waves of his voice as support; can use his voice as a type of sonar; using sonic scream, can create mind-affecting vibrations that will disrupt a person's equilibrium or cause a person to fall unconscious by disrupting the liquids in the inner ear.

SECURITY BRIEF

Sean Cassidy was born the heir to a small fortune and owner of a castle in Cassidy Keep, Ireland. While still a young man, he married Maeve Rourke and accepted a job at Interpol. During a period while Sean was away on a long mission, Maeve discovered she was pregnant and gave birth to a daughter, Theresa. Soon afterwards, Maeve was killed by an IRA bomb.

Unable to contact Sean, Sean's cousin, Tom, took care of Theresa. When Sean returned and discovered that Maeve had been killed, he exploded in anger and knocked Tom off a bridge, laming him. Tom decided to raise Theresa himself, never revealing her existence to Sean.

Forced to commit criminal acts by the villainous Factor Three, Sean was saved by Professor X and the X-Men. Several years later, the Professor invited Sean to join his new X-Men team. Sean, now called Banshee, accepted. It was then that he met Xavier's friend and ally, Dr. Moira MacTaggert, and they fell in love.

Several years later, Sean discovered how his cousin, who had become known as the mutant Black Tom Cassidy, had fooled him with regard to his daughter. Theresa had developed her own sonic powers and had taken the name, Siryn. Later, father and daughter were reunited.

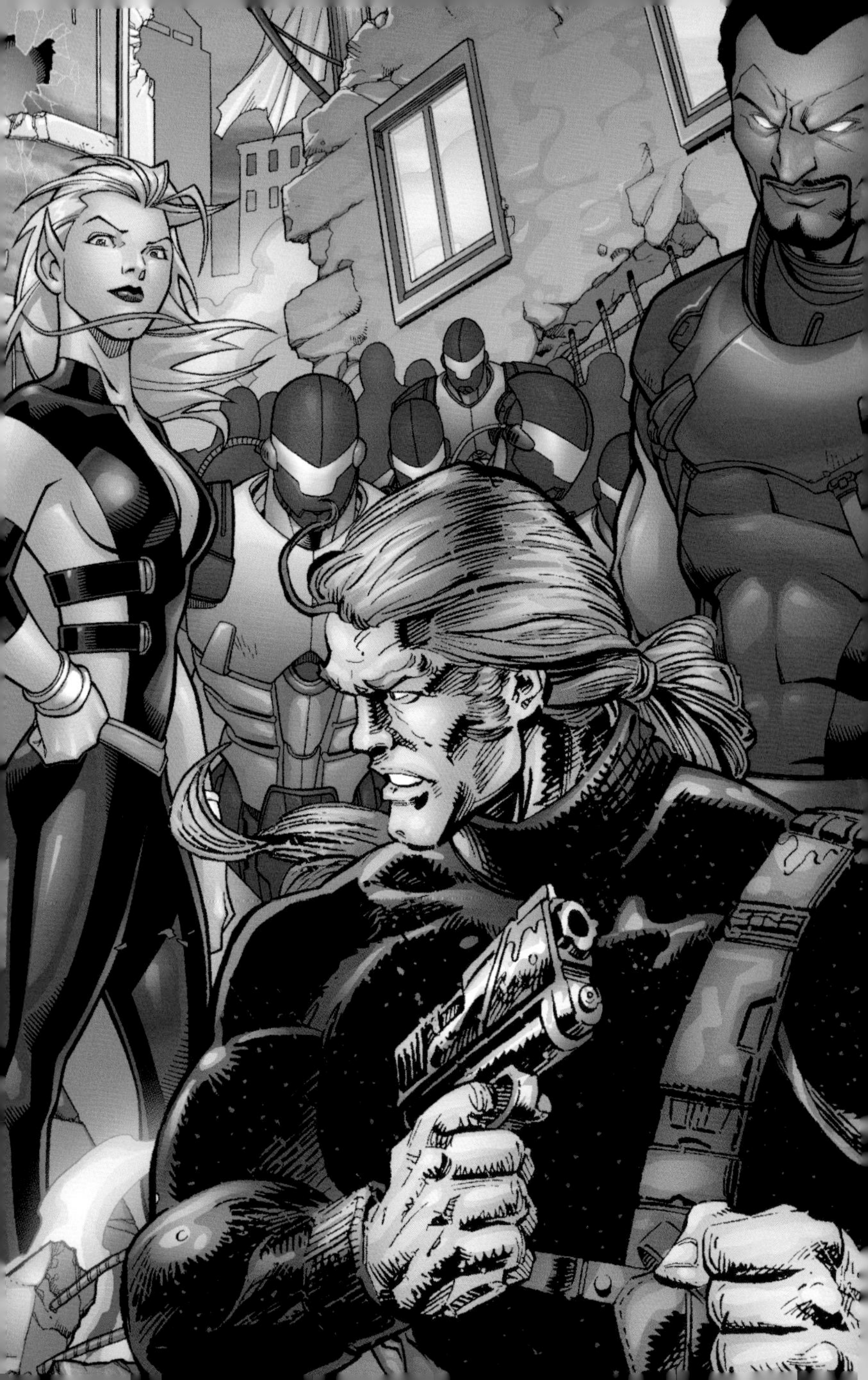

Left: ***Banshee with Moses Magnum***

Recently, Moira MacTaggert died in an explosion while working on a cure for the mutant plague known as the Legacy Virus. Her death led to Sean leaving the X-Men to start the X-Corps a paramilitary mutant group. The true force behind the team was the shape-shifting mutant, Mystique. When finally discovered, she destroyed the Corps and cut Sean's throat. At present, he's recovering in a hospital. But whether his sonic powers remain is uncertain.

SECRETS

- Sean worked as a member of Interpol and later as an officer for the New York Police Department.
- Factor Three forced Banshee to work for them by putting an explosive headband around his skull.

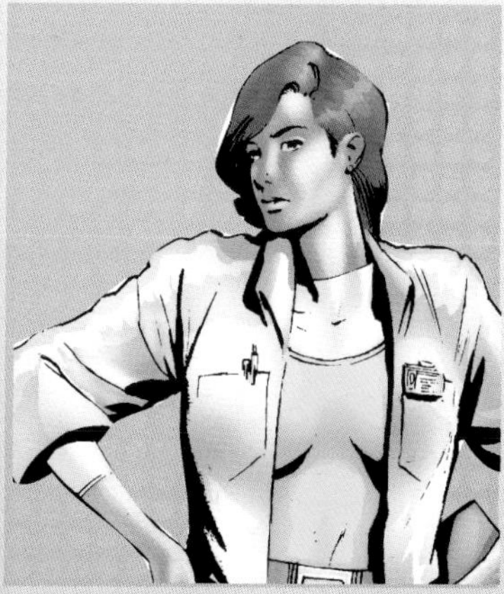

Moira MacTaggert

- When mutant Moses Magnum tried to destroy Japan by using psionic power waves to cause a gigantic earthquake and tsunami, Banshee used his sonic power to cancel Magnum's force waves. The effort cost him the use of his voice for months.
- Banshee worked for several years as co-headmaster at the Massachusetts Academy with Emma Frost, where he taught young mutants how to use their powers.

STATUS Inactive

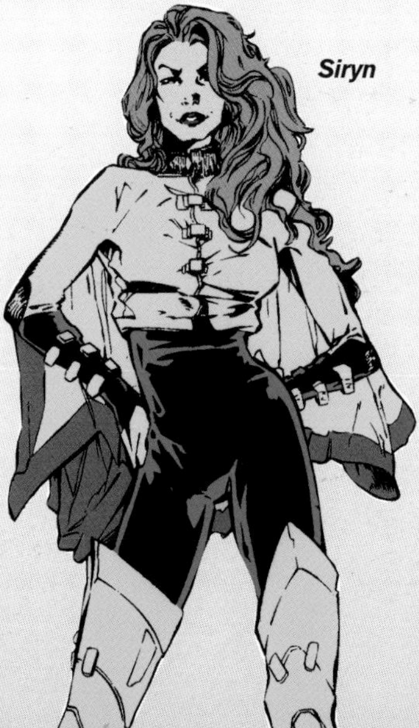

Siryn

BEAST

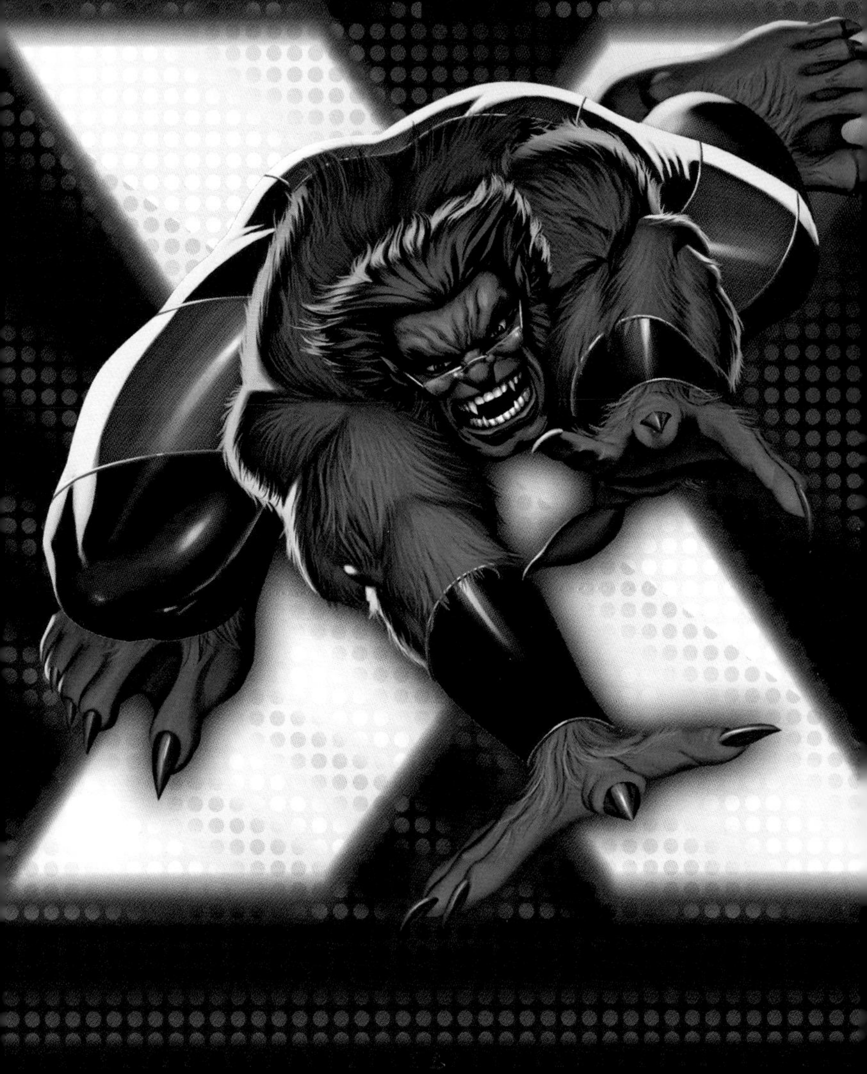

POWERS

Has superhuman agility, incredible strength, tremendous endurance, astonishing stamina; is a brilliant scientist who is an expert in genetics and chemistry; is one of the leading biochemists in the world today.

SECURITY BRIEF

As a young man working at a nuclear power plant, Norton McCoy was exposed to high levels of radiation during an accident at the facility. This radiation affected his genes, and his son, Henry, was born with super mutant powers. Unlike most mutants, Henry displayed signs of his mutant heritage from birth: he had unusually large hands and feet as well as superhuman speed and agility. As a teenager, Hank McCoy became a star football player, attracting the attention of Professor X, and the criminal mutant who called himself El Conquistador. El Conquistador tried to blackmail Hank into assisting him in his crimes by taking his parents hostage. With the help of Professor X, Hank defeated the villain. He then became a member of the original X-Men team, adopting the name Beast.

Hank completed his doctoral studies under instruction from Professor X, specializing in human genetics. While working for the Brand Corporation, he developed an elixir that activated latent mutations. Using himself as a subject, McCoy drank the serum, which resulted in massive physical changes. He grew fur over his entire body and developed even greater agility, strength, and speed.

Professing an interest in helping humanity, Hank resigned from the Brand Corporation and became a member of the superhuman team, the Avengers. After serving with that team for years, he decided to form his own group, the Defenders. Both Iceman and Angel, members

**B
E
A
S
T**

**Real name
Henry (Hank) McCoy**

Height 5 ft. 11 in.

Weight 402 lbs.

Eyes Blue

**Hair
Brown (originally);
Blue-black (currently)**

**Group Affiliations
X-Men, X-Factor**

ACTIVE

of the original X-Men team, joined with him as part of the new team.

The Defenders disbanded following the apparent deaths of several team members in battle. Beast, along with Cyclops, Angel, and Iceman, started a new group, which they called X-Factor. Supposedly, their mission was to track down and neutralize violent new mutants. In reality, they hunted young mutants so that they could teach them how to survive in a world that knows what terrible deeds they can accomplish.

Over the last few years, Beast has returned to the X-Men as an active member. He also works as a genetics researcher at the Xavier Institute for Higher Learning.

SECRETS

- Beast has had an unstable long-term relationship with TV news reporter, Trish Tilby.

- Dark Beast—a duplicate of Beast who had all his intellect and physical powers but who was totally amoral— lived in the parallel universe, the Age of Apocalypse. When the Age of Apocalypse universe collapsed, Dark Beast somehow crossed over to our world.

- Beast is able to crawl up brick walls by wedging his fingers and toes into small cracks like a mountain-climber.

STATUS Active

Dark Beast

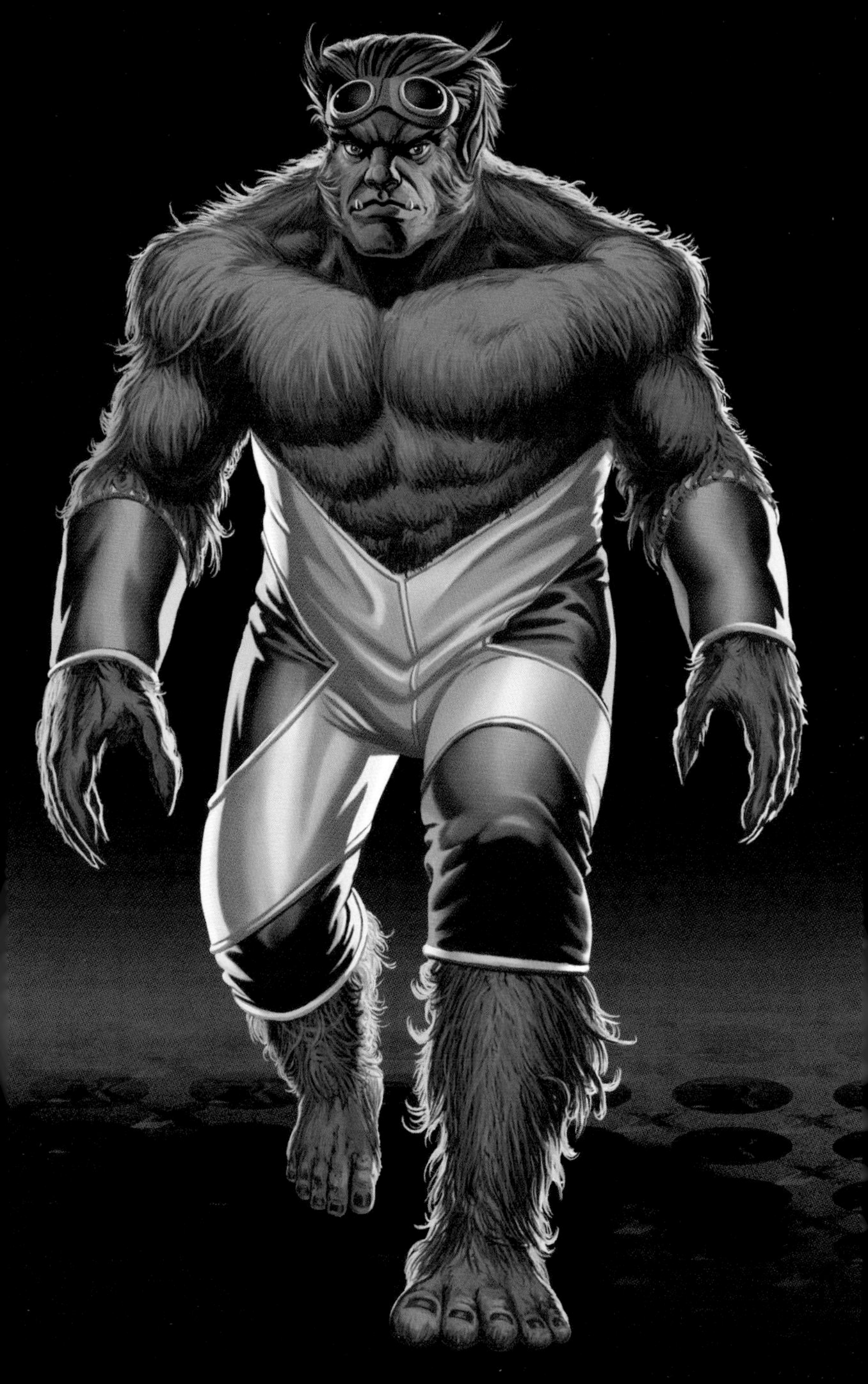

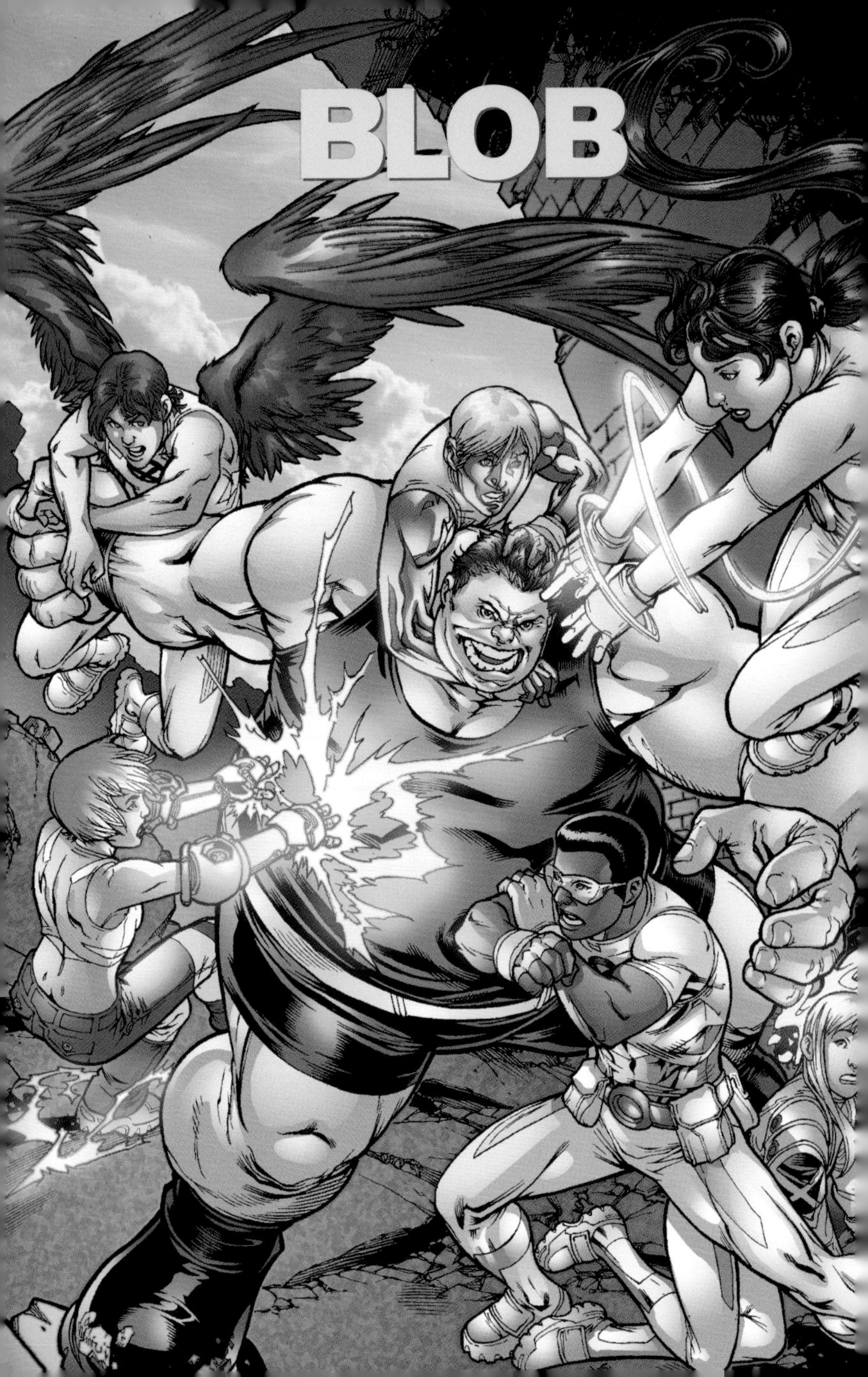
BLOB

POWERS

Huge, obese mutant who can make himself immovable; uses personal gravity to bond himself to the ground beneath him; invulnerable to most injuries; skin is nearly indestructible; has evolved further over past few years, greatly increasing in height, weight, and strength.

SECURITY BRIEF

Blob started out as a circus performer unaware of his mutant status. He was contacted by Professor Xavier and invited to the X-Mansion where he was told he was a mutant. Xavier asked Dukes to join the X-Men team, but the circus entertainer refused because he felt he was better than the rest of the X-Men.

Instead, Dukes later joined Magneto's Brotherhood of Evil Mutants. He remained a member of the group through their history. When Mystique took over the Brotherhood and changed it into the government agency, Freedom Force, Dukes worked with them. When Freedom Force dissolved, Dukes returned to his old ways and once more became a member of the newly reunited Brotherhood.

SECRETS

- Blob's skin is nearly invulnerable to injury. It can't be cut, ripped, torn, or damaged by any disease.

- Blob's major weakness as a fighter is his short temper. He is not very smart and is fairly easy to manipulate.

- Despite his huge size, Blob has the same balance and agility of a normal man.

STATUS Active

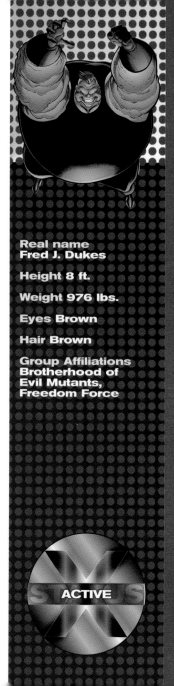

**B
L
O
B**

**Real name
Fred J. Dukes**

Height 8 ft.

Weight 976 lbs.

Eyes Brown

Hair Brown

**Group Affiliations
Brotherhood of
Evil Mutants,
Freedom Force**

ACTIVE

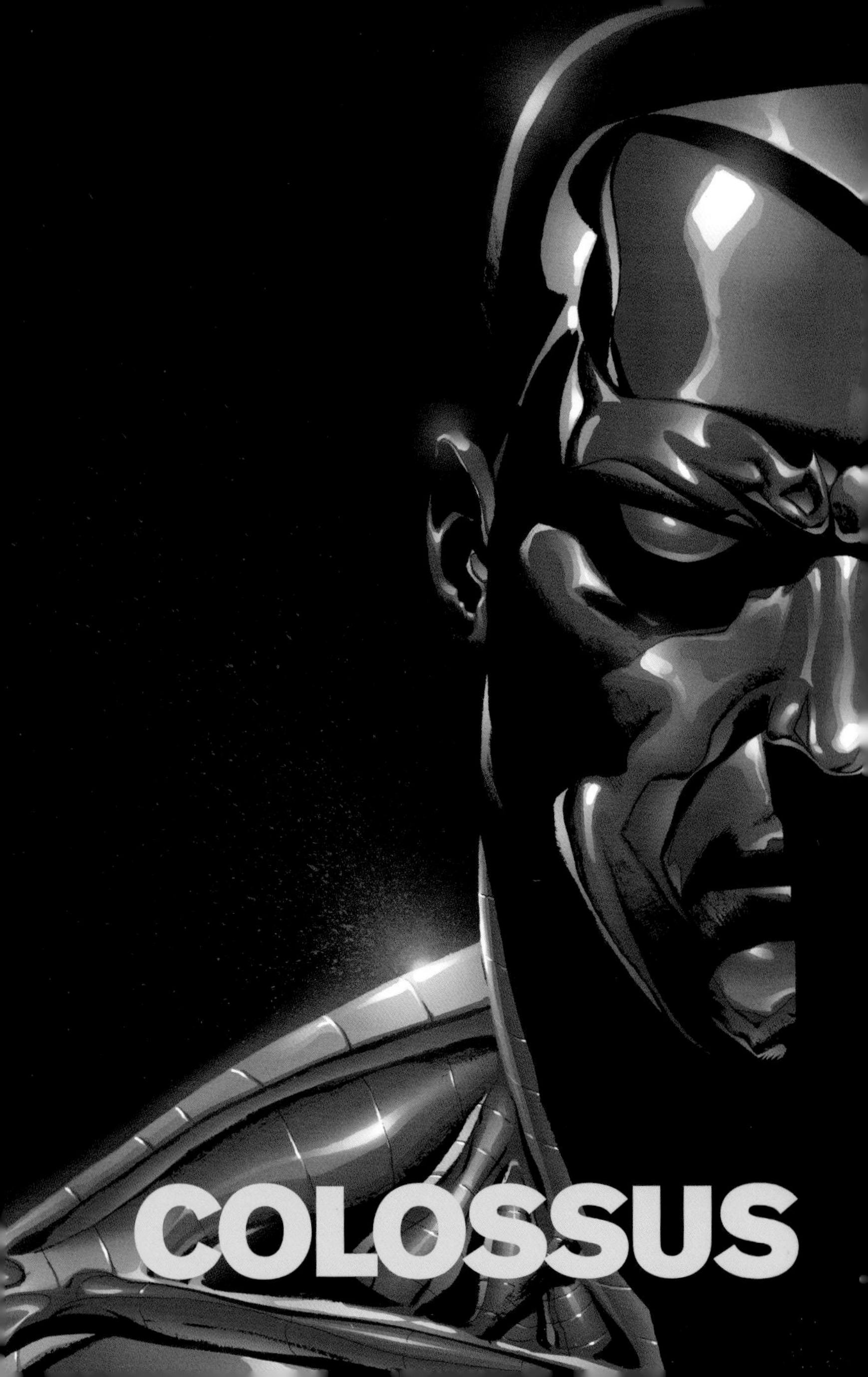
COLOSSUS

POWERS

Can transform his body into an unknown type of organic steel; when this happens, he grows bigger and his body mass more than doubles (how he does this is unknown); in armored state, possesses superhuman strength and stamina; nearly invulnerable and does not seem to need air; cannot transform only part of his body—must transform entirely; if knocked unconscious in his armored form, returns to his human shape.

SECURITY BRIEF

Piotr Rasputin was born and raised on a collective farm in Russia. His older brother, Nikolai, and his younger sister, Illyana, were also mutants. Professor X recruited Piotr for the X-Men when the original team was captured by the mysterious living island, Krakoa. He adopted the name Colossus.

Piotr fell in love with one of his teammates and began a difficult relationship. His girlfriend over the years has been Kitty Pryde, known as Shadowcat with whom his sister Illyana became best friends. When Illyana died of the Legacy Virus, Piotr briefly joined Magneto and his band of mutants.

Piotr eventually rejoined the X-Men. When Beast found a cure for the Legacy Virus, the only way it could be activated was by the death of a mutant. Colossus sacrificed himself so no other mutant had to die.

After Colossus died, Shadowcat left the X-Men. Recently, she returned and on a mission with the team, found Colossus still alive in the clutches of an alien scientist, Ord. Shadowcat saved Colossus, and he has since rejoined the X-Men.

COLOSSUS

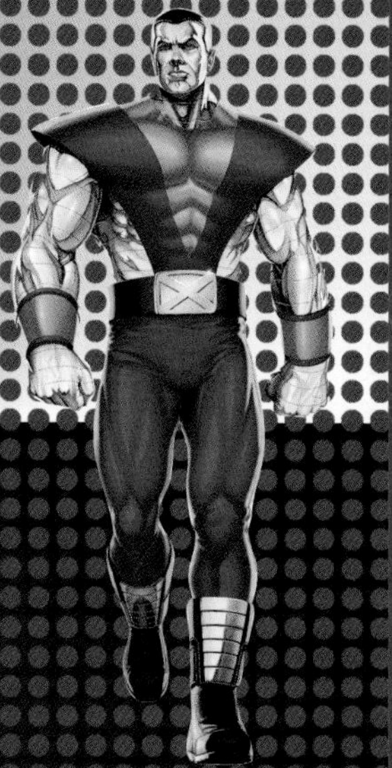

Real name
Piotr Rasputin

Aliases **Peter Nicolas, Proletarian**

Height
(normal) 6 ft. 6 in., (armored) 7 ft. 5 in.

Weight
(normal) 250 lbs., (armored) 500 lbs.

Eyes **Blue, (transformed) Silver**

Hair **Black**

Group Affiliations
X-Men, Brotherhood of Evil Mutants

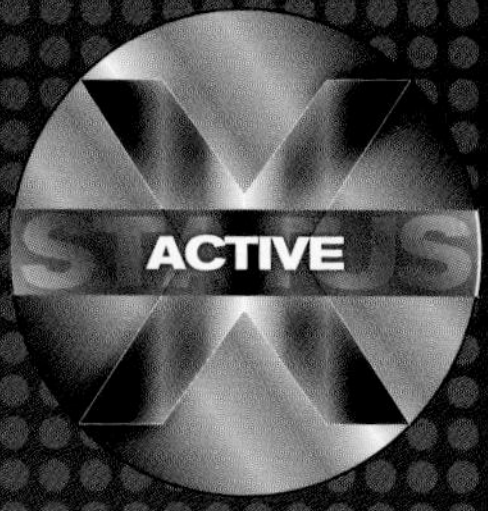
STATUS
ACTIVE

SECRETS

- Colossus's older brother, Mikhail, is also a mutant. Mikhail is a cold, self-centered schemer. Over the years he has teamed up with Apocalypse, Mr. Sinister, Omega Red, and others. Mikhail is able to teleport through space and other dimensions. He can fire destructive power blasts from his hands.

- Colossus's younger sister, Illyana, was kidnapped by demons and taken to the dimension of Limbo. She was raised there and taught magic. When she finally escaped, Illyana returned to Earth years older, though no time had passed since her disappearance. She took the code name, Magik and joined the New Mutants.

- Colossus served for a time as a member of the British-based mutant team, Excalibur.

STATUS Active

Magik

Mikhail

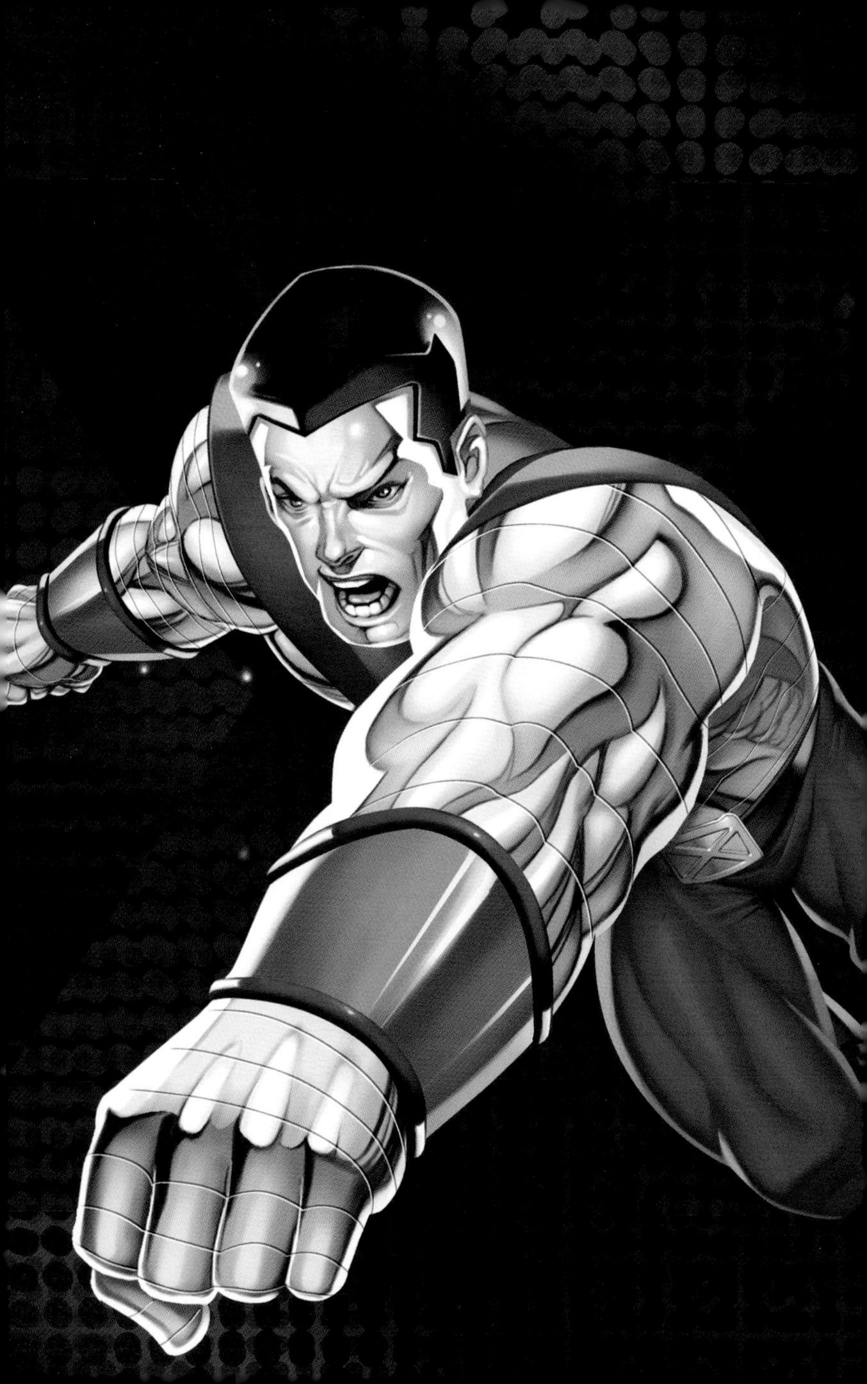

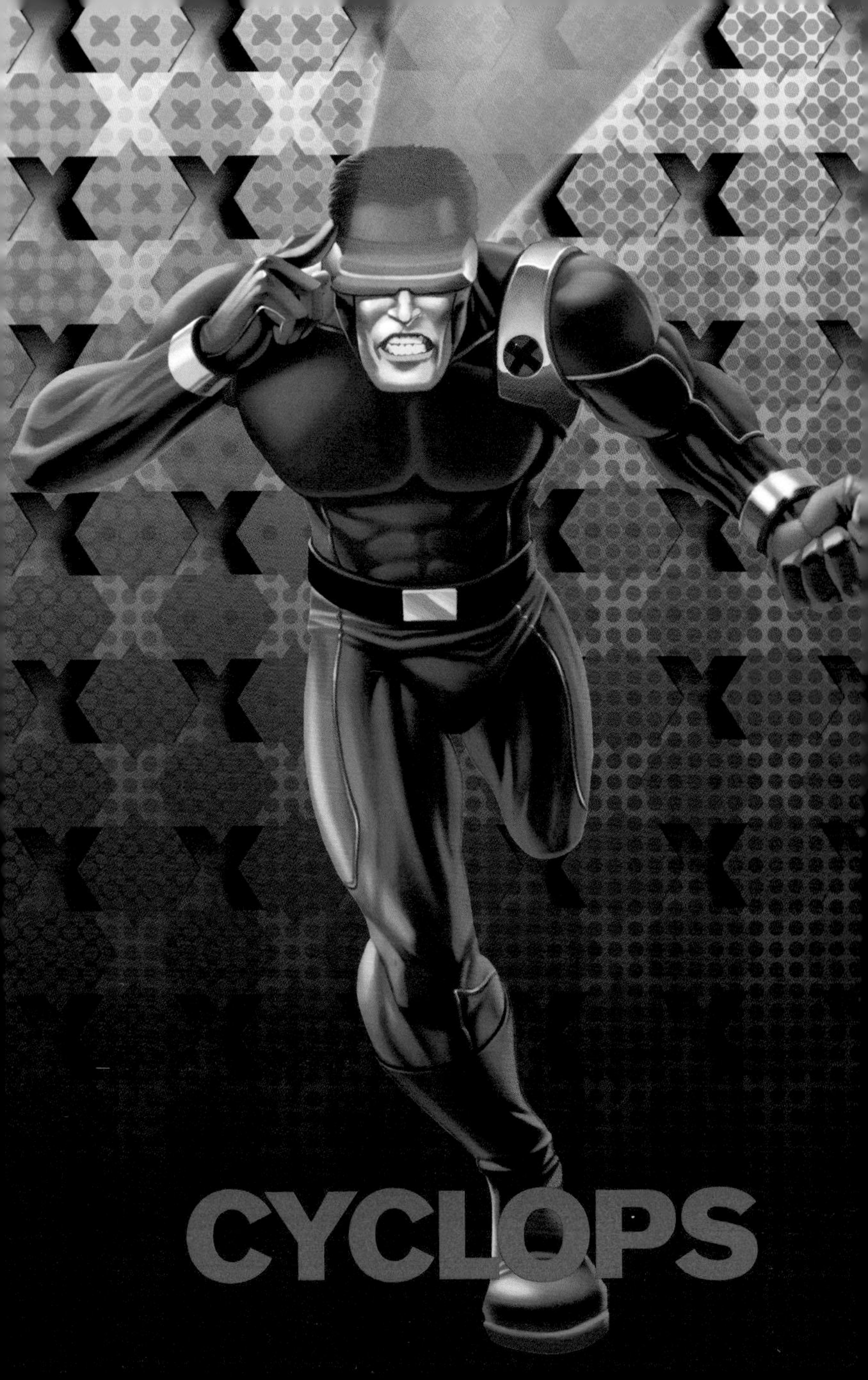
CYCLOPS

CYCLOPS

POWERS

Can focus energy from another universe through eyes into heatless but intensely destructive optic blasts; effective range of blasts is approximately 2,000 feet; uses eyes as interdimensional apertures; controls apertures through body's absorption of sunlight and other ambient energy; regulates width of optic blasts through reflexive ability of eyes to focus; generates self-protective psionic field that automatically repels other dimensional energies of optic blasts and inures body to their harmful effects.

SECURITY BRIEF

Scott Summers was born and raised in Anchorage, Alaska, the son of Katherine Summers and U.S.A.F. Major Christopher Summers. One afternoon, when the Major took his family on an airplane flight, it was attacked by an alien spaceship. The plane caught fire but Scott and his younger brother, Alex, escaped by parachute. Scott hit his head on landing, causing an injury that made it impossible to control his optic blasts. He also suffered a severe case of amnesia.

Unsure of his true identity, Scott grew up in an orphanage in Nebraska secretly run by the diabolical scientist, Mr. Sinister. At sixteen, Scott was discovered by Professor X and became the first member of the X-Men. Over the next few years, now named Cyclops, he had a tempestuous relationship with Jean Grey.

After Jean Grey's apparent death, Scott left the X-Men. He returned months later when the team needed his help to fight rival mutant, Magneto. Shortly afterwards, he met Madelyne Pryor, a young woman who seemed a near exact duplicate of Jean. Scott and Madelyne married and had a son, Nathan. Then, Jean returned: she had not died.

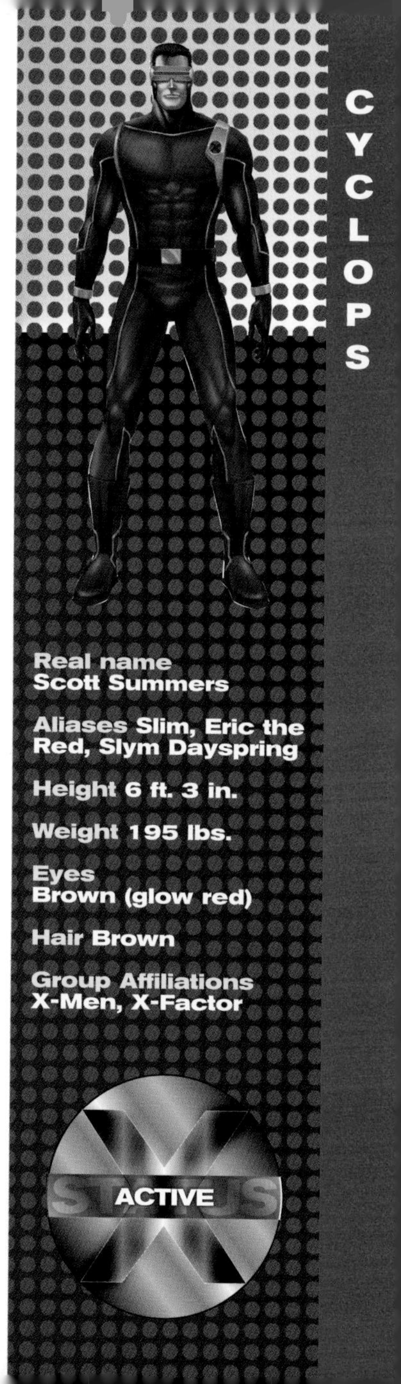

Real name
Scott Summers

Aliases Slim, Eric the Red, Slym Dayspring

Height 6 ft. 3 in.

Weight 195 lbs.

Eyes
Brown (glow red)

Hair Brown

Group Affiliations
X-Men, X-Factor

STATUS **ACTIVE**

Scott left Madelyne and Nathan for Jean. Teaming with a number of the other original X-Men, they formed a new mutant action group, X-Factor.

Madelyne, overwhelmed with rage at being abandoned by Scott, transformed into the demonic Goblyn Queen and nearly destroyed Nathan before committing suicide. Soon afterwards, the arch-villain, Apocalypse, infected baby Nathan with a techno-organic virus. The only way to save Scott's son was to allow him to be taken into the future by a mysterious sisterhood known as the Askani.

A few years later, Scott and Jean finally married. During their honeymoon, their personalities were brought into the far future and under the identities of Slim and Redd raised Nathan for the first twelve years of his life. When they finally returned to their normal bodies in the present, Jean began to manifest the Phoenix powers again.

Recently Scott, who feels threatened by a wife more powerful than he is, has drifted into a relationship with Emma Frost a reformed member of The Hellfire Club also known as the White Queen, who had joined the X-Men. At present, Scott and Emma serve as headmasters of Professor Xavier's school.

Despite his tumultuous personal life, Scott Summers still remains the undisputed leader of the X-Men.

SECRETS

- Cyclops can block his optic blasts simply by closing his eyelids. However, because the interdimensional energies he channels are "on" all the time, he regularly wears a visor made of synthetic ruby quartz crystal resonant with his personal psionic field to prevent accidental destruction. The visor helps him to regulate the height of his optic blasts.

- Scott thought his parents were killed when the alien Shi'ar spaceship attacked their airplane. In fact, they were taken prisoner by the alien raiders and sold into slavery. Katherine Summers died in captivity, but Christopher Summers escaped and under the identity Corsair, became leader of an interstellar freedom force known as the Starjammers. Scott didn't learn his father was still alive until many years later.

- Scott's son, Nathan, was raised two thousand years in the future where he became the freedom fighter known as Cable. In a twist of fate, Cable returned to the present as a much older man than his father.

STATUS Active

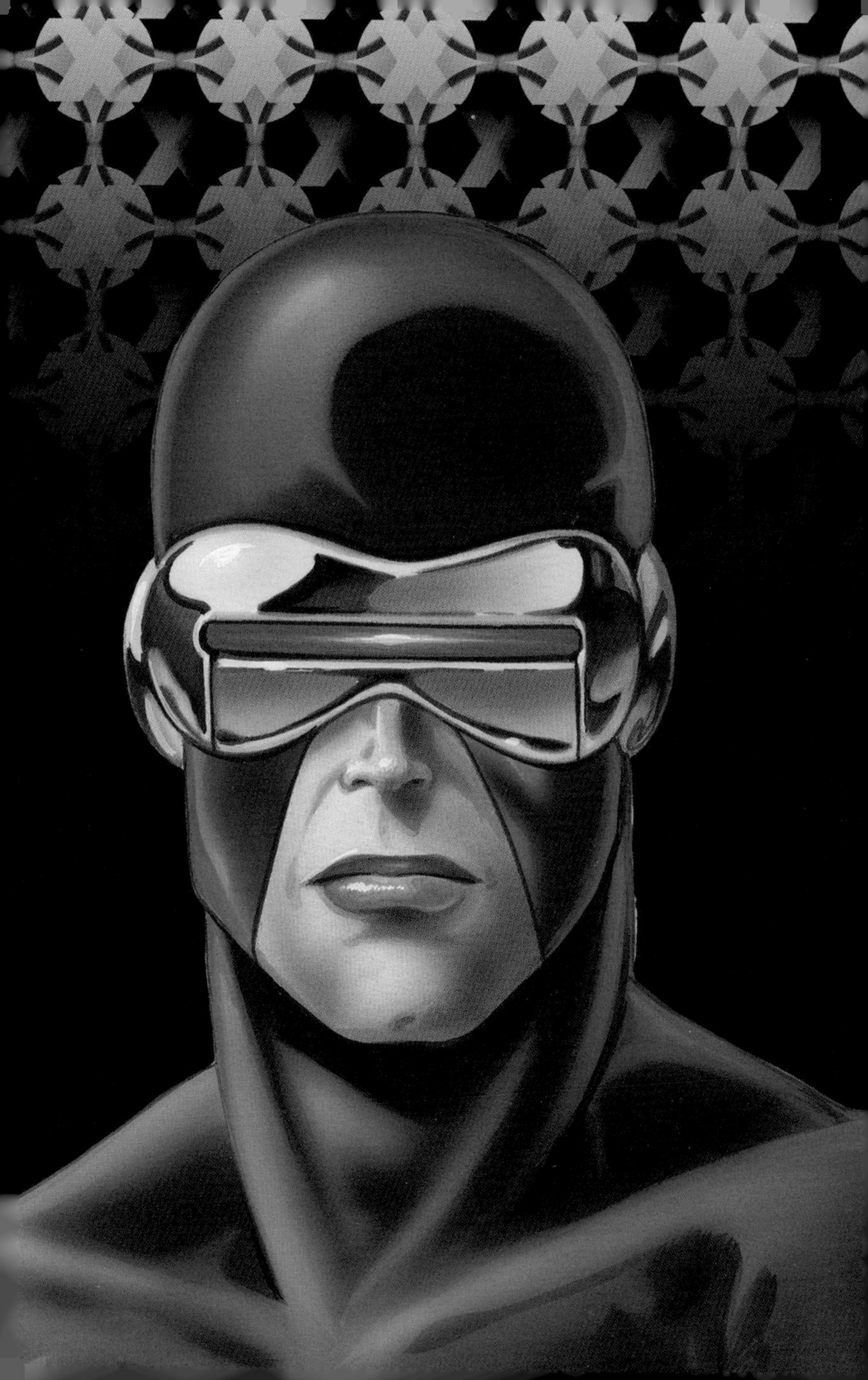

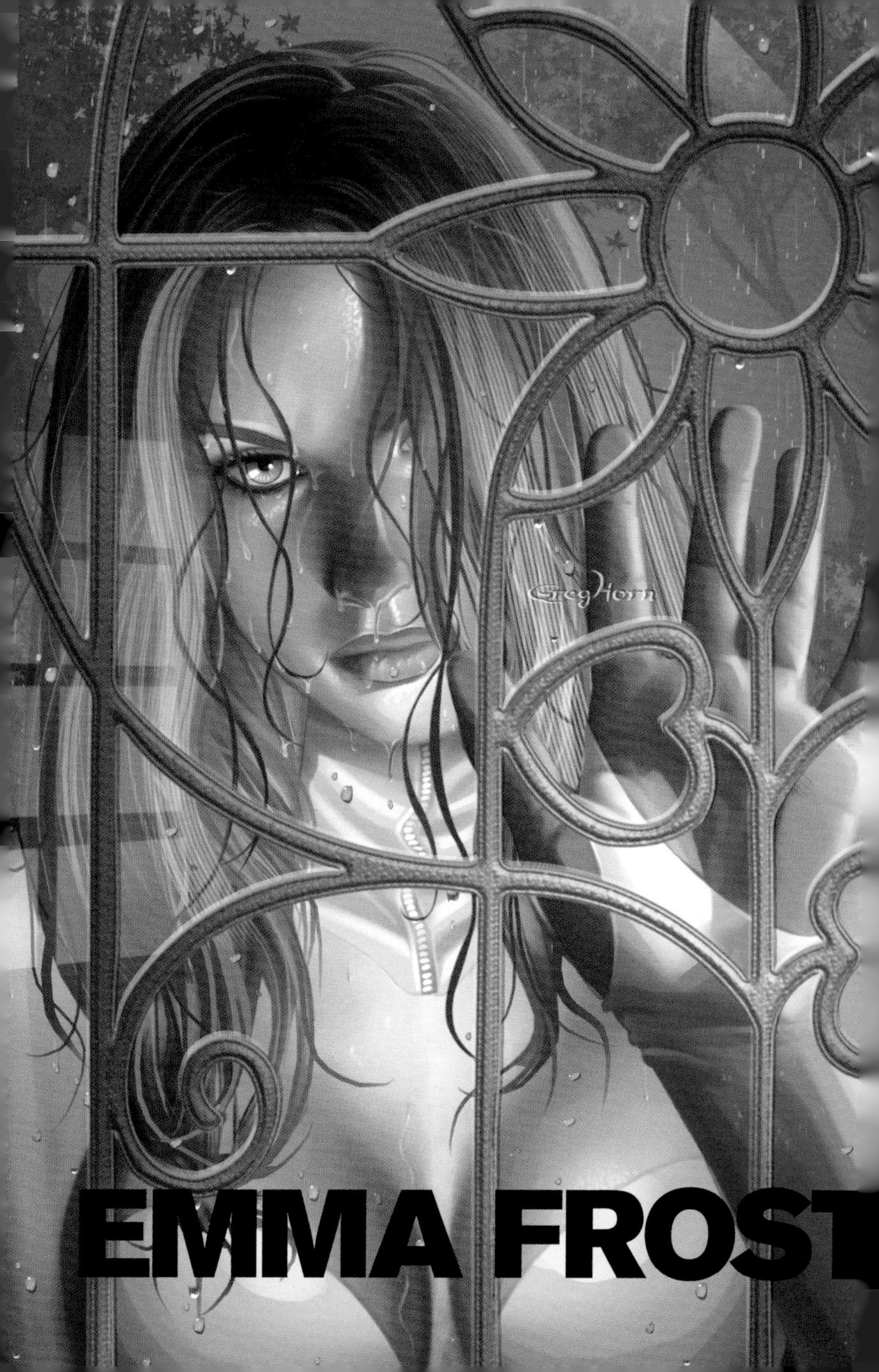
Greg Horn
EMMA FROST

POWERS

Extremely powerful telepath; can project her thoughts and listen to other people's thoughts; can command others to do what she wants; can erase memories of others; can make people believe that they see things that aren't there; can transform herself into a flexible, diamond-like substance which can't be damaged (in this state she cannot use her telepathic powers but she has increased strength and endurance).

SECURITY BRIEF

Emma Grace Frost was born a rich and privileged member of a wealthy Boston society family. Exploiting her beauty and intelligence, she expanded the family business into a multibillion dollar empire. Emma also employed a secret weapon: she was a mutant with extraordinary powers of telepathy who could change people's minds at will. Emma's success brought her to the attention of the Hellfire Club. She was invited to join and quickly rose to the position of White Queen

While a member of the Club, Emma also ran the Massachusetts Academy, a school for mutants established by the Hellfire Club. Emma's students were known as the Hellions, and they often fought Professor X's teenage group, the New Mutants. When Jean Grey visited the Hellfire Club, Emma engaged her in a psychic duel but was badly beaten.

Several years later, Emma and the Hellions were attacked by a group of Sentinels. The Hellions were killed and Emma was badly hurt. When she recovered, she teamed with Banshee to train the mutant group, Generation X. When that group disbanded, Emma traveled to the island of Genosha and taught mutants at a school there.

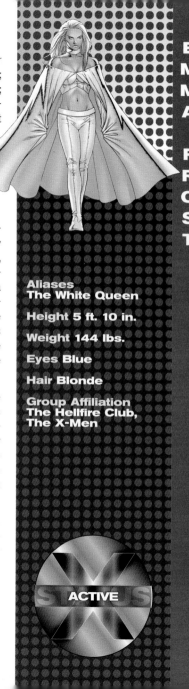

E M M A   F R O S T

Aliases
The White Queen

Height 5 ft. 10 in.

Weight 144 lbs.

Eyes Blue

Hair Blonde

Group Affiliation
The Hellfire Club,
The X-Men

ACTIVE

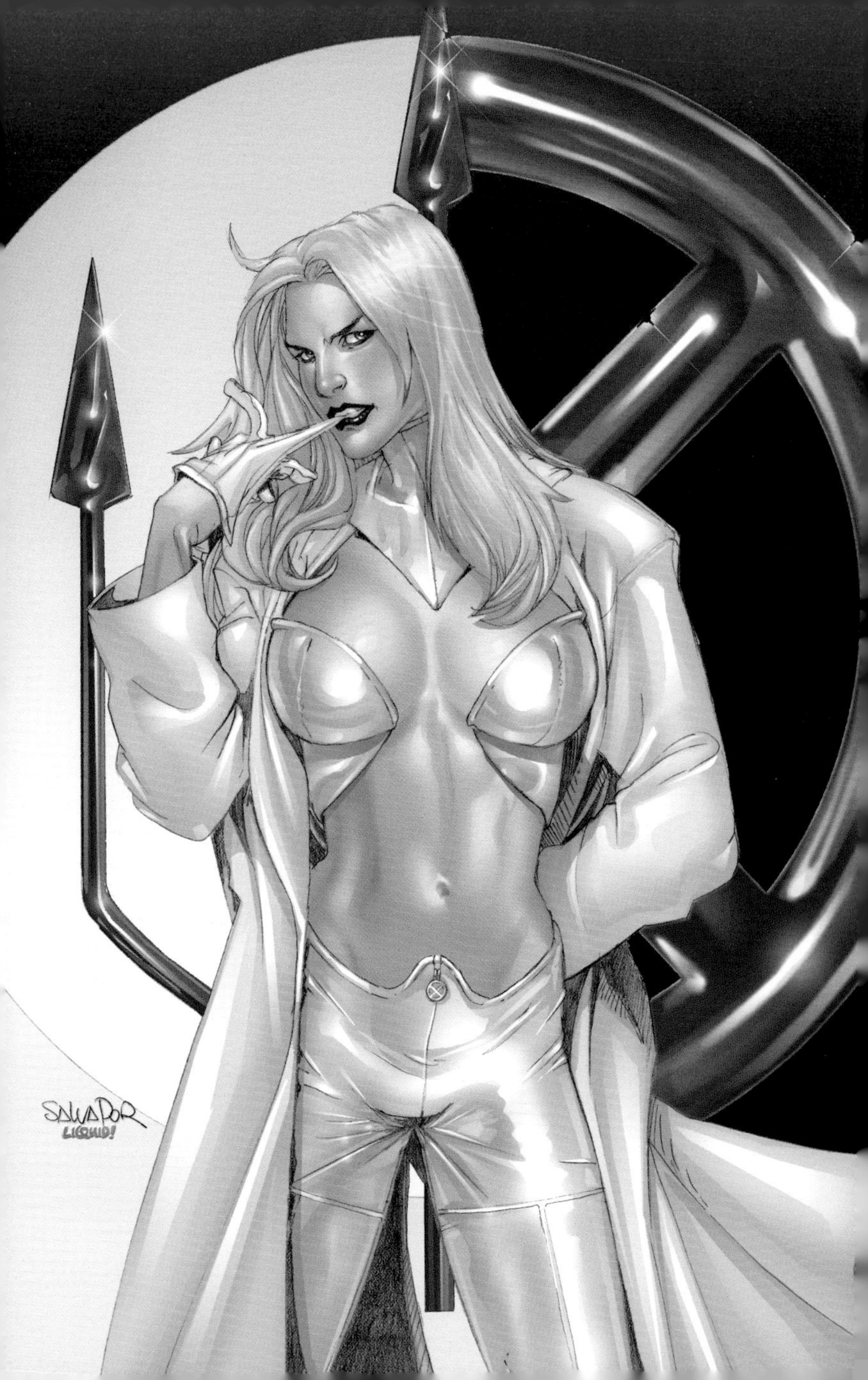

When Sentinels under the command of Cassandra Nova attacked Genosha and killed most of the island's population, Emma survived by turning into an indestructible diamond-like substance. Afterwards, she returned to the United States, and, with Cyclops, took control of Professor X's Institute for Higher Learning.

A number of the X-Men still do not trust Emma, who for years was one of their most dangerous enemies.

SECRETS

- Emma once designed a special device that enabled her to switch minds for a short time with any individual. She used it to exchange minds with Storm.

- Though Emma Frost was an enemy of the X-Men, she willed the care of the Massachusetts Academy to Professor X if she was ever injured. When the mutant, Trevor Fitzroy, killed the Hellions and nearly killed Emma, Xavier took over running the other school.

- Emma's estranged sister, Adrienne, planted a bomb at the Massachusetts Academy that killed Synch, one of Emma's students. Emma tracked down and murdered Adrienne.

- While working at Professor X's Academy, Emma trained a group of telepathic quintuplets known as the Stepford Cuckoos.

STATUS Active

Stepford Cuckoos

GAMBIT

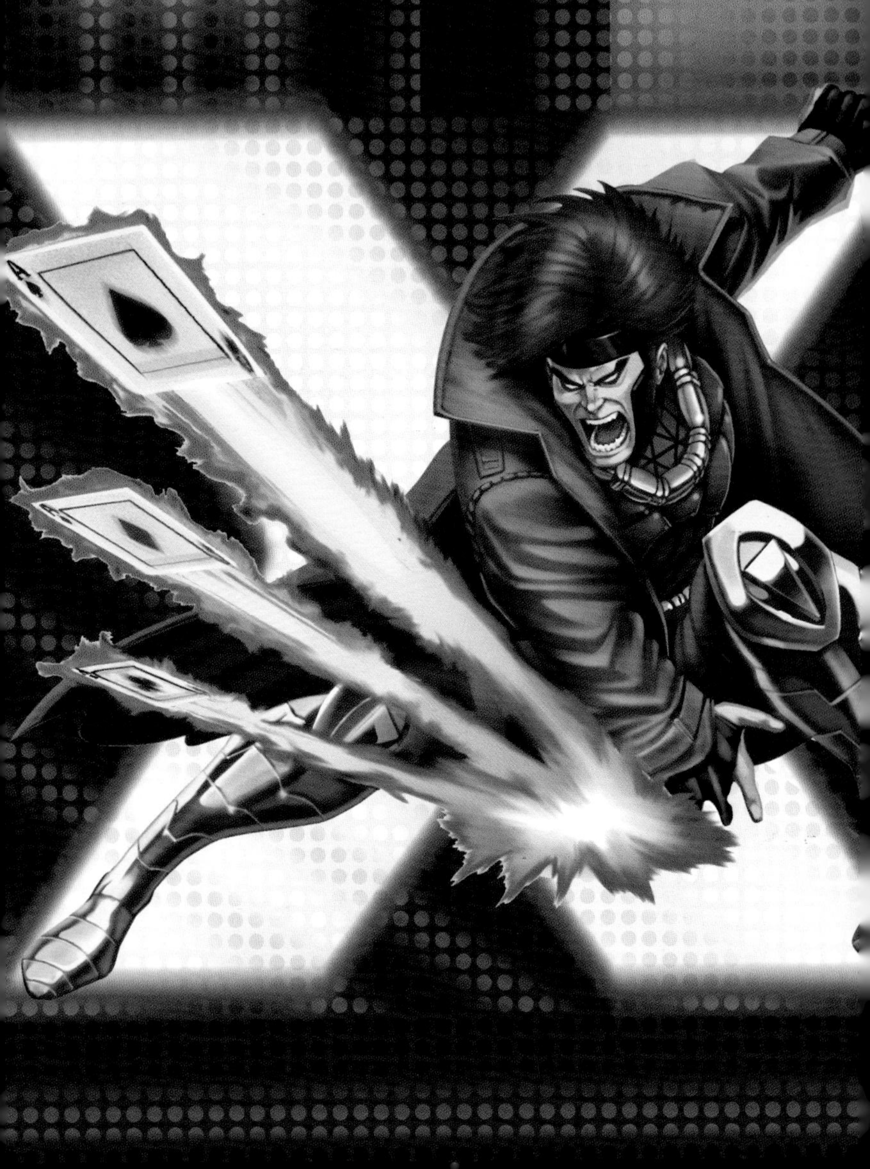

POWERS

Able to explosively charge inanimate objects which he then can use as bombs (for example, if he throws a deck of cards he can turn each card into a powerful explosive); invulnerable to psychic attacks because of the charged energy stored in his body; an agile fighter and an expert thief.

SECURITY BRIEF

As a baby, Remy LeBeau was found abandoned in New Orleans. His bright red eyes earned him the title of *le diable blanc*—the White Devil. Remy was taken in and raised by the Thieves Guild, becoming a master thief. An ancient prophecy predicted that he would unite the warring Thieves and Assassin's Guild. Acting to fulfill the prophecy, Remy married Bella Donna Boudreaux, the daughter of the head of the Assassins. The prophecy might have come true had Remy not slain Bella Donna's brother in a duel the same day. Remy was exiled from New Orleans and his marriage was annulled.

Remy wandered the world as a thief, meeting all sorts of unsavory characters. During this time, he encountered Mr. Sinister who promised to help Remy gain control over his wild powers. Remy agreed and Sinister operated on him. He was cured, but he owed Sinister favors in return and had to perform several missions for him.

Sinister had Remy lead a group of mutant mercenaries including the bestial Sabretooth, into the headquarters beneath New York City of a group of underground mutants known as the Morlocks. Remy thought the mercenaries were only going to kidnap some Morlocks. Instead, they began slaying them. This event became known as the Mutant Massacre and forever tainted Remy's image.

GAMBIT

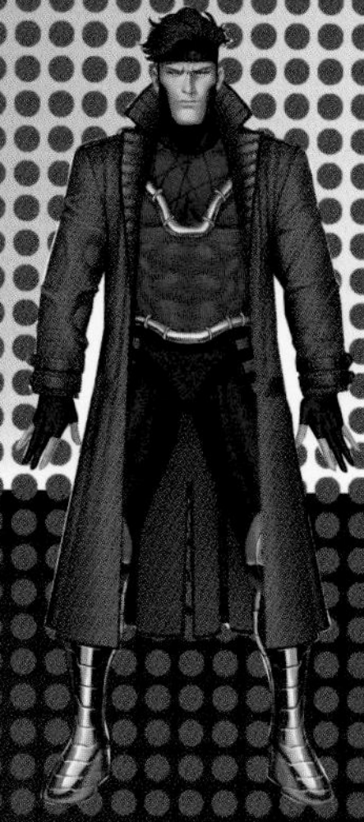

Real name
Remy LeBeau

Height 6 ft. 1 in.

Weight 179 lbs.

Eyes Red

Hair Brown

Group Affiliation
X-Men

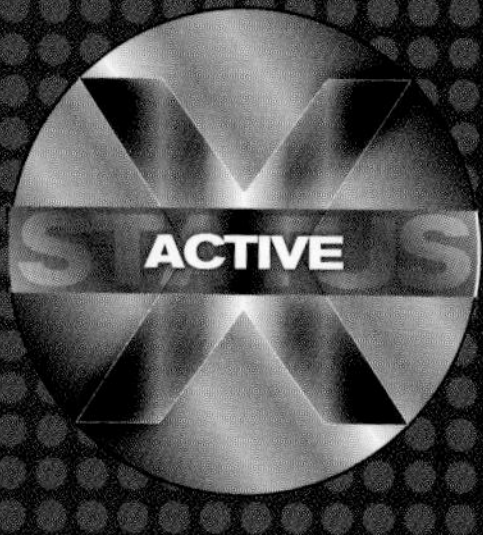
STATUS
ACTIVE

Much later, Remy rescued Storm who had been turned into a child by The Nanny. It was Storm who brought him to the X-Men, which he joined. Though he had his quarrels with individual group members, Remy became one of its most valuable participants.

Though normally a loner, Remy fell in love with one of his teammates, Rogue, despite the fact that Rogue cannot touch anyone without her absorbing their powers and eventually killing them. Over the years, Remy and Rogue have stayed true to each other, though more than once their relationship has been challenged by outer-space villains or rival mutants on Earth.

Recently, Remy (as Gambit) lost his powers and retired with Rogue from the X-Men. However, another mutant named Sage was able to restore Gambit's gift and currently he and Rogue are again members of the X-Men team.

SECRETS

• A deadly mastermind, the New Sun, fought Remy for several years, finally hiring a superhuman group of assassins to kill him. When Remy confronted the New Sun, the villain turned out to be an alternate reality version of Remy, whose out-of-control powers had destroyed his world. Remy managed to control his powers while defeating the New Sun.

• Remy once won a fighting match with Wolverine in the Danger Room of the X-Men headquarters. Knowing his opponent's incredible fighting skills, Remy actually rigged the fight.

• Remy has the ability to charm people with what seems to be a mild form of hypnosis.

STATUS Active

Sage

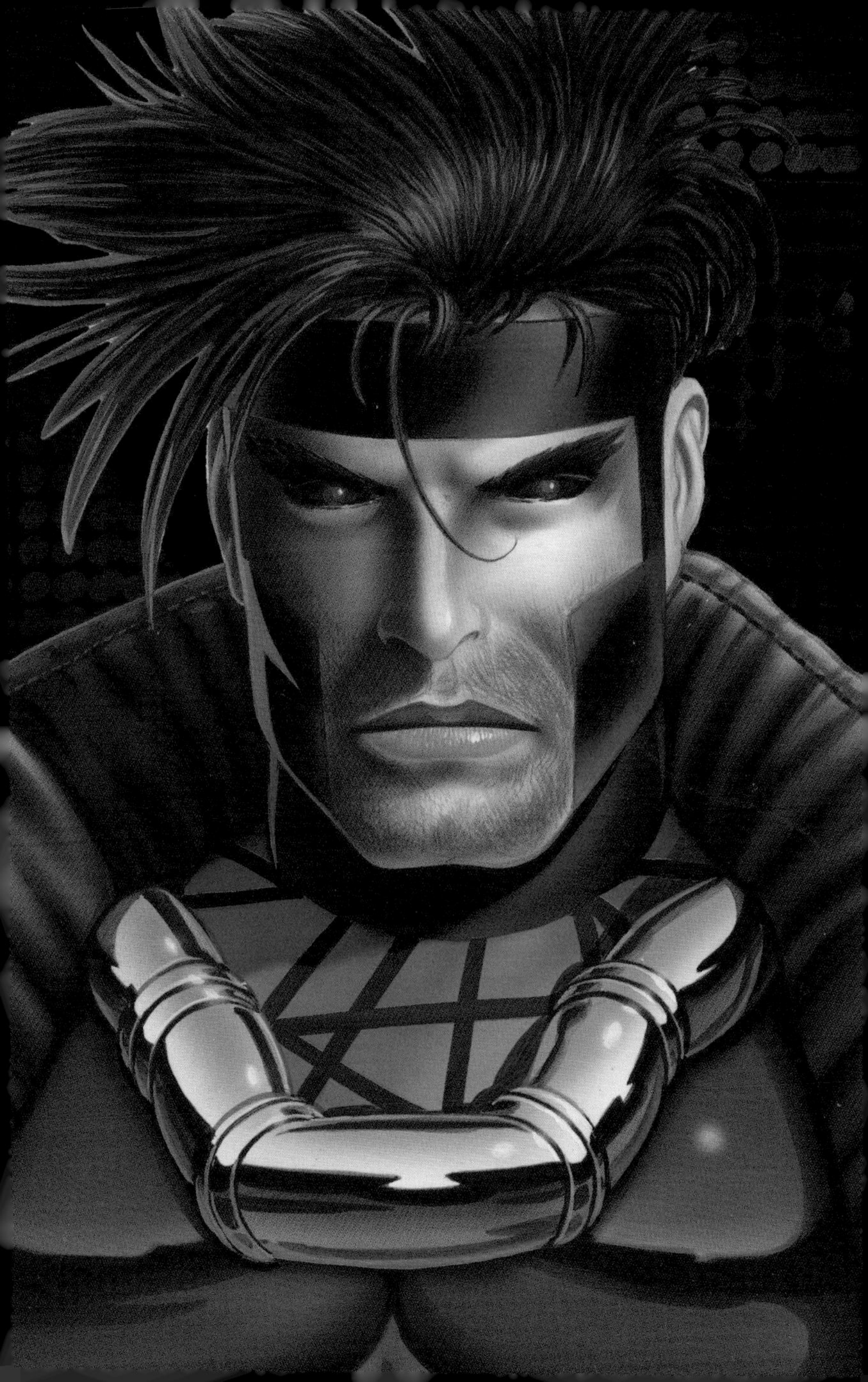

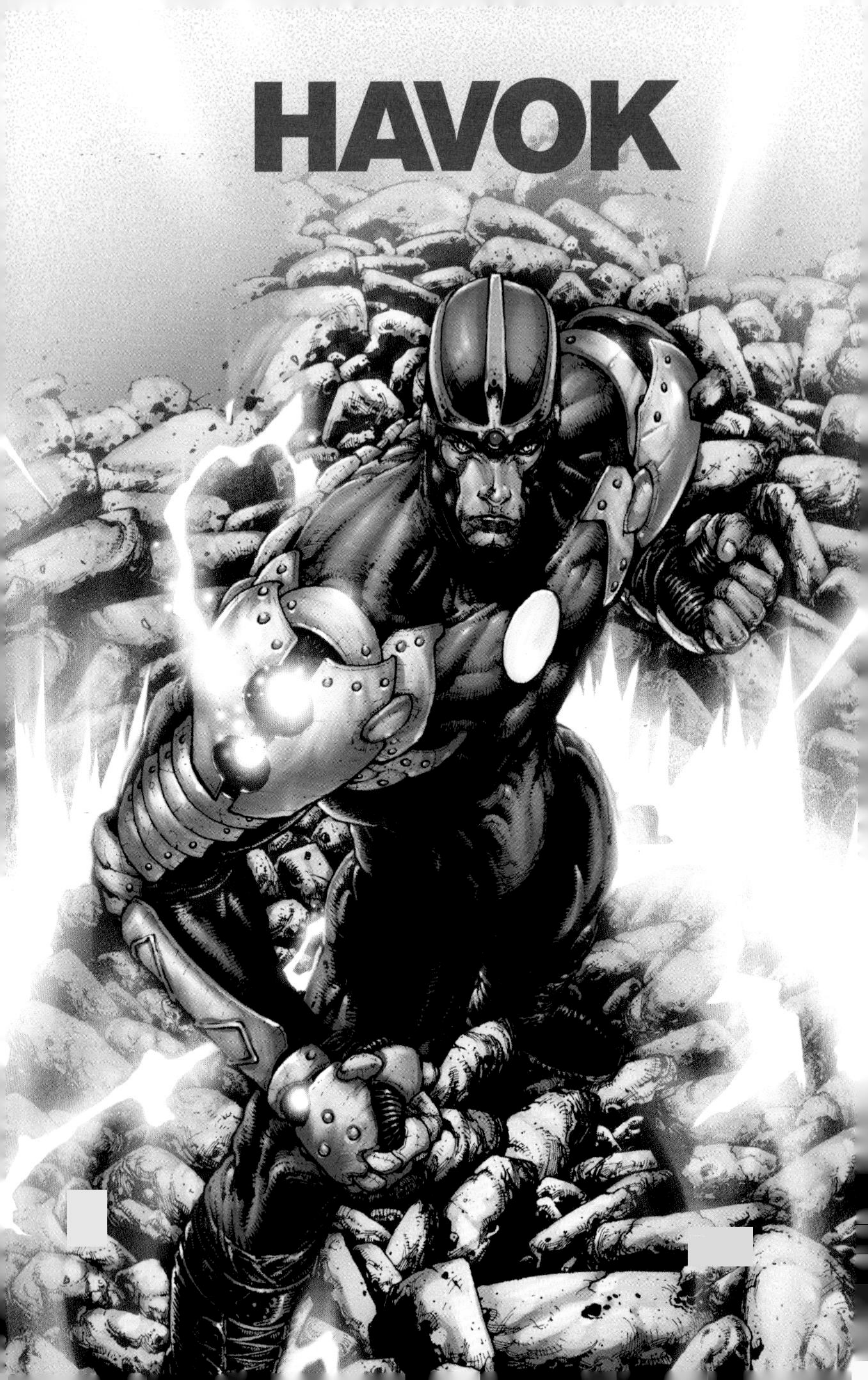
HAVOK

HAVOK

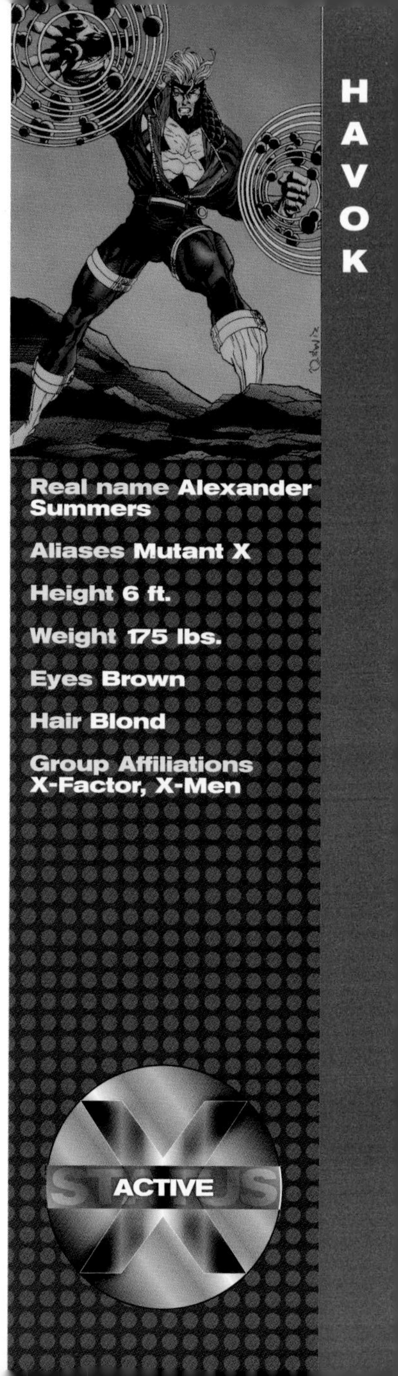

Real name Alexander Summers

Aliases Mutant X

Height 6 ft.

Weight 175 lbs.

Eyes Brown

Hair Blond

Group Affiliations X-Factor, X-Men

STATUS ACTIVE

POWERS

Absorbs energy from solar rays, processes it in his cells, then discharges it from his body in waves of plasma; plasma waves explode in all directions unless channeled by Havok along the length of his arms; focused ray of hot plasma hitting an object results in a huge rise in temperature that causes the object to disintegrate; immune to his own energy blasts as well as those of his brother, Cyclops.

SECURITY BRIEF

As children, Alex Summers and his older brother, Scott, survived an alien spaceship attack that they thought had killed their parents. The two boys were put in an orphanage and Alex was soon adopted by the Blandings family. Years later, when Scott Summers became leader of the X-Men, he sought out his younger brother and they discovered that Alex had the power to wield plasma blasts. But Alex had problems learning how to control his gift.

Alex joined the X-Men, taking the code name, Havok. While a member of the team, he fell in love with Lorna Dane, the mutant known as Polaris. Their long and difficult relationship has endured over the years.

Havok became close friends with Wolverine and had several adventures with him, including battling Meltdown. Soon afterwards, Havok fell in love with Madelyne Pryor, the ex-wife of his brother, Cyclops. Madelyne, in the guise of the Goblyn Queen, wanted to use Havok's energy powers to take over the world and convert it into a realm of demons. Havok finally realized what she was doing and abandoned Madelyne, who later on committed suicide when she discovered she was a clone of Jean Grey.

When the original X-Men left X-Factor, Havok became leader of the group. After experiencing

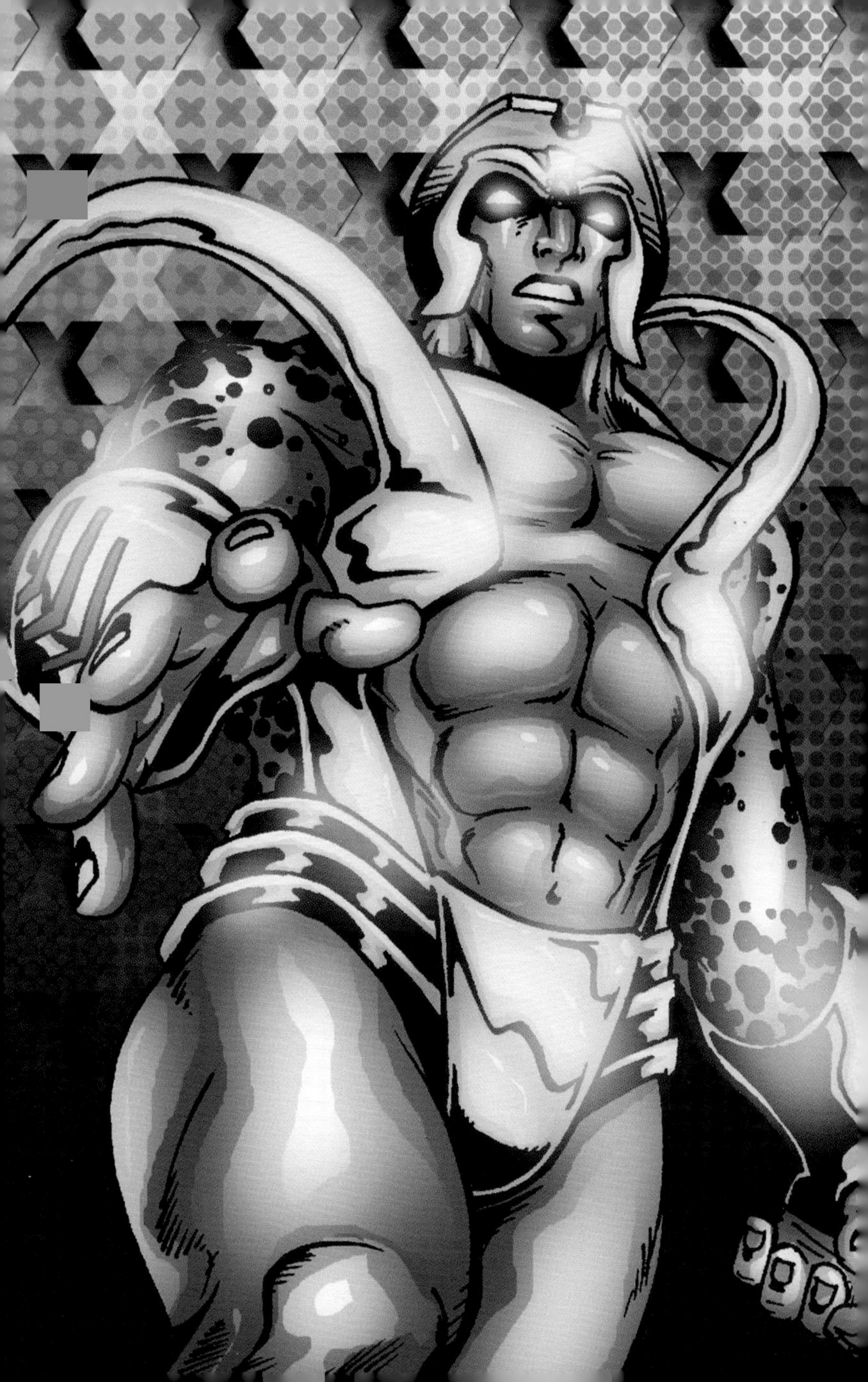

a mental breakdown caused by Dark Beast, Havok decided to work on his own. When Havok was on an airplane that exploded, his friends thought he had perished. In fact, an imperfect time machine hurtled him into an alternate reality.

In this parallel world, Havok led a group of X-Men known as The Six. Married to Madelyne Pryor, and father of a son named Scotty, Havok fought to save his new home from destruction by Captain America and the Beyonder. Havok triumphed, though most of the Six were killed and he was thrust back into normal reality in a coma.

After a long, complex recovery, Havok now leads an X-Men team consisting of Iceman, Polaris, Wolverine, Rogue, and Gambit.

SECRETS

- The Living Pharaoh used Alex's energy absorbing abilities to transform himself into the Living Monolith. When the Living Monolith was defeated by the X-Men, Alex was freed.

- Alex lost his memory traveling through the Siege Perilous, an extra-dimensional gateway that causes amnesia and physical transformations in those who pass through it. He ended up in Genosha, a country where mutants were used as slaves. During a fight with his brother, Scott, Alex regained

his memory but told no one. That enabled him to catch the evil leader of Genosha, Cameron Hodge, by surprise and kill him.

- Havok joined with Dark Beast, to form a mutant terrorist organization they called the Brotherhood. According to Havok, he was working undercover to sabotage Dark Beast's evil ambitions.

- After Havok returned to this reality, he remained in a coma for a year. During that time, Carter, the mutant son of his nurse, Annie, used his telepathic powers to cause Alex and his mother to fall in love in their dreams. When Havok awakened, the dream love affair broke up his romance with Polaris.

STATUS Active

Polaris

Left: *Living Monolith*

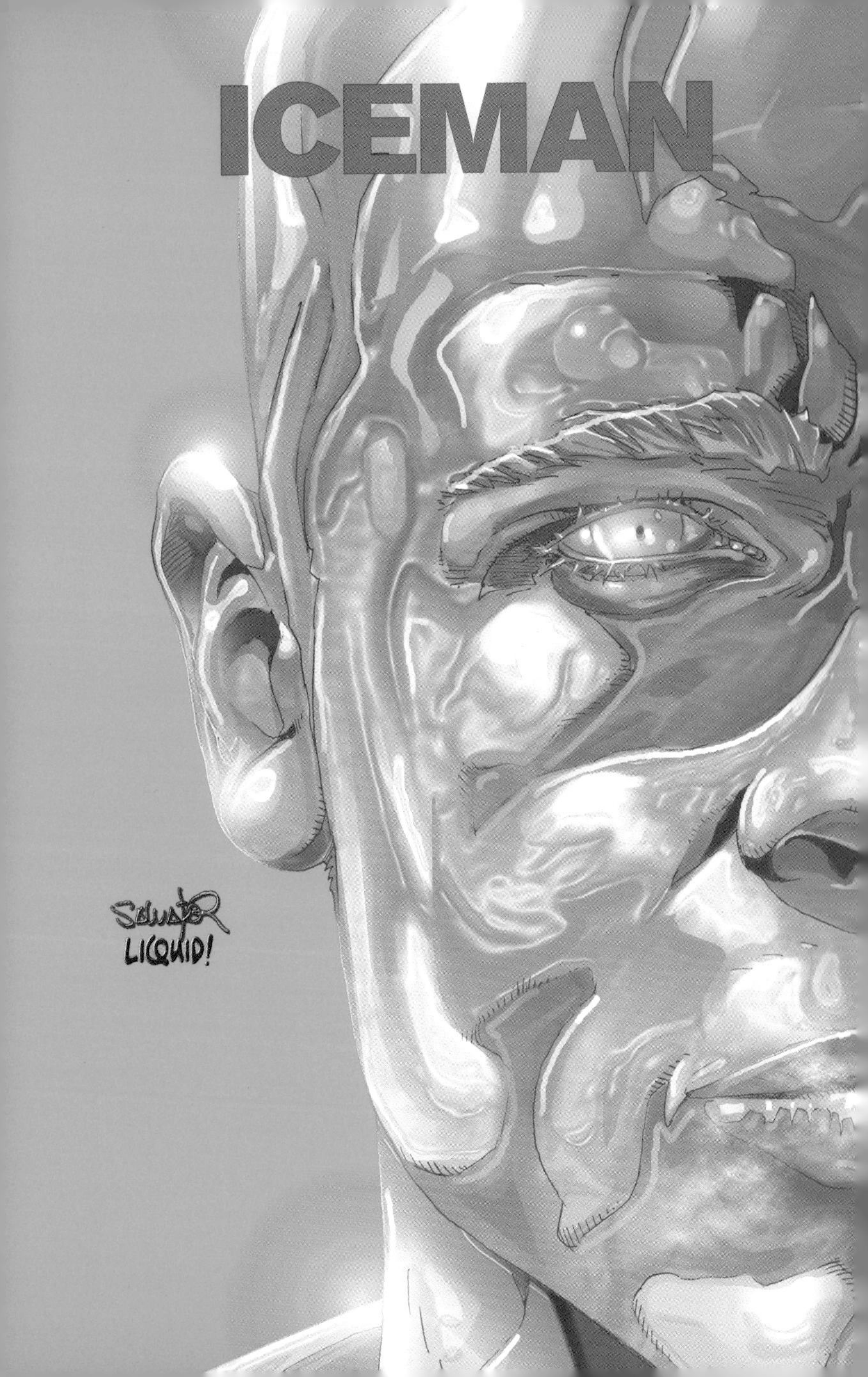
ICEMAN
LICQUID!

POWERS

Possesses the power to freeze moisture in the air and turn it into any form he desires; can form barriers and bridges of ice seemingly out of nowhere; can completely cover his body in a layer of ice but still move freely; has learned to control his body on a molecular level and transform himself into a being entirely of ice; can travel great distances through water and reform his body after turning it into vapor.

SECURITY BRIEF

Bobby Drake was the second teenager recruited by Professor X to be one of the X-Men. The youngest member of the team, he often got into trouble due to his immature antics. For a short time, Bobby was romantically involved with Lorna Dane, the young mutant who became known as Polaris. When Lorna spurned Bobby for Cyclops's brother, Alex Summers, the mutant known as Havok, Bobby angrily left the X-Men for months but he did return.

After being rescued from Krakoa, Bobby and the rest of his teammates other than Cyclops, left Professor Xavier's school. Together with Angel, Bobby formed the Champions. When that team disbanded, Bobby enrolled in college as a full-time student. Later he joined Angel and Beast as a member of the Defenders. When the Defenders parted ways, Bobby returned to normal life and started working as an accountant. Needless to say, he did not remain at that job very long. Along with the other original members of the X-Men, Iceman became part of the new mutant team, X-Factor.

When Professor Xavier returned from a long period of recuperation in outer space, Bobby Drake and the rest of the members of X-Factor rejoined the X-Men.

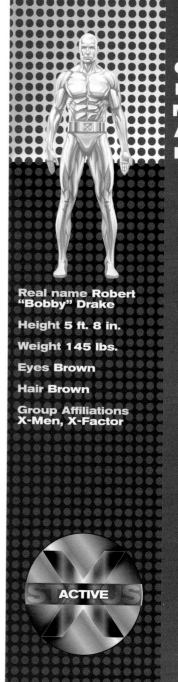

ICEMAN

Real name Robert "Bobby" Drake

Height 5 ft. 8 in.

Weight 145 lbs.

Eyes Brown

Hair Brown

Group Affiliations X-Men, X-Factor

ACTIVE

SECRETS

- When Bobby Drake first revealed his ice powers, an angry mob tried to lynch him. The local sheriff put Bobby in a jail cell for his own protection. Professor X sent Cyclops to rescue Bobby, but Bobby didn't trust him and refused to leave. The two mutants started fighting and didn't stop until they both were exhausted. That's when the mob reappeared and nearly hung them both.

- Professor Xavier erased all memories of Bobby's mutant powers from the minds of the townspeople who nearly killed him.

- The Norse God, Loki, once increased Bobby's freezing powers so much that he froze everything he touched.

- Due to a massive power surge and an unexpected problem with a Shi'ar device, Iceman and Emma Frost's minds were switched for several days. During the period when she controlled Iceman's body, Emma pushed his abilities in new and unexpected directions. Afterwards, she refused to reveal to Bobby how she used his talent, forcing him to learn the new powers on his own.

STATUS Active

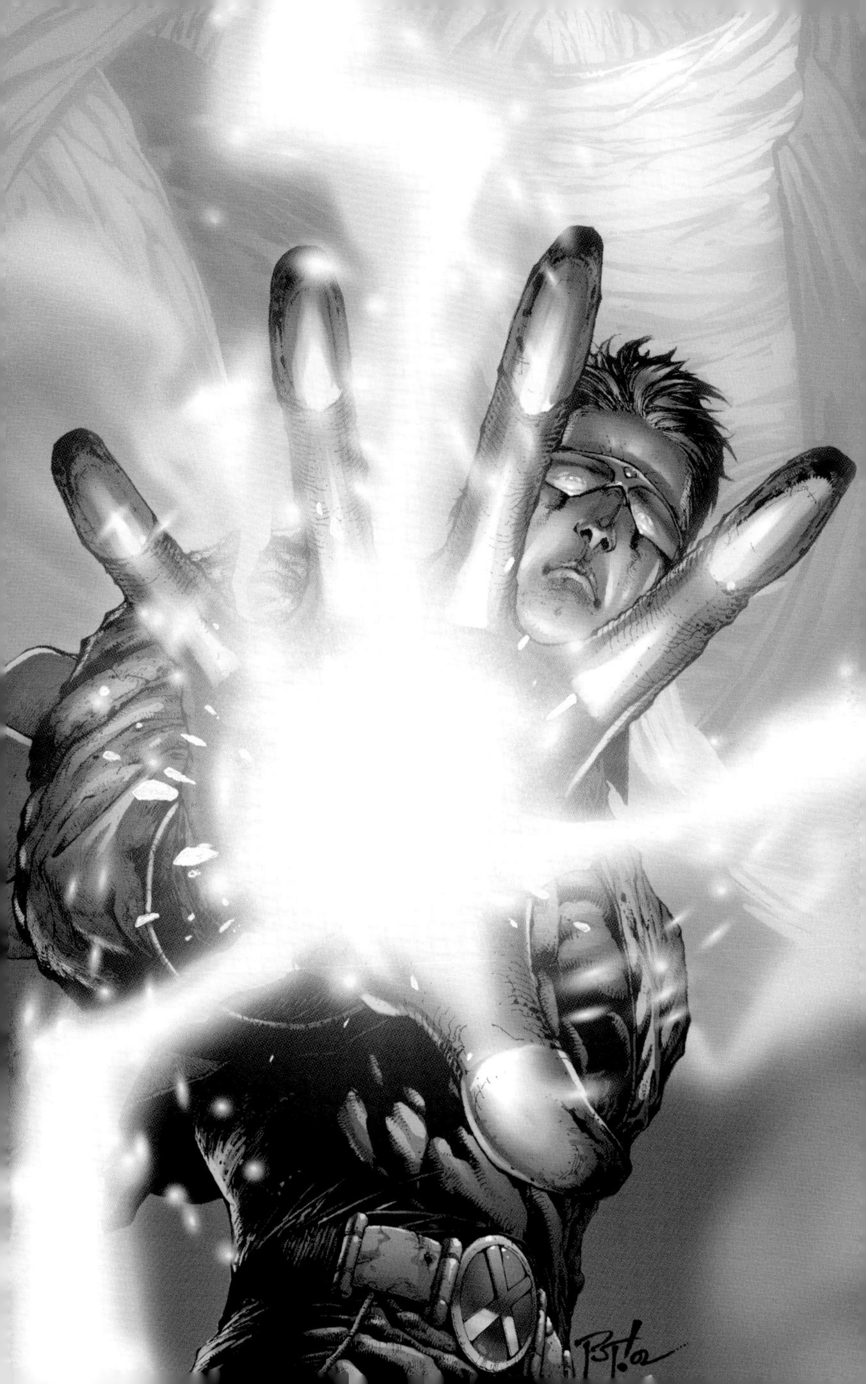

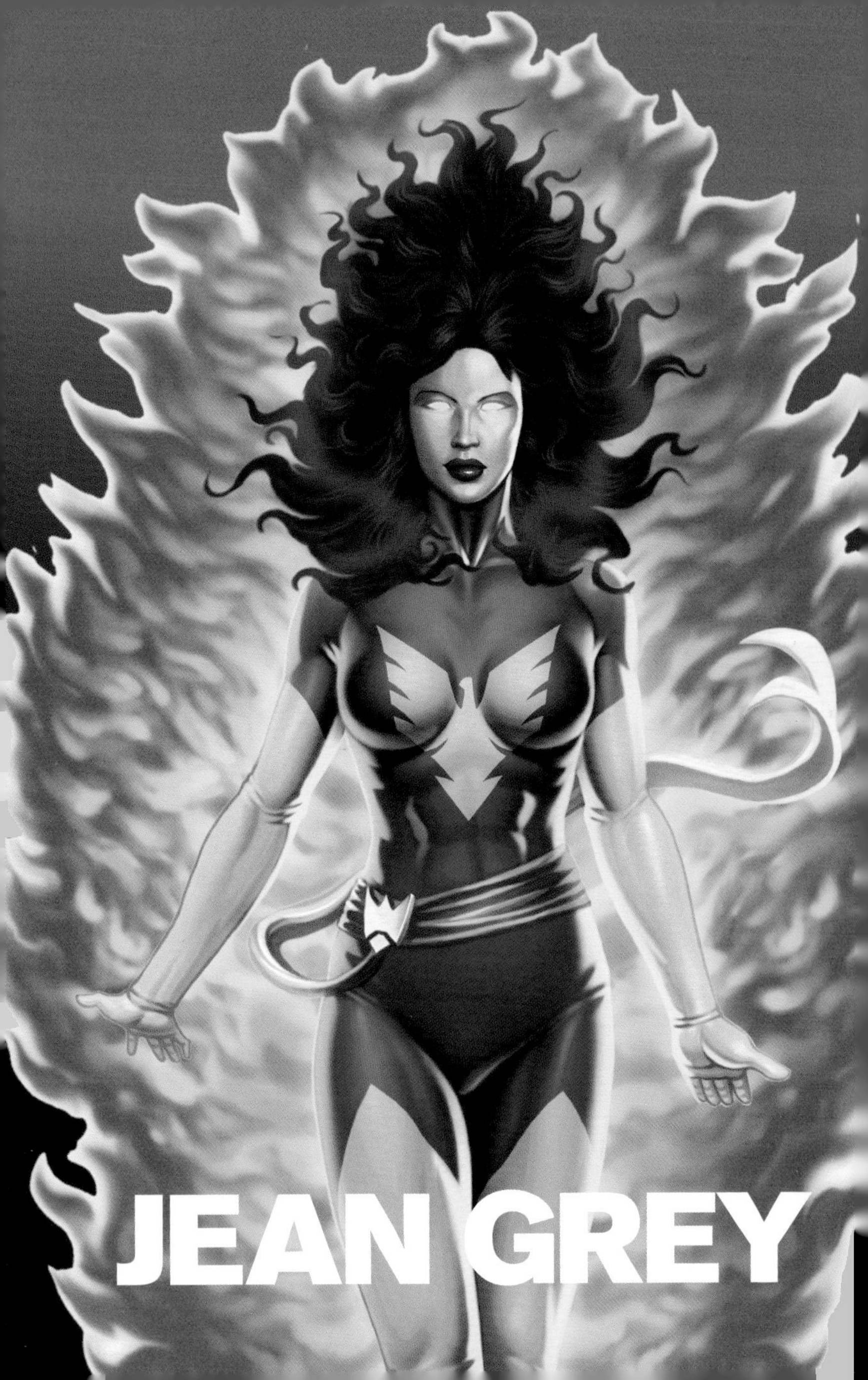
JEAN GREY

POWERS

Telekinetic abilities enable her to levitate and move people or objects; telepathic; can read minds; can project thoughts into the minds of other people and stun enemies with a telepathic mind bolt.

SECURITY BRIEF

Jean Grey's mutant telepathic powers were unleashed when she was only ten years old and witnessed her best friend being hit by a car. Without knowing what she was doing, Jean linked with the mind of her friend and thus experienced the trauma of dying. Jean went into a catatonic state from which she could not be revived for years.

Finally, Jean was discovered by Professor X. He blocked her telepathic ability so that she could learn how to use her power at a more subdued rate. Jean recovered and the Professor tutored her for years on the use of her mutant abilities. When Xavier started his secret School for Gifted Youngsters, Jean joined the X-Men, becoming the first woman to do so.

While Jean dated several of the X-Men, it was Cyclops who appealed to her the most and the two began dating. In the meantime, Jean served with the X-Men, attended college and eventually earned her degree.

When the original team was trapped by the living island, Krakoa, Professor X assembled a new team to rescue them. Afterwards, most of the first team left to pursue their own goals. Much later Jean, Wolverine, and Banshee were kidnapped by Sentinels and taken to a space station. With the help of the other X-Men, the team escaped in a space shuttle with Jean as pilot. Unshielded radiation nearly killed her. Before that could happen, unknown to anyone, a cosmic entity known as the Phoenix saved Jean, putting her in a healing cocoon beneath

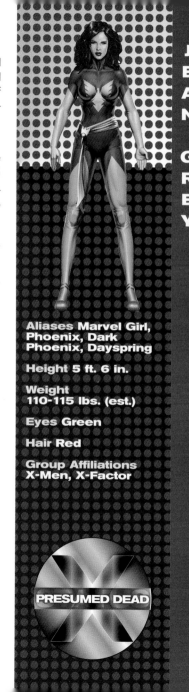

JEAN GREY

Aliases Marvel Girl, Phoenix, Dark Phoenix, Dayspring

Height 5 ft. 6 in.

Weight 110-115 lbs. (est.)

Eyes Green

Hair Red

Group Affiliations X-Men, X-Factor

PRESUMED DEAD

Jamaica Bay, and replacing her as an exact duplicate on the shuttle. The Phoenix succeeded in convincing everyone that she was the real Jean.

Because the Phoenix had a difficult time accommodating human emotions, she transformed after months into the Dark Phoenix. In this form, the cosmic being destroyed a Shi'ar spaceship, then caused the star that heated the D'Bari solar system to turn nova, killing five billion D'Bari.

The X-Men confronted the being they thought was Jean Grey on the Moon, and Phoenix committed suicide before it could do any more harm. Then, the Phoenix tried to revive Jean but was rejected by Jean's mind because of the destruction the Phoenix had caused. Instead, the Phoenix Force accidentally awakened Jean's clone, Madelyne Pryor.

The X-Men assumed Jean was dead and mourned her. Cyclops met Madelyne Pryor, a young woman with an astonishing likeness to Jean and married her. They had a son, Nathan.

Several years after Jean's death, the Avengers found a life pod buried in the mud beneath Jamaica Bay. They brought it to the Fantastic Four who opened it and found the real Jean Grey inside. It took Jean time to recover and realize exactly what happened to her. But, she did and with the other original X-Men formed a new team, X-Factor.

After the death of Madelyne Pryor, Jean and Scott Summers finally married. Jean became known as Phoenix. However, that name signaled new problems. Jean started developing the powers of the Phoenix again, and she began having marital problems with Scott.

Scott's worries about Jean drove him into the arms of Emma Frost, now one of the X-Men. Jean and Emma fought and Scott left them both. He returned just as Xorn, who was disguised as Magneto, attacked the X-Men. Attacking the iron in Jean's bloodstream, Xorn caused Jean to have a stroke. She died this time in Scott's arms.

Still, the question of whether she is really dead, merely absorbed into the Phoenix Force, or *is* the Phoenix Force remains open.

SECRETS

- Jean dated Archangel before dating Scott.
- After Jean graduated college, she worked for a while as a model. It was during this time that she met the mutant, Lorna Dane, who later became known as Polaris. Jean also met Alex Summers, Scott's younger brother, the mutant known as Havok.

STATUS Presumed Dead

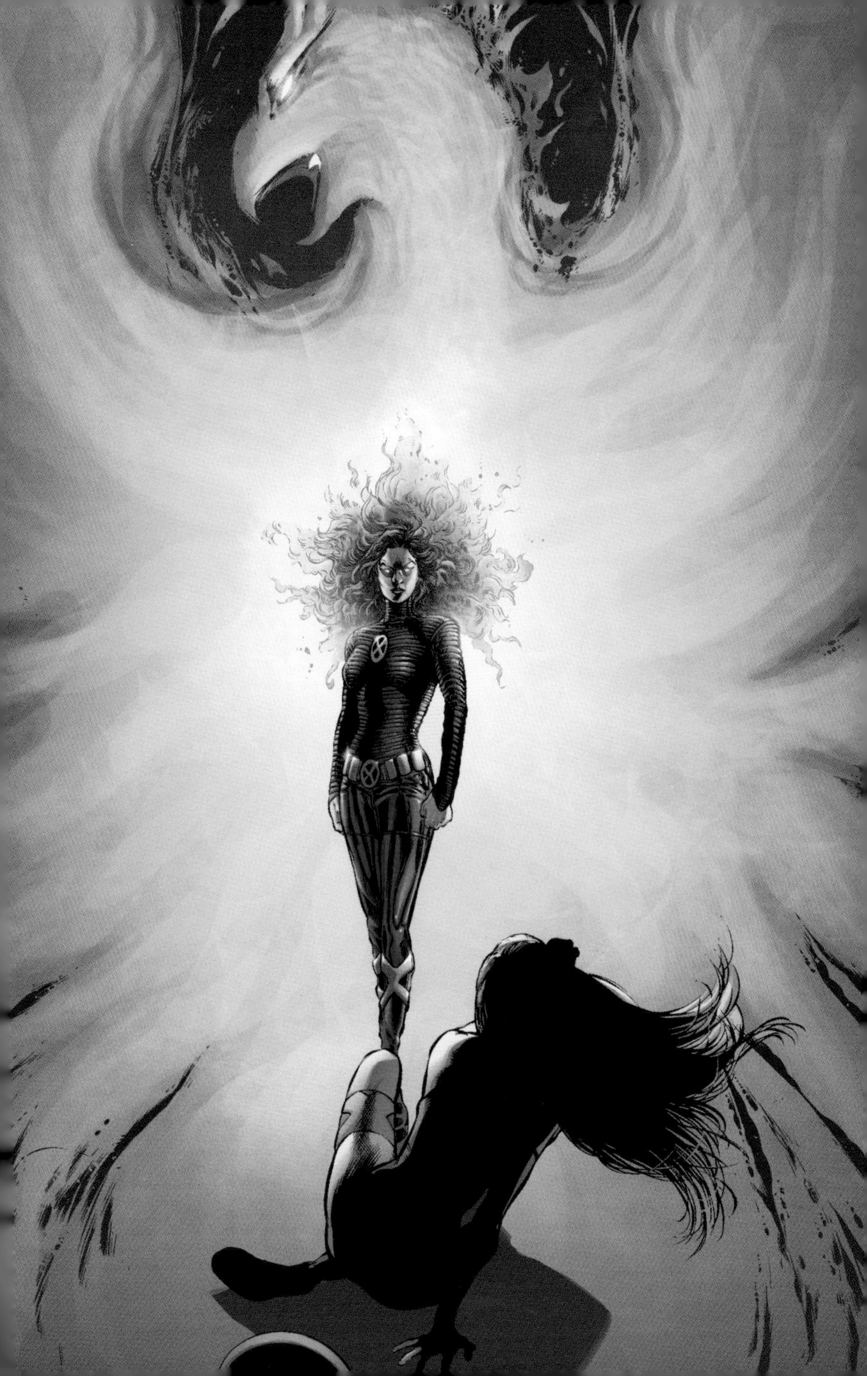

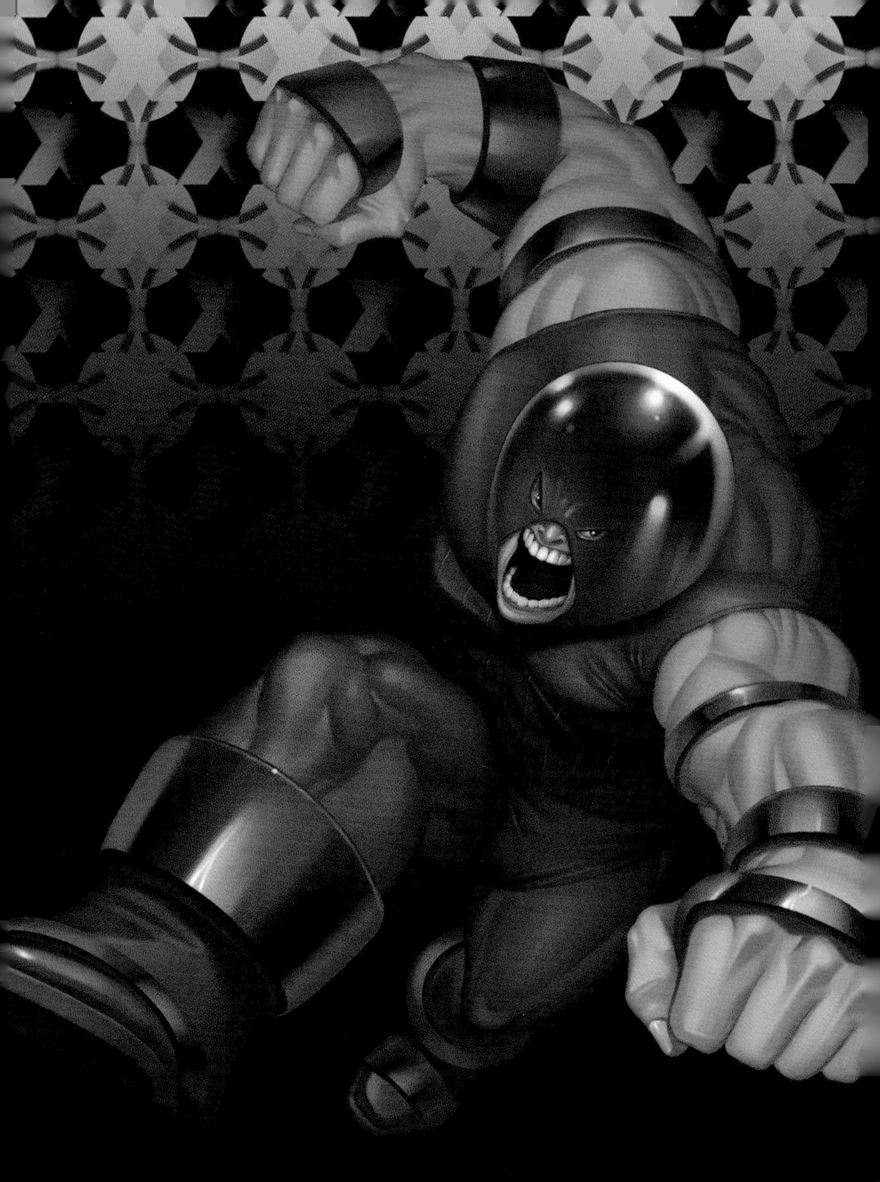

JUGGERNAUT

JUGGERNAUT

POWERS

Possesses superhuman strength, endurance, and durability owing to mystical energies absorbed during years of exposure to the Crimson Ruby of Cyttorak; upper limit of supernatural powers has yet to be measured.

SECURITY BRIEF

Cain Marko is the stepbrother of Professor X, the founder of the X-Men. Marko's father, Kurt, married Charles's mother after her first husband died. Cain was a brutal sibling and his father sent him to military school. Both he and Charles fought as soldiers in the Korean War. It was there that the two found the ancient temple of Cyttorak, and on its altar the Crimson Ruby of Cyttorak. Cain took the mystic gem and was transformed by it supernaturally into a human juggernaut.

When the temple collapsed, Charles escaped but it took Cain weeks to dig himself free. Angered at his abandonment, Cain set out to hurt his brother and anyone else who got in his way.

Under the influence of the mystical powers of the Crimson Ruby of Cyttorak, Juggernaut was nearly indestructible and virtually invulnerable to earthly forces. Plasma cannons or mountains of rock could only slow, but not stop, his advance. He could survive indefinitely without food, air, or water, and could shield himself from injury with a mentally generated force field that drew strength from his mystical energies. Even the X-Men had a difficult time keeping him from attacking their mentor.

Recently, Juggernaut was stripped of the energies that enhanced his strength and sustained his personal force field. He has since made peace with his brother and, in a startling shift of loyalties, has became one of the X-Men.

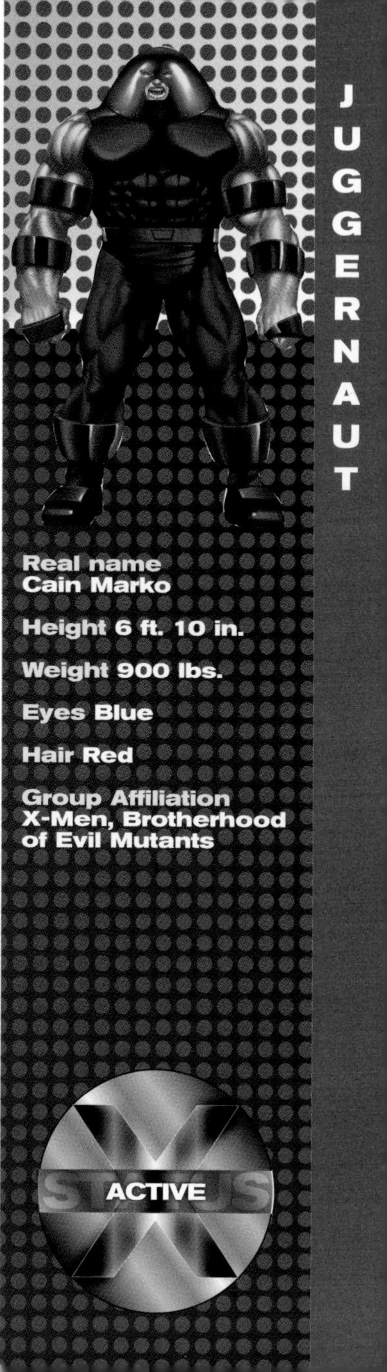

Real name
Cain Marko

Height 6 ft. 10 in.

Weight 900 lbs.

Eyes Blue

Hair Red

Group Affiliation
X-Men, Brotherhood of Evil Mutants

STATUS
ACTIVE

Black Tom Cassidy

SECRETS

- The one mutant powerful enough to hurt Juggernaut is the mysterious being known as Onslaught.

- Juggernaut served as the human avatar for the mystic being, Cyttorak. When seven other avatars, known as Examplars, built a machine to take control of mankind, only Juggernaut stood against them. He defeated the Examplars and then destroyed their device.

- For many years, Juggernaut's only friend was the mutant, Black Tom Cassidy. Then, a young boy named Sammy became friends with him and helped convince him to reform.

- Juggernaut rejoined a new Brotherhood of Mutants started by Black Tom Cassidy, but did so planning to sabotage the group. When Black Tom killed Sammy, Juggernaut went berserk and tried to kill his one-time friend.

STATUS Active

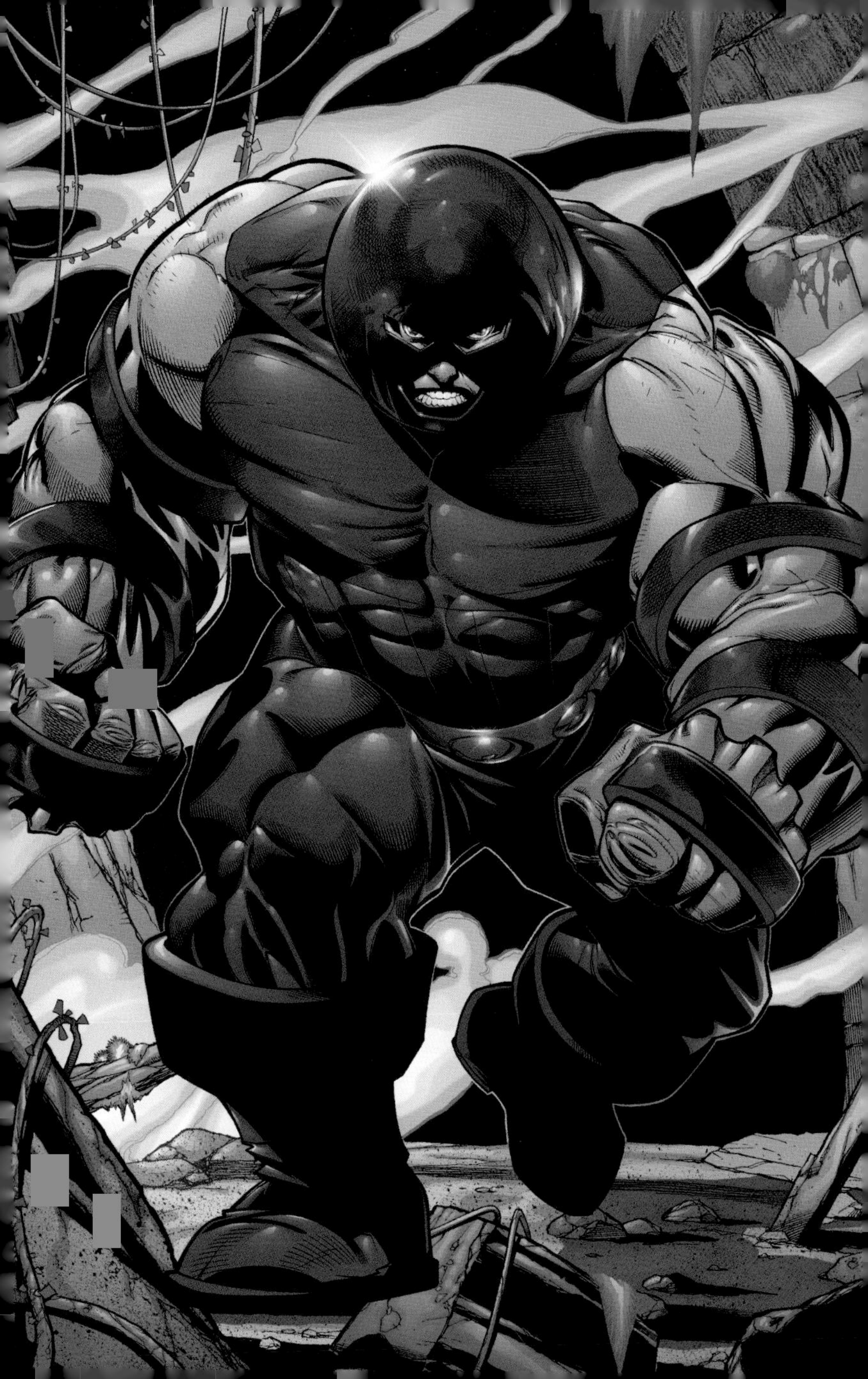

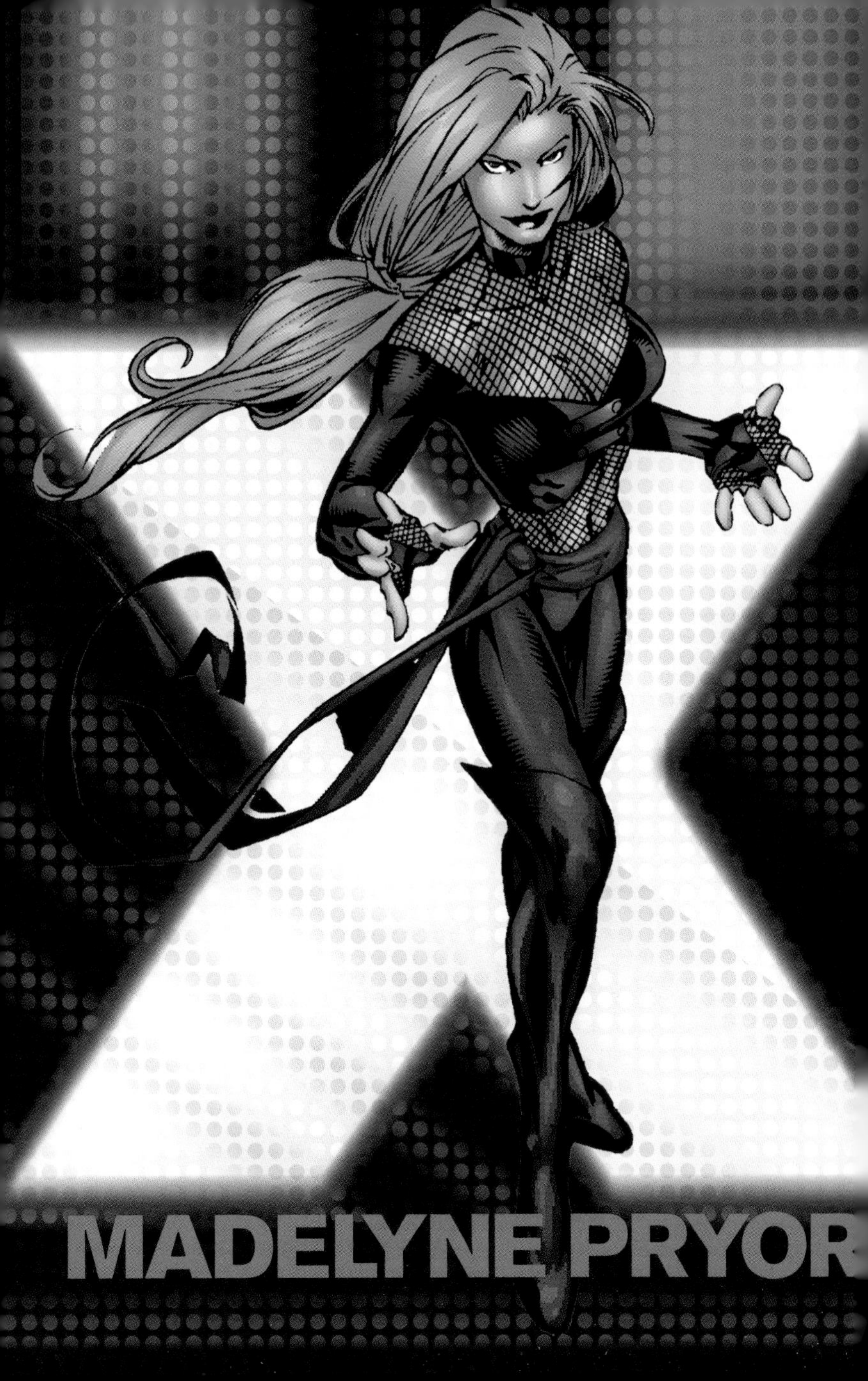
MADELYNE PRYOR

POWERS

Madelyne Pryor was a clone of Jean Grey, created by Mr. Sinister, but she did not have any mutant powers. When Madelyne became the Goblyn Queen, she gained control of a number of supernatural powers.

SECURITY BRIEF

Madelyne Pryor was a clone of Jean Grey created by the geneticist, Mr. Sinister. She was brought to life by the Phoenix Force, which had been pretending to be Jean and committed suicide on the Moon. Sinister sent Madelyne to Alaska with no memory of who she actually was. She met Scott Summers, the mutant known as Cyclops; there, they fell in love and got married. Soon afterwards, Scott retired from the X-Men.

Madelyne gave birth to a child she and Scott named Nathan Summers. All seemed to be going well until Scott discovered that Jean Grey had been found alive. Scott left Madelyne and his son to be with Jean. Soon afterwards, baby Nathan was kidnapped by mercenaries working for Mr. Sinister.

Given the chance by demonic creatures from the dimension of Limbo to get even with Scott for leaving her and Nathan, Madelyne accepted and was transformed into the Goblyn Queen.

It was one of the demons who revealed to Madelyne that she was merely a clone of Jean Grey and not a real person. Linking telepathically with Jean Grey, Madelyne killed herself, hoping that Jean would die as well. Jean survived and saved baby Nathan from the demons.

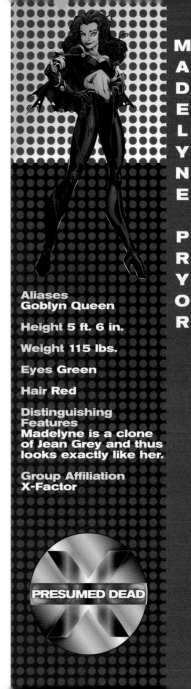

M A D E L Y N E   P R Y O R

Aliases
Goblyn Queen

Height 5 ft. 6 in.

Weight 115 lbs.

Eyes Green

Hair Red

Distinguishing Features
Madelyne is a clone of Jean Grey and thus looks exactly like her.

Group Affiliation
X-Factor

PRESUMED DEAD

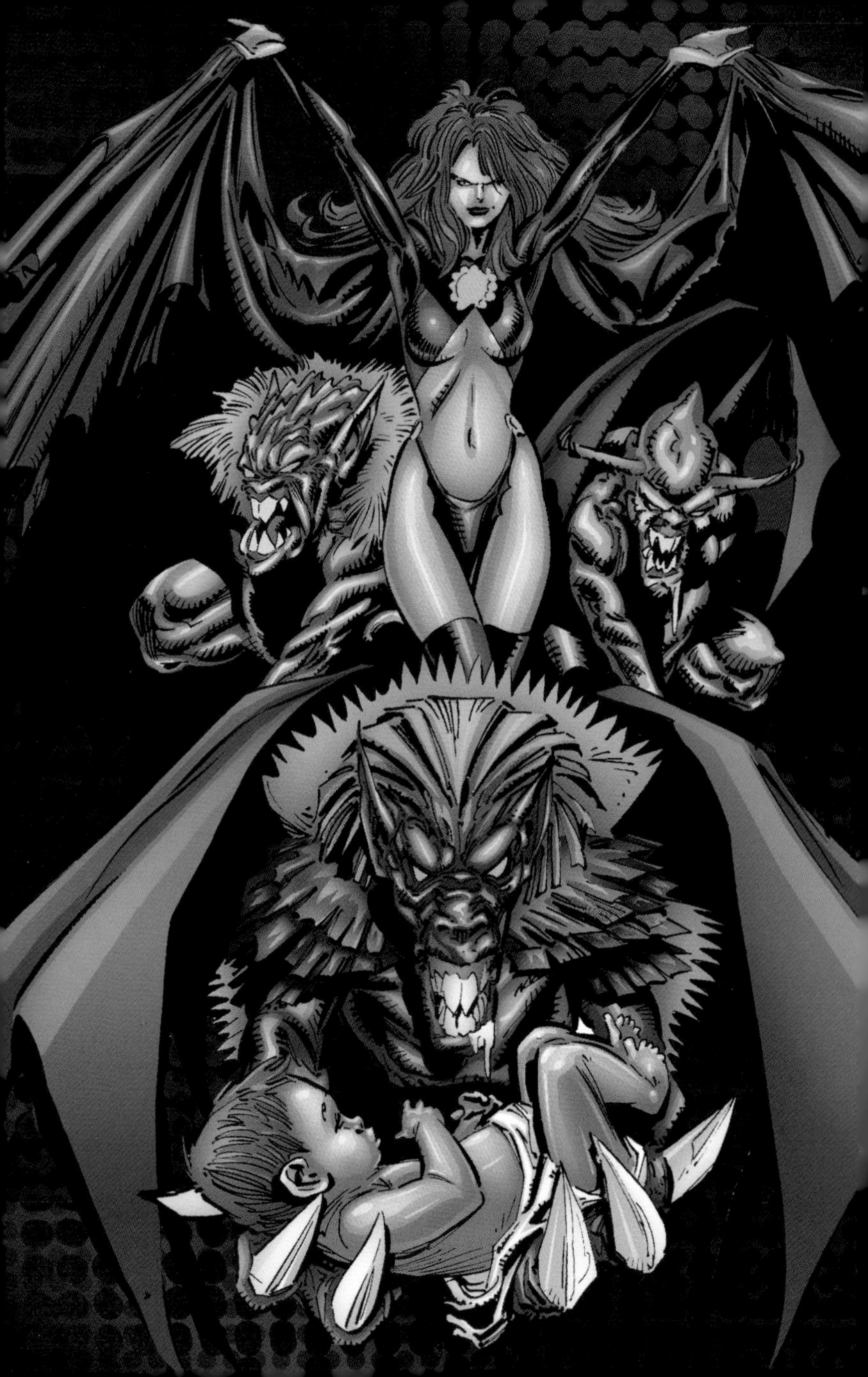

SECRETS

- Madelyne's son, Nathan, was later taken into the future where he became the freedom fighter known as Cable.
- Professor X was unable to read Madelyne's mind though she was not a mutant.
- Madelyne survived a terrible plane crash in Alaska the day the Phoenix Force committed suicide on the Moon.
- Madelyne was with the X-Men when they were supposedly killed in Dallas and were resurrected in Australia.

STATUS Presumed Dead

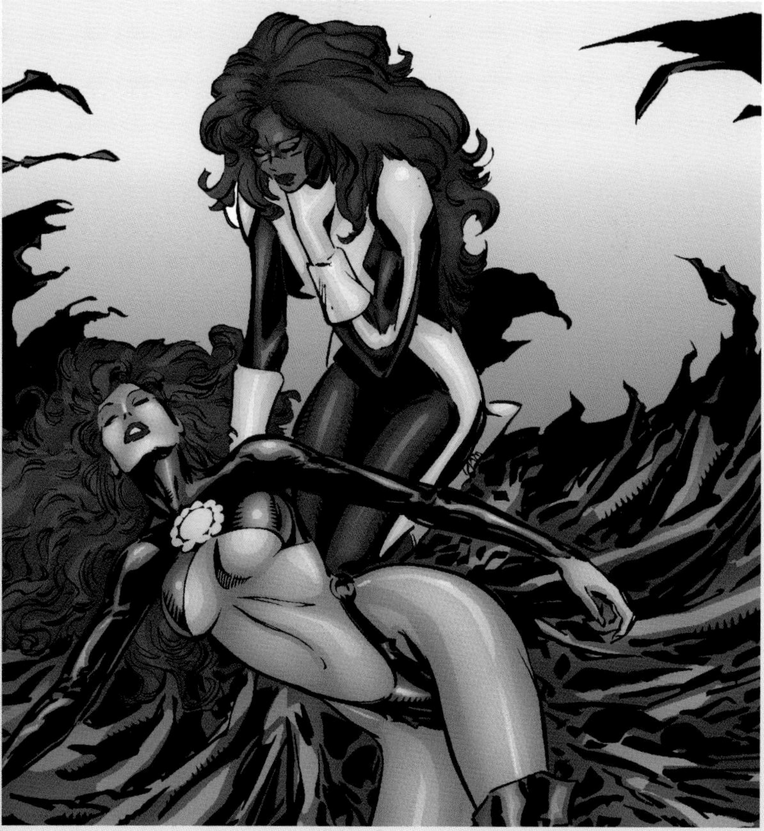

Goblyn Queen with Jean Grey

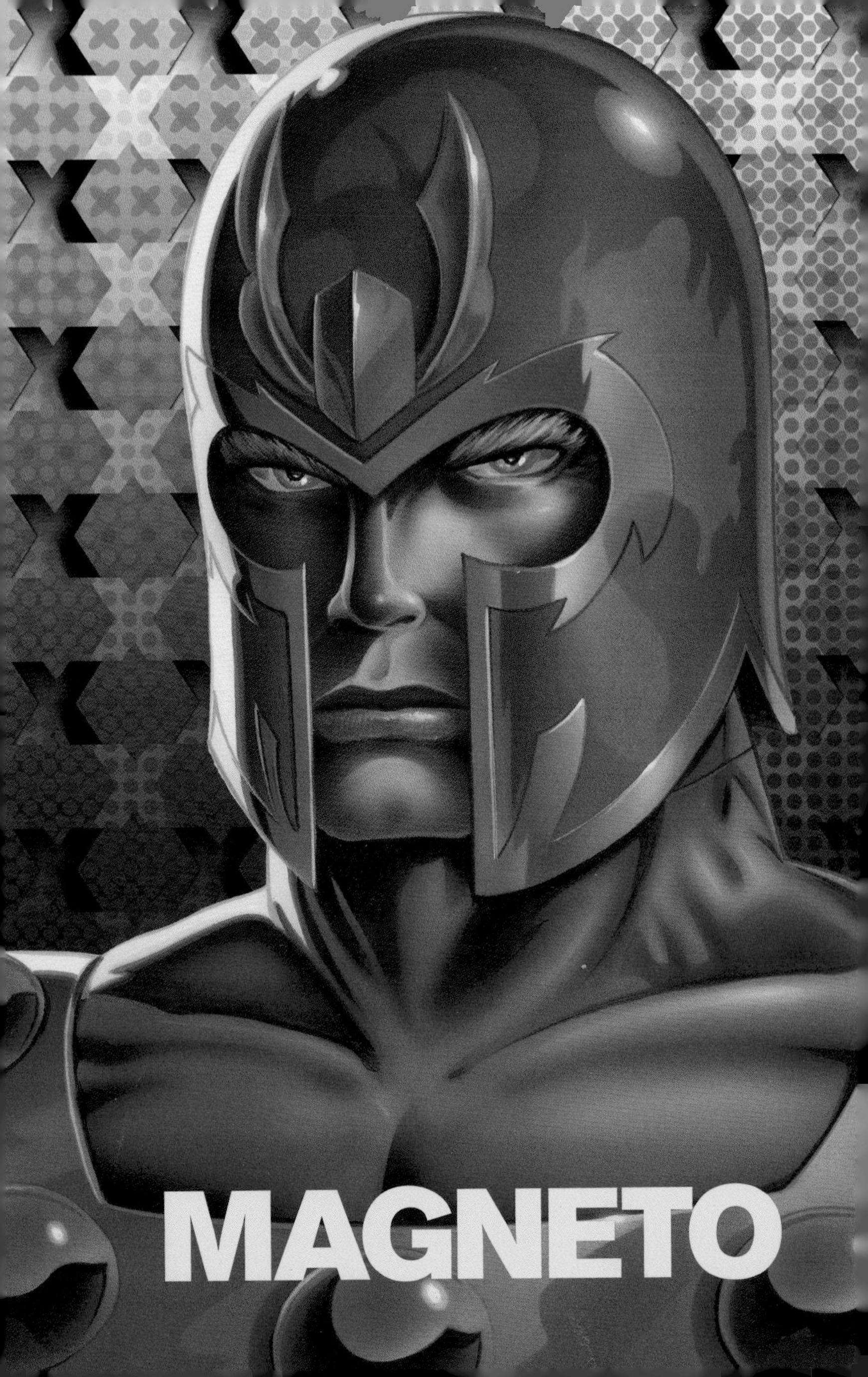
MAGNETO

POWERS

Able to manipulate magnetic fields that exist naturally or artificially; can possibly generate his own magnetic fields as a result of prodigious psionic powers; can project or manipulate any and all energies that are part of the electromagnetic spectrum including visible light, radio waves, gamma rays, and forms of ionizing radiation; has shown evidence of being able to manipulate different types of electromagnetic energy simultaneously for different purposes; can create anti-gravity fields that allow him to levitate and move non-magnetic objects; able to generate virtually impenetrable magnetic force field for self-protection; has mastered astral projection, telepathy, and possibly mind control; ability to manipulate and apply electromagnetic and other energies is directly proportional to his state of physical well-being (injury or exhaustion weaken his powers); has superior intelligence; is an expert at genetics and cloning who is able to mutate humans in order to endow them with superhuman powers; is a brilliant engineer who has designed advanced spaceships, robots, and complex computers.

SECURITY BRIEF

As a child, before his mutant powers were fully functional, Magneto and his family were imprisoned in the Auschwitz concentration camp because they were Jews. Magneto alone survived. After the war he married a gypsy, Magda, a fellow survivor. They had a daughter, Anya.

When a fire swept Magneto's home, he saved his and Magda's lives by using his mutant powers, but an angry crowd prevented him from rescuing his daughter. Magneto attacked the crowd in revenge, and ultimately came to the realization that normal people would never accept mutants among them.

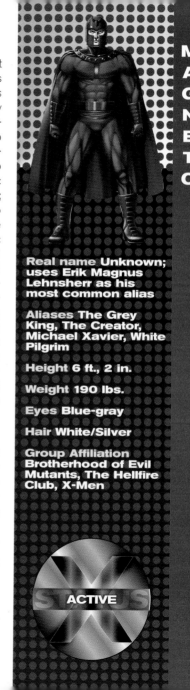

MAGNETO

Real name Unknown; uses Erik Magnus Lehnsherr as his most common alias

Aliases The Grey King, The Creator, Michael Xavier, White Pilgrim

Height 6 ft., 2 in.

Weight 190 lbs.

Eyes Blue-gray

Hair White/Silver

Group Affiliation Brotherhood of Evil Mutants, The Hellfire Club, X-Men

ACTIVE

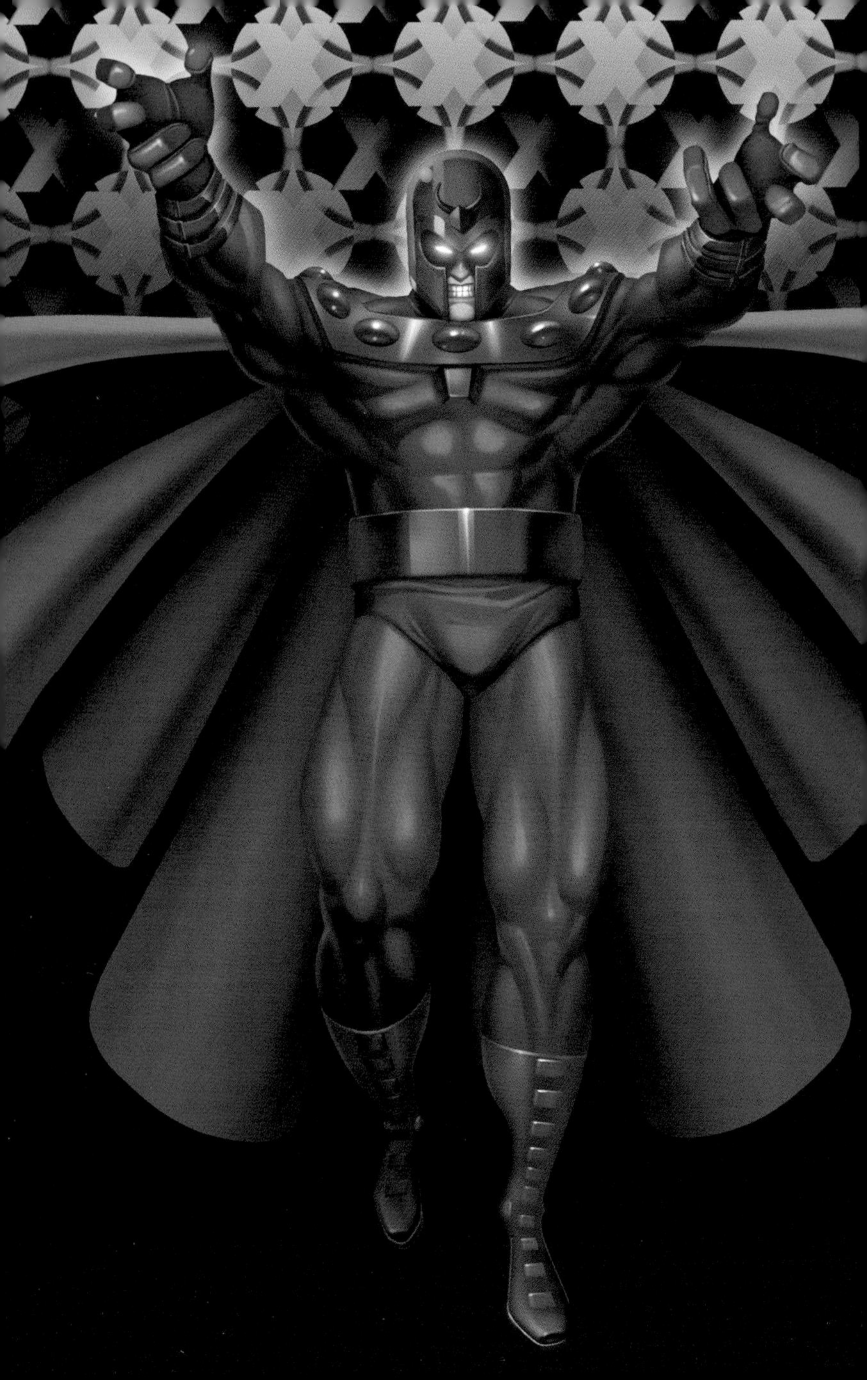

Magda fled and later discovered that she was pregnant with twins. She died giving birth to Quicksilver and the Scarlet Witch, two mutants who were raised by gypsies. Magneto and the twins did not learn of their relationship until many years later.

Magneto worked in a hospital in Israel for some time, where he met and became friends with Charles Xavier. The two men both worried how mutants would survive in the future. Professor X felt that they needed to coexist with mankind; Magneto believed that the only way mutants would be safe was by ruling mankind.

Afterwards, the two men pursued their separate visions. Xavier started the X-Men, while Magneto founded the Brotherhood of Evil Mutants. Magneto proved to be a cunning and capable leader, a man with boundless ambition and determination. After years of trying to conquer the world, he decided, instead, that a safe haven for mutants would be enough. At first, he envisioned a giant asteroid in outer space where mutants could live without fear of anyone on Earth. When that plan proved impractical, he came up with the idea of a separate country for mutants, a refuge similar to what Israel had provided for the Jews after World War II. Magneto selected the island of Genosha, off the African coast, for this safe haven. After blackmailing the United Nations with huge magnetic disruptions, the organization agreed to his demands. Genosha has been used ever since as a mutant haven.

SECRETS

- While searching for his wife, Magneto realized his name was known to his enemies. He quickly paid a forger to create a new identity for him, that of Erik Magnus Lehnsherr. No one knows Magneto's true name.

- Magneto created a large base of operations inside an asteroid he called Asteroid M. He lived there for several years while conducting missions on Earth.

- Magneto joined with Professor X and the X-Men when a group of heroes and villains were abducted by an alien being, the Beyonder, to a far planet to participate in the Secret Wars.

STATUS Active

Magneto

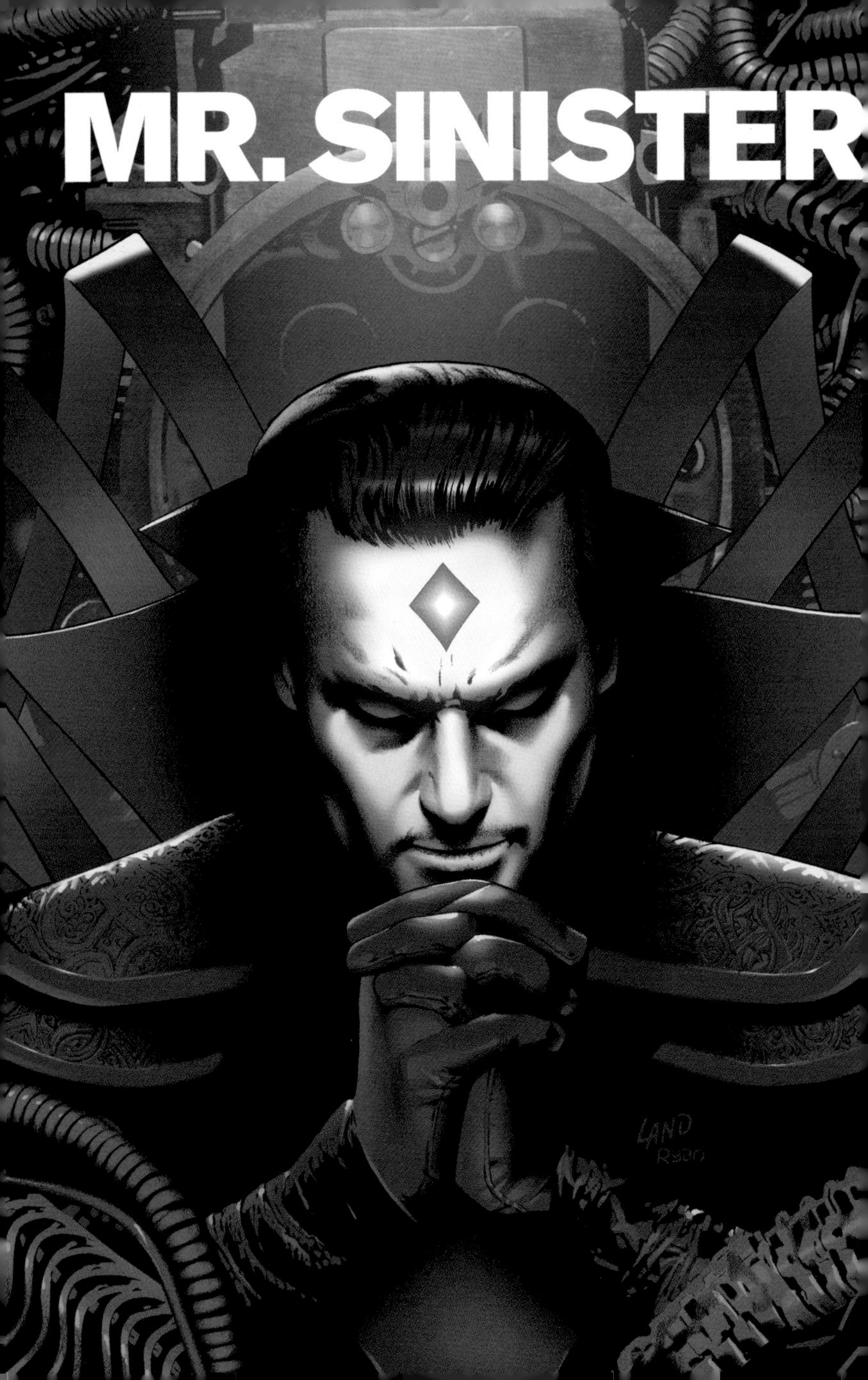
MR. SINISTER

POWERS

Has control over every molecule in his body; is difficult to injure and has incredible regenerative powers—he once had a large hole shot in his head and was badly injured a number of times, but in all cases survived and afterwards showed no signs of any wound; is extremely strong, which may also be a result of his shapeshifting power; has demonstrated minor telepathic and telekinetic skills and is able to fire concussive plasma blasts from his hands; is a brilliant geneticist and surgeon.

SECURITY BRIEF

Dr. Nathaniel Essex was a 19th-century scientist in England who was obsessed with mutations, which were caused by "Essex Factors" in the human genetic code. His theories were ridiculed, and this contributed to his cold and bitter personality. Essex performed experiments on ordinary people, all of whom were kidnapped by a hired band of thugs, the Marauders. He even performed experiments on the body of his son, who died at age four.

Entirely by accident, the Marauders awakened Apocalypse, an ancient mutant in suspended animation. When Essex explained the science of evolution to Apocalypse, the two formed an uneasy partnership. Apocalypse made Essex immortal and awakened a number of mutant powers in his body. Essex, now calling himself Mr. Sinister, agreed to help Apocalypse conquer the world.

When Apocalypse ordered Sinister to create a plague that would wipe out all the weak of the earth, Sinister did create the plague, but its only victim was Apocalypse, who lapsed back into suspended animation following exposure to it.

Near the end of the 19th-century, Sinister moved from England to the United States. It

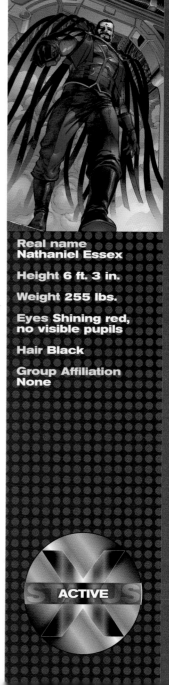

Real name Nathaniel Essex

Height 6 ft. 3 in.

Weight 255 lbs.

Eyes Shining red, no visible pupils

Hair Black

Group Affiliation None

ACTIVE

was here that he conducted numerous experiments in genetics and mutation, influencing the work of many other scientists interested in the same subject.

Sinister tracked the genetic lines of certain families over the course of a century, trying to create mutants with incredible powers. It was through his efforts that Scott Summers, better known as the mutant Cyclops, married Madelyne Pryor, a clone of Jean Grey, whose son grew up to be the mutant named Cable. Sinister also interfered with the life of the mutant Gambit, helping him control his powers, but at a high price.

It was Sinister who sent his new band of Marauders to wipe out the band of mutants who lived in tunnels beneath New York City and called themselves the Morlocks. This was known as the Mutant Massacre.

When Jean Grey and Cable destroyed Apocalypse, they set Sinister free from his bargain with the ancient mutant and his plans to conquer the world. No longer needing to worry that Apocalypse might be searching for him, Sinister can do what he wants as far as genetic research and experimenting with mutants. He is completely self-interested and amoral.

SECRETS

• Essex named himself Sinister after the last word his dying wife used to describe his experiments.

• Sinister relies on a group of mutant Marauders to perform criminal work. He keeps DNA records of these agents so that whenever one is killed, he can create a clone to replace him.

• During World War II, Mr. Sinister worked with the Nazis. They called him "Nosferatu," after the famous vampire, because of his pale skin and his habit of taking blood samples from everyone he met.

STATUS Active

Morlocks Group

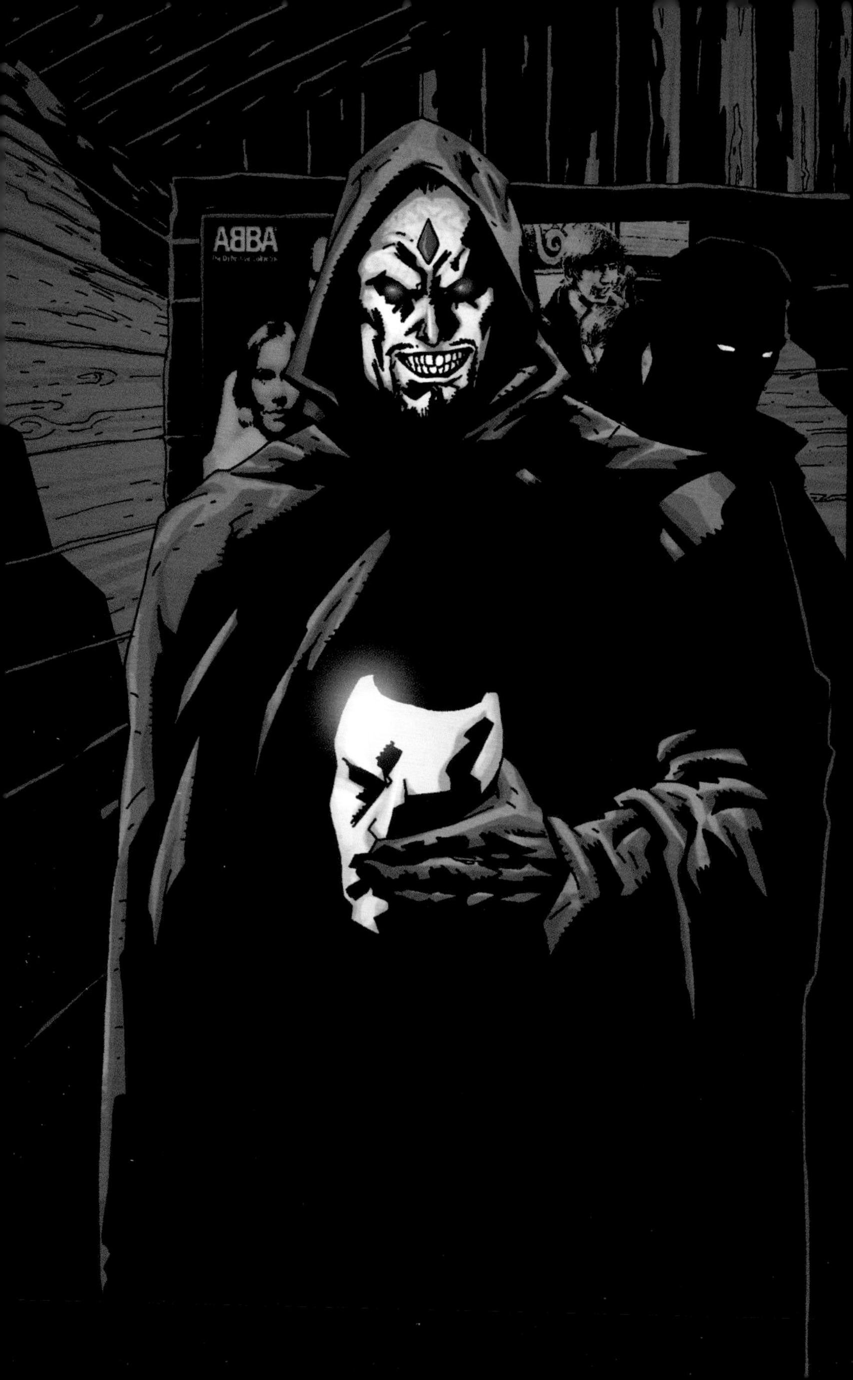
ABBA

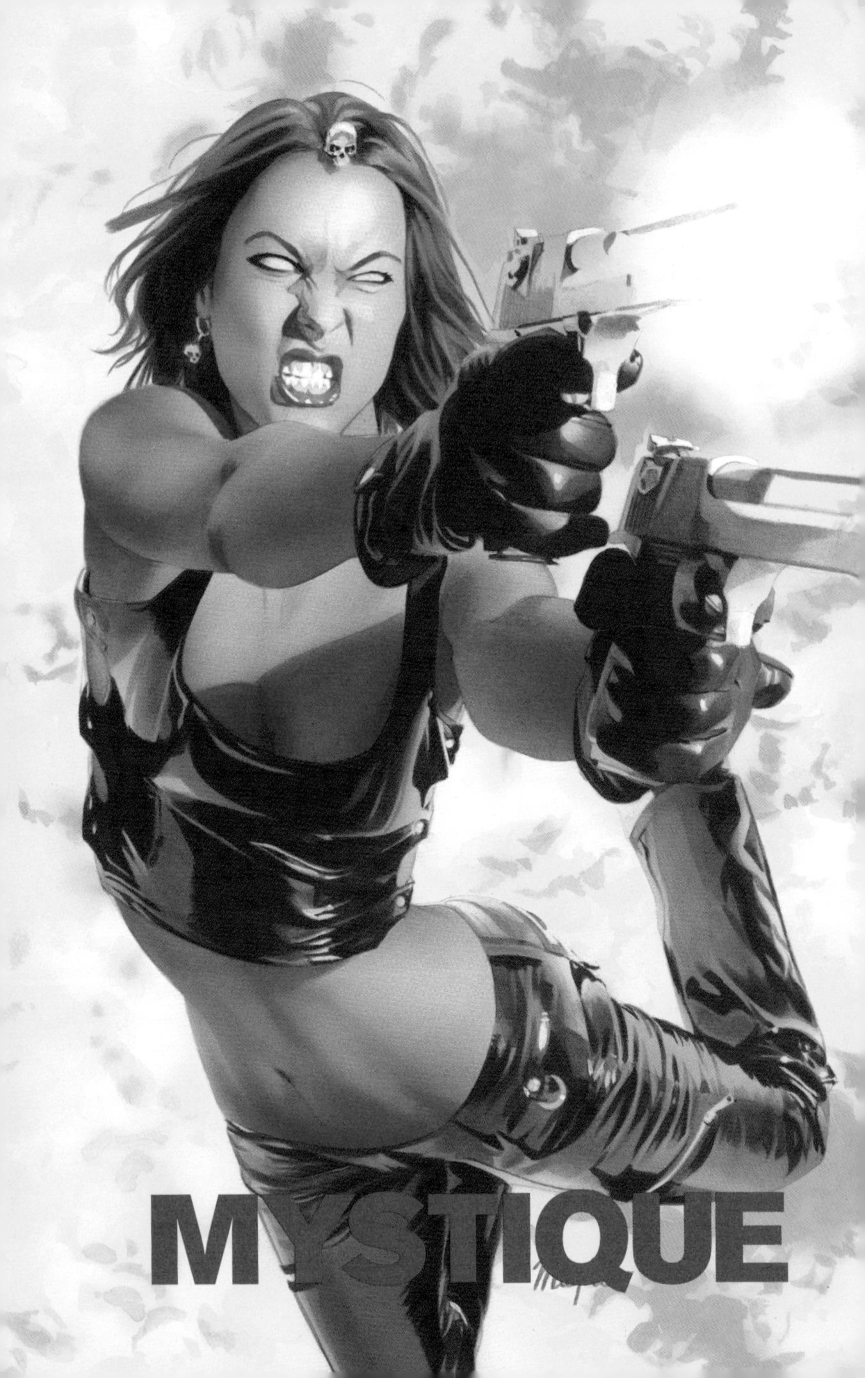
MYSTIQUE

POWERS

Can shift shape and change her appearance at will, although the duplication is only superficial—cannot assume powers of any mutant she replicates; as a result of recent radiation exposure has undergone a complex mutation that allows her to add wings, grow body armor, boost natural night vision, extend talons from fingers, and adopt other physical modifications; heals at a faster rate than humans; is immune to most poisons.

SECURITY BRIEF

The known history of Raven Darkhölme, the mutant who goes by the code name Mystique, is as enigmatic and ambiguous as might be expected for a shapeshifter able to change physical features and identities at will. She was alive as far back as the 19th century. At the turn of the 20th century she assisted the mutant Destiny in the deciphering of her prophetic diaries and with her attempted to prevent the worst of their predictions from coming true. In the guise of German spy Leni Zauber, she met and befriended the mutant known as Sabretooth, with whom she had a non-mutant child, Graydon Creed. Later, she gave birth as well to mutant Kurt Wagner, a.k.a. Nightcrawler, whom she has twice tried to kill.

Mystique's ability to deceive and beguile through physical transformation has allowed her to infiltrate unusually powerful public offices. She was working in the Department of Defense as Assistant Secretary of Defense Research Planning Agency when she encountered the mutant Rogue, whom she adopted and raised as her own child. She enlisted Rogue in her own version of the Brotherhood of Evil Mutants, which made its first strike at the botched assassination attempt on Robert Kelly during his now infamous anti-mutant speech

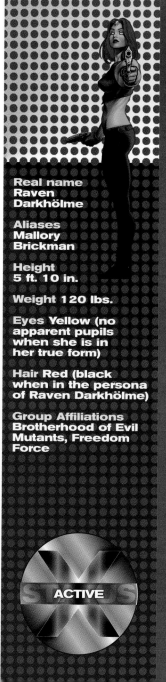

MYSTIQUE

Real name
Raven Darkhölme

Aliases
Mallory Brickman

Height
5 ft. 10 in.

Weight 120 lbs.

Eyes Yellow (no apparent pupils when she is in her true form)

Hair Red (black when in the persona of Raven Darkhölme)

Group Affiliations
Brotherhood of Evil Mutants, Freedom Force

ACTIVE

on the floor of the U.S. Senate. Only Mystique and Rogue escaped, and eventually Rogue defected to seek help with her mutant absorption powers from Professor X.

With anti-mutant sentiments intensifying around the world, Mystique made a novel proposal to the United States government: in exchange for conditional pardons and amnesty, members of her Brotherhood would serve as Freedom Force, a team tasked with policing and apprehending mutants. Various troubles after the disbanding of Freedom Force resulted in Mystique being captured by Homeland Security. She was saved from execution by Professor X, who offered her a mission too sensitive for the X-Men to undertake. Later, she participated in an assassination plot against Professor X.

Mystique is the ultimate double agent. In her many guises, she has worked with the X-Men and against them, has cooperated with Professor X only to betray him, has waylaid mutants whom she has befriended, and has denied her own progeny. Self-interest and survival are her prime motivations.

SECRETS

- Mystique's non-mutant son, Graydon Creed, became the presidential candidate of the Anti-Mutant political party.
- On a trip to Europe, Mystique took the form of a blonde-haired woman for a day at the beach. A famous fashion photographer came up to her and told her he wanted to make her the next big fashion model. Mystique accepted his offer and shortly became a top model in New York.
- Recently, Mystique applied for membership in the X-Men. After confrontations with Rogue and Nightcrawler, she decided it wasn't a good idea and left before a vote could be taken. She never learned that the group had decided to award her a probationary membership, dependent on her future behavior.

STATUS Active

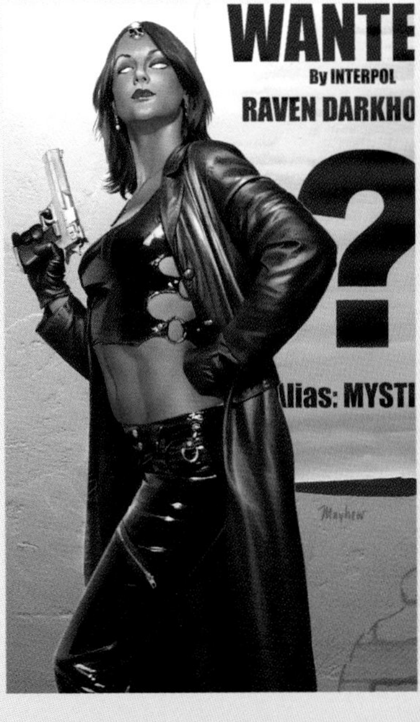
WANTE
By INTERPOL
RAVEN DARKHO
?
lias: MYSTI
Mayhew

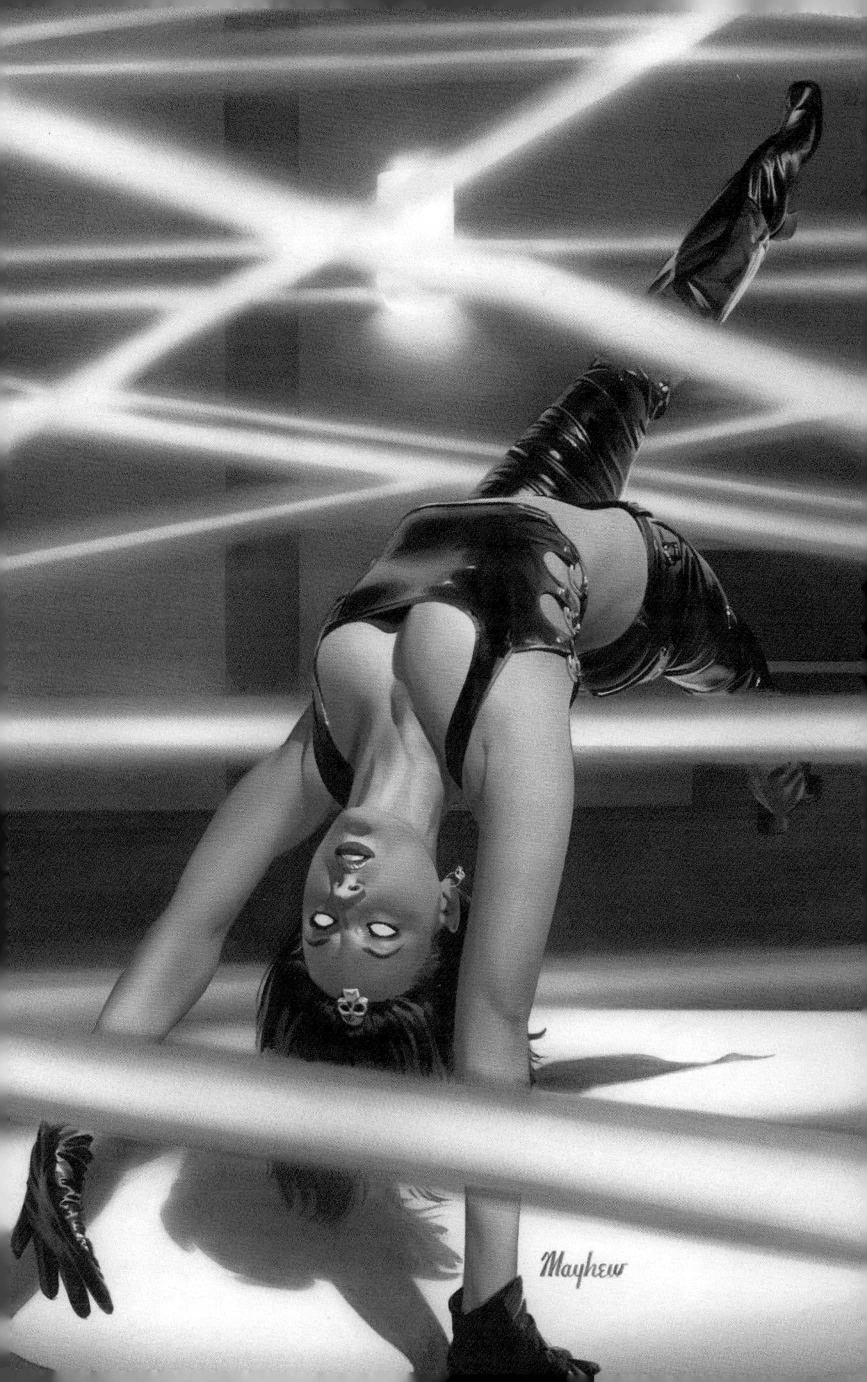
Mayhew

NIGHTCRAWLER

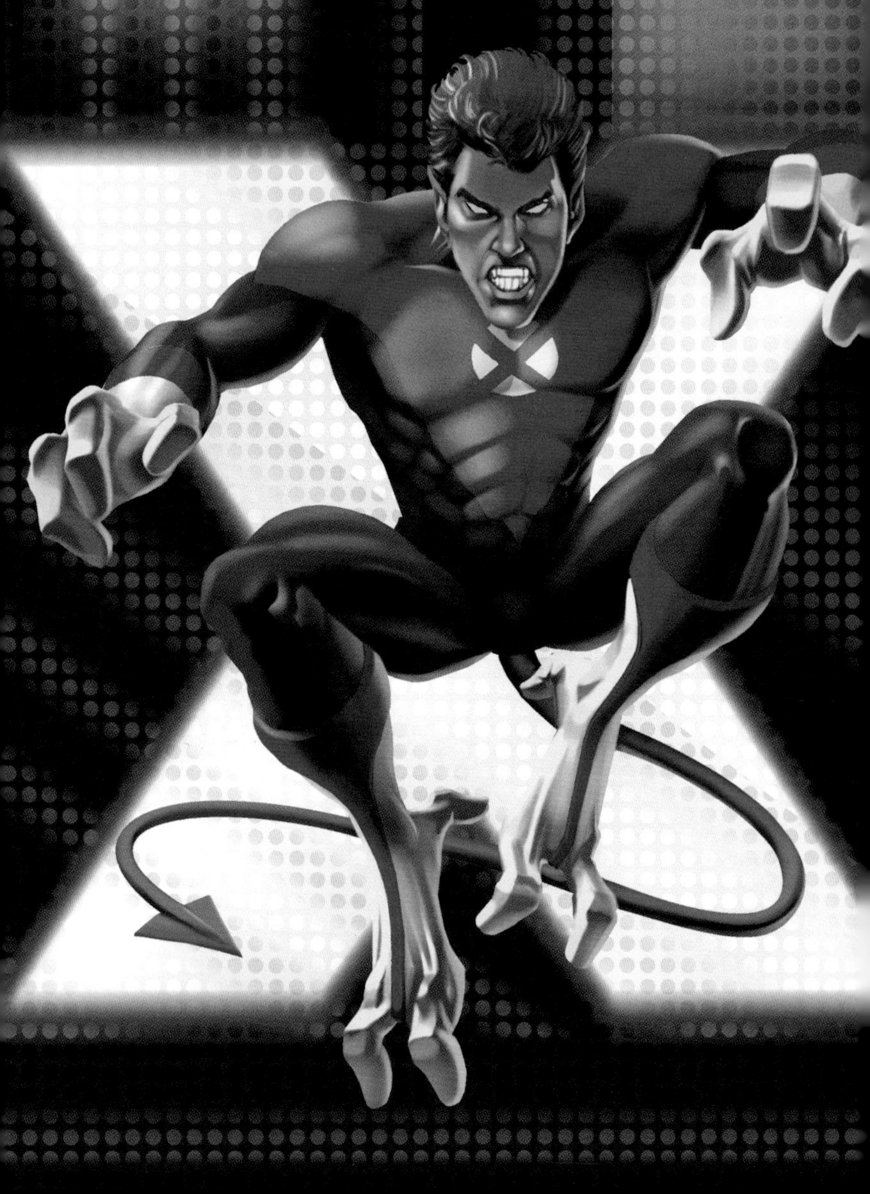

POWERS

Able to teleport from one location to any nearby location he has seen before; has an awareness of space so he does not reappear in solid objects; possesses incredible athletic abilities, amazing reflexes, and superhuman agility.

SECURITY BRIEF

Born in Germany, Kurt Wagner was the son of the mutant rebel, Mystique, and Azazel, a mutant demon. Abandoned by his real parents, Kurt was raised by gypsies. As a teenager, Kurt worked in a circus in Munich until Professor X rescued him from an angry mob and recruited him as one of the X-Men.

As a member of the X-Men, Kurt became close friends with fellow mutant, Wolverine. He also became the team joker, a role enhanced by his ability to teleport from place to place in the blink of an eye. It was during this period that Kurt became romantically involved with the sorceress, Amanda Sefton (a.k.a. Jimaine), who was in reality his foster sister.

Kurt was badly hurt in a fight with the mutant group, the Marauders. While he and Shadowcat were recovering at Professor X's school, the rest of the X-Men supposedly died on a mission to Dallas. Alone, the two mutants joined with a group of heroes in Britain to form Excalibur. Over a period of months, Kurt gradually became leader of the group. Excalibur broke up after a number of adventures when two of the team members married and Shadowcat and Kurt learned that the X-Men were still alive.

At present, Kurt Wagner is a member of the Uncanny X-Men.

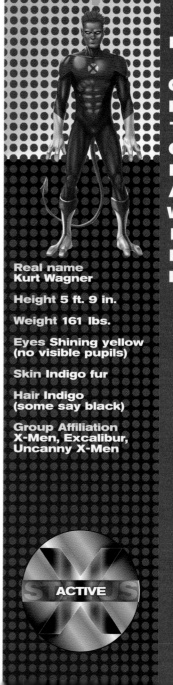

NIGHTCRAWLER

Real name
Kurt Wagner

Height 5 ft. 9 in.

Weight 161 lbs.

**Eyes Shining yellow
(no visible pupils)**

Skin Indigo fur

**Hair Indigo
(some say black)**

**Group Affiliation
X-Men, Excalibur,
Uncanny X-Men**

ACTIVE

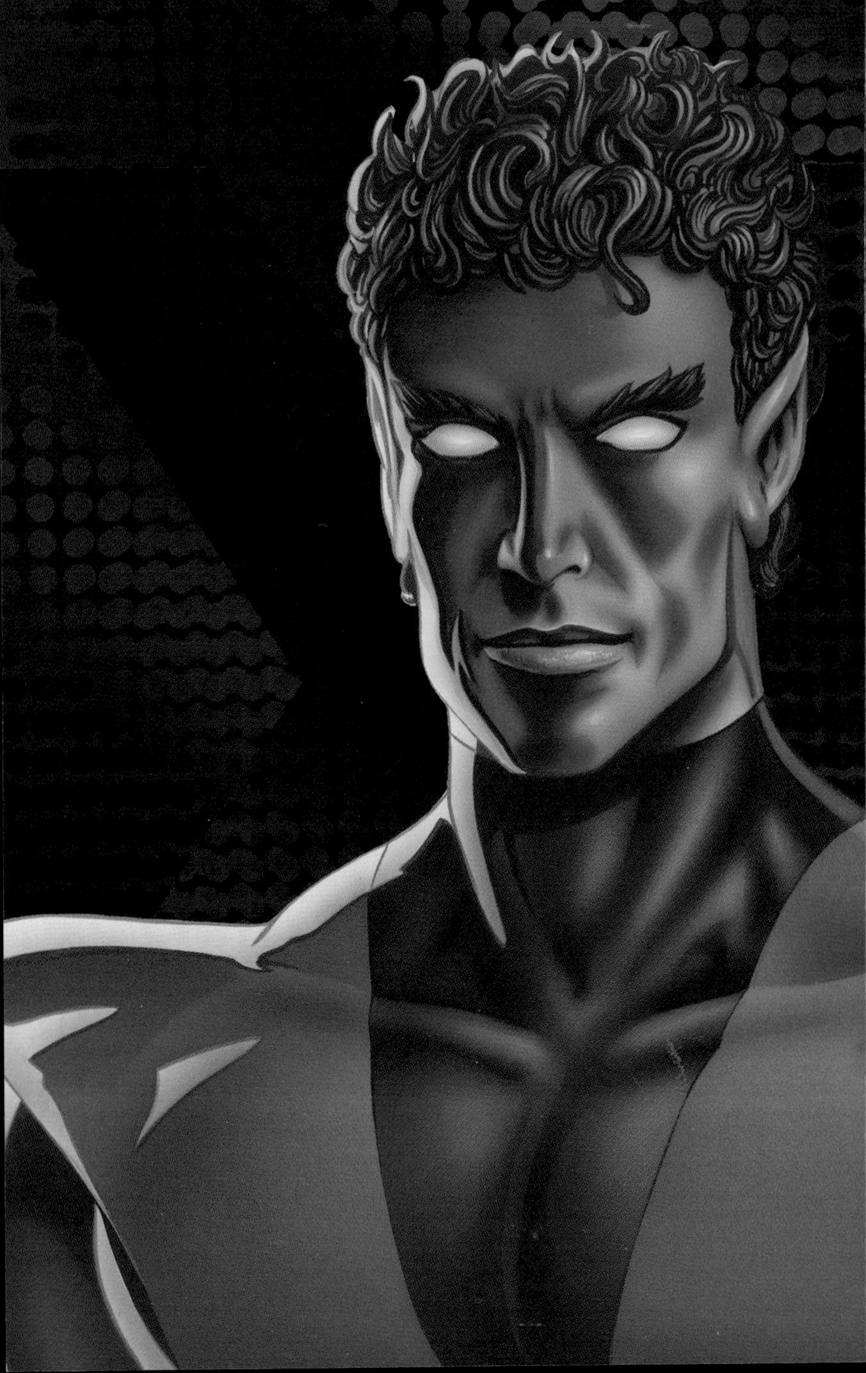

SECRETS

- Kurt was extremely agile even as a child, and he was a star acrobat in the circus. Audiences always assumed he was a normal person wearing a bizarre costume.
- When Kurt teleports, he enters another dimension and then leaves at his desired location. When he teleports, he leaves a smell of brimstone behind, the odor originating from the alternate dimension.
- Though he closely resembles a demon, Kurt is the most religious of all the X-Men, and at one time, studied to become a priest.
- Kurt's tail is strong enough to support the weight of his body.

STATUS Active

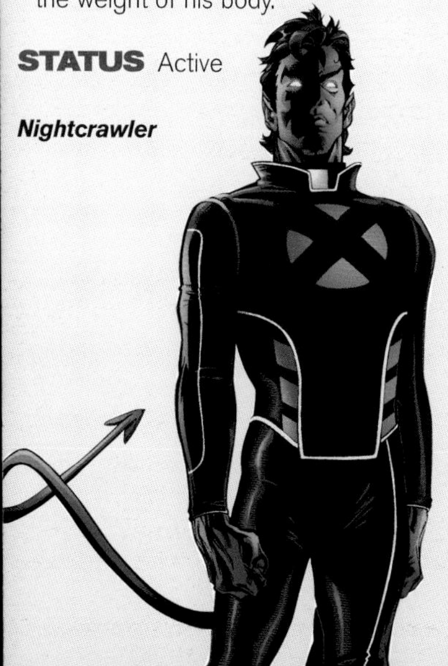

Nightcrawler

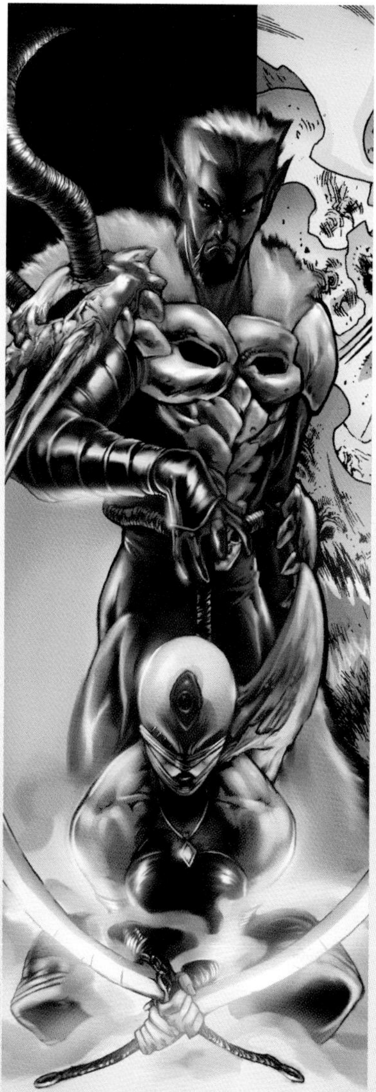

Azazel and Ginniyeh

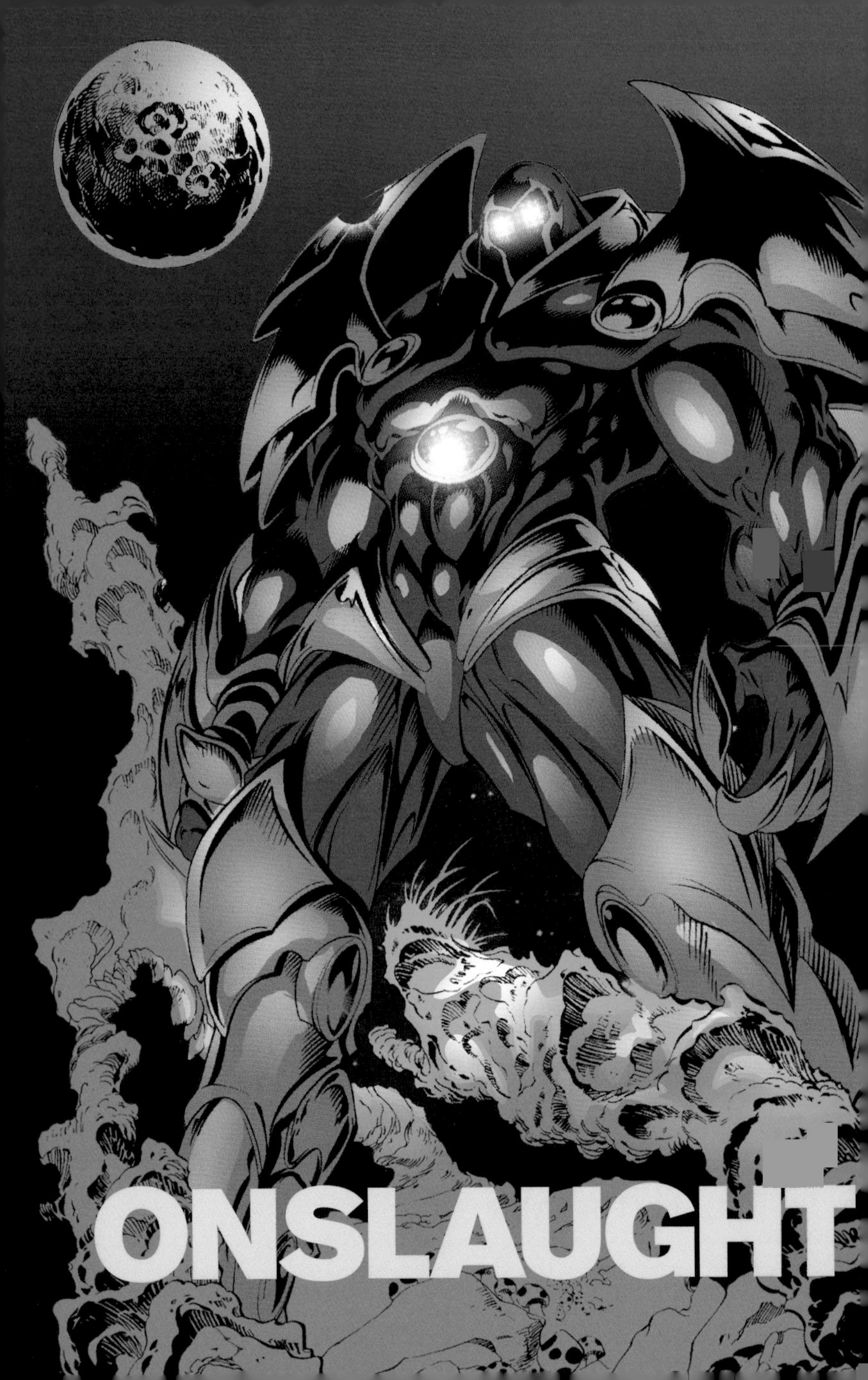
ONSLAUGHT

POWERS

Combines the mutant powers of Professor X and Magneto; can project illusions, induce amnesia, and cause mental or physical paralysis; can fire powerful mental bolts at nearby mutants; can shape and manipulate magnetic fields; one of the most powerful psionic beings in the universe; can use its powers to lift 100 tons; virtually indestructible; possesses nearly limitless strength; powerful enough to hurt the otherwise invulnerable Juggernaut.

SECURITY BRIEF

Onslaught came into being as the result of a battle between the X-Men and Magneto's band of mutants known as the Acolytes. When Magneto threatened to kill a bunch of innocent people, Wolverine attacked him, freeing the hostages. Angered at seeing his plans thwarted, Magneto used his full powers of concentration and pulled every bit of adamantium metal from Wolverine's skeleton and bones, nearly killing Wolverine. Acting in retribution, Professor X telepathically shut down Magneto's mind. As this took place, a flawed part of Magneto's mind settled into a repressed area of Professor X's ego. This combination of ostensibly "good" and "evil" forces evolved into Onslaught.

Onslaught's actual manifestation as a quasi-physical being occurred as a result of the parallel world known as the Age of Apocalypse dissolving into the multi-verse of possible worlds. A young man named Nate Grey emerged from it and, when Professor X attempted to scan Grey's brain to verify exactly what dimension he came from, Nate accidentally pulled Professor X's astral form out of his body. The accident freed the composite psi creature inside Xavier.

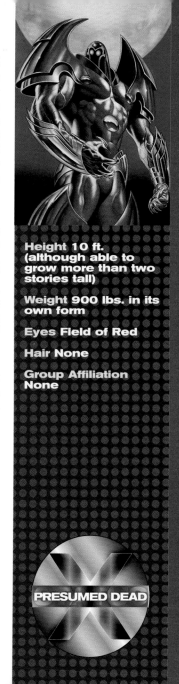

O N S L A U G H T

Height 10 ft. (although able to grow more than two stories tall)

Weight 900 lbs. in its own form

Eyes Field of Red

Hair None

Group Affiliation None

PRESUMED DEAD

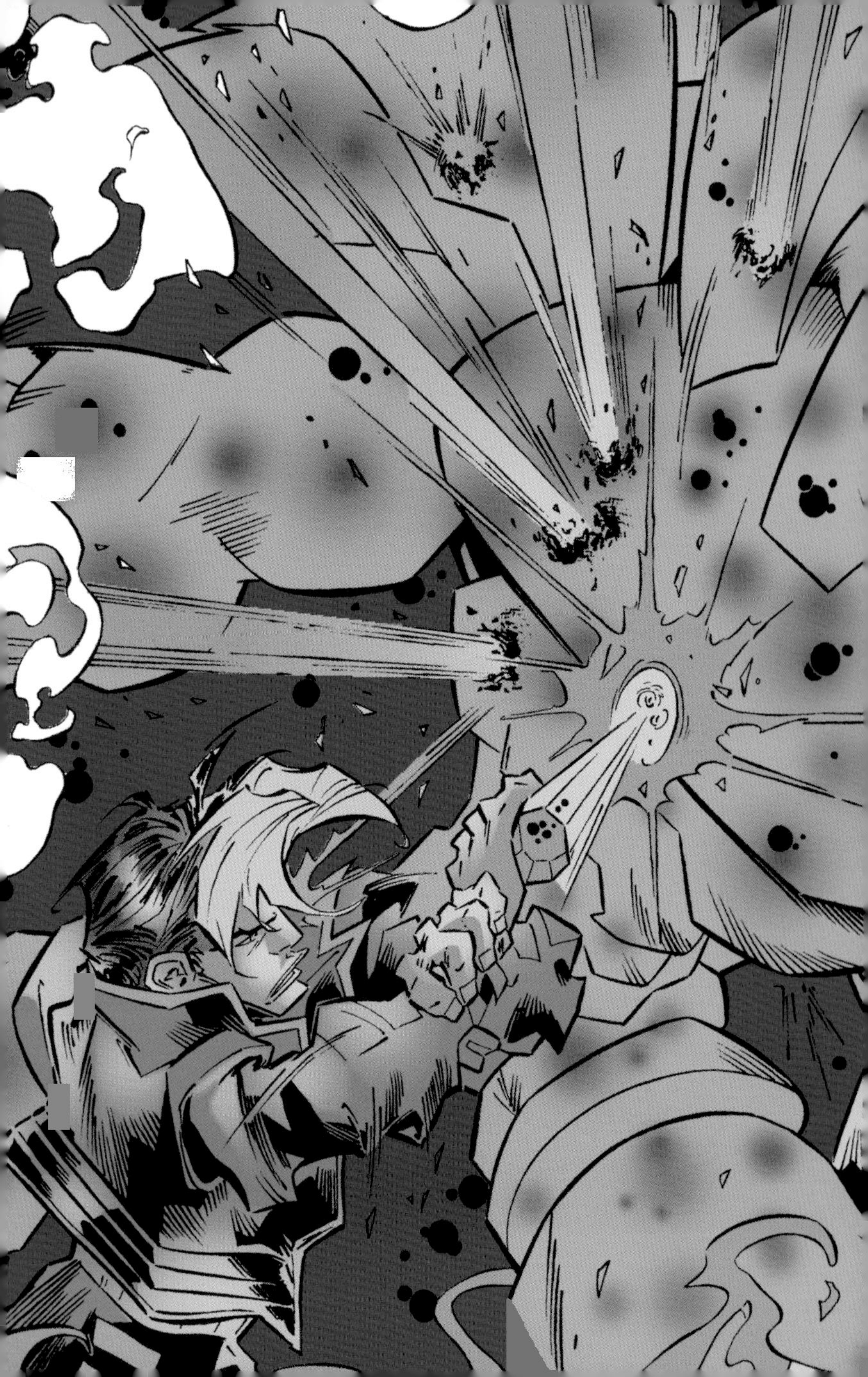

Left: *Nate Grey fighting*

Thus freed, Onslaught set out to gain absolute mastery over mankind. It first kidnapped the only two mutants capable of rewriting reality: Nate Grey, known as X-Man, and Franklin Richards, the son of Sue and Reed Richards of the Fantastic Four. Onslaught imprisoned the two in a citadel he created in New York City so that he could control their powers.

Initially Onslaught was regarded as a mysterious character whom no one knew anything about, and whose origin was unknown, even though it wore a uniform similar to Magneto's. However, it was considered a formidable adversary: it was enormous, extremely intelligent, possessed tremendous mental and magnetic powers, and was clearly capable of defeating other mutants.

Once it was revealed to be a composite life-form made from parts of Magneto's and Xavier's minds, Onslaught was defeated by the combined power of the X-Men, the Fantastic Four, the Avengers, the Hulk, and Doctor Doom.

SECRETS

- Onslaught was awakened inside Professor Xavier when a group of mutant-hating humans killed a young mutant near the Xavier institute.

- Onslaught's first battle was with Professor Xavier's stepbrother, Cain Marko, in the guise of Juggernaut.

STATUS Presumed Dead

Acolytes

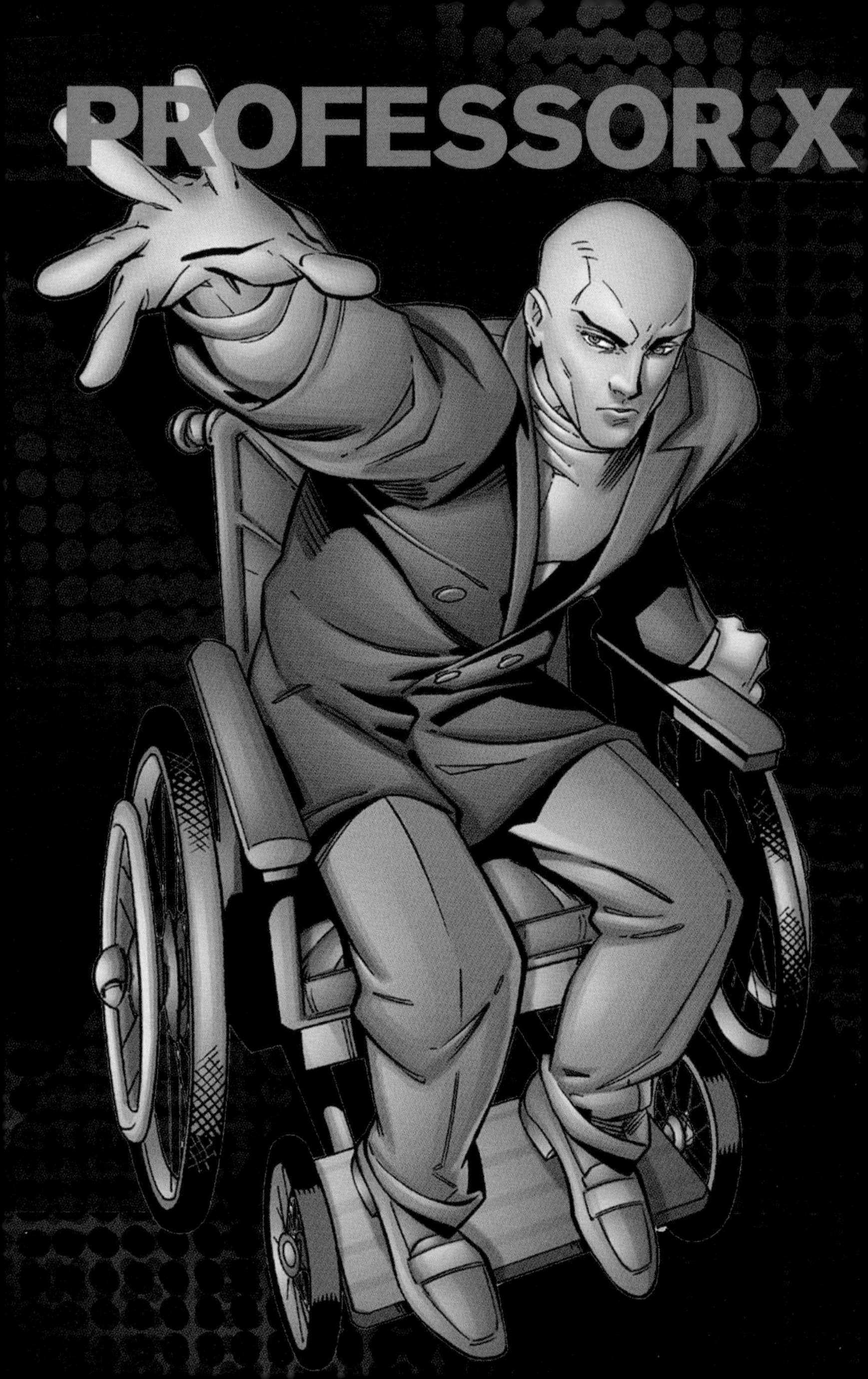
PROFESSOR X

POWERS

Possesses a full range of psionic powers; can read, control, and influence human minds; one of the world's most powerful telepaths, regarded as a top authority on genetics, mutations, and psionic powers; designed and built much of the equipment used at X-Men headquarters.

SECURITY BRIEF

Charles Francis Xavier was the son of wealthy parents, Brian and Sharon Xavier. After Charles's father died in a nuclear accident, his mother married Brian's business partner, Kurt Marko. The union was unhappy and ended with the separate deaths of both parents, leaving Charles and his psychotic stepbrother, Cain (Juggernaut), very wealthy. It was about that time that Xavier's telepathic powers began to develop. A brilliant scholar and gifted athlete, Charles attended Bard College and then Oxford.

After enlisting in the military, he spent several years touring the world. In Egypt, he encountered the telepath, Shadow King, whom he defeated in a psychic duel.

In a clinic in Israel Charles met Holocaust survivor, Erik Magnus Lehnsherr who was working as an orderly. The two became close friends though they disagreed on how mutants would be treated by humanity. Erik believed that the only solution to mutant persecution was for mutants to dominate humanity. Charles had no idea that Erik would become his greatest foe, the mutant called Magneto.

Soon after the two friends parted, Charles encountered an alien being, Lucifer, who plotted to invade Earth. Xavier disrupted the alien's plans. The creature retaliated by dropping a huge boulder on Charles, crushing his legs and leaving him a paraplegic.

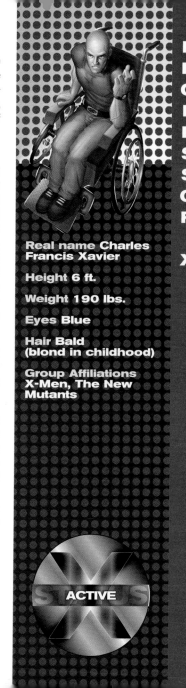

P
R
O
F
E
S
S
O
R

X

Real name Charles Francis Xavier

Height 6 ft.

Weight 190 lbs.

Eyes Blue

Hair Bald
(blond in childhood)

Group Affiliations
X-Men, The New Mutants

ACTIVE

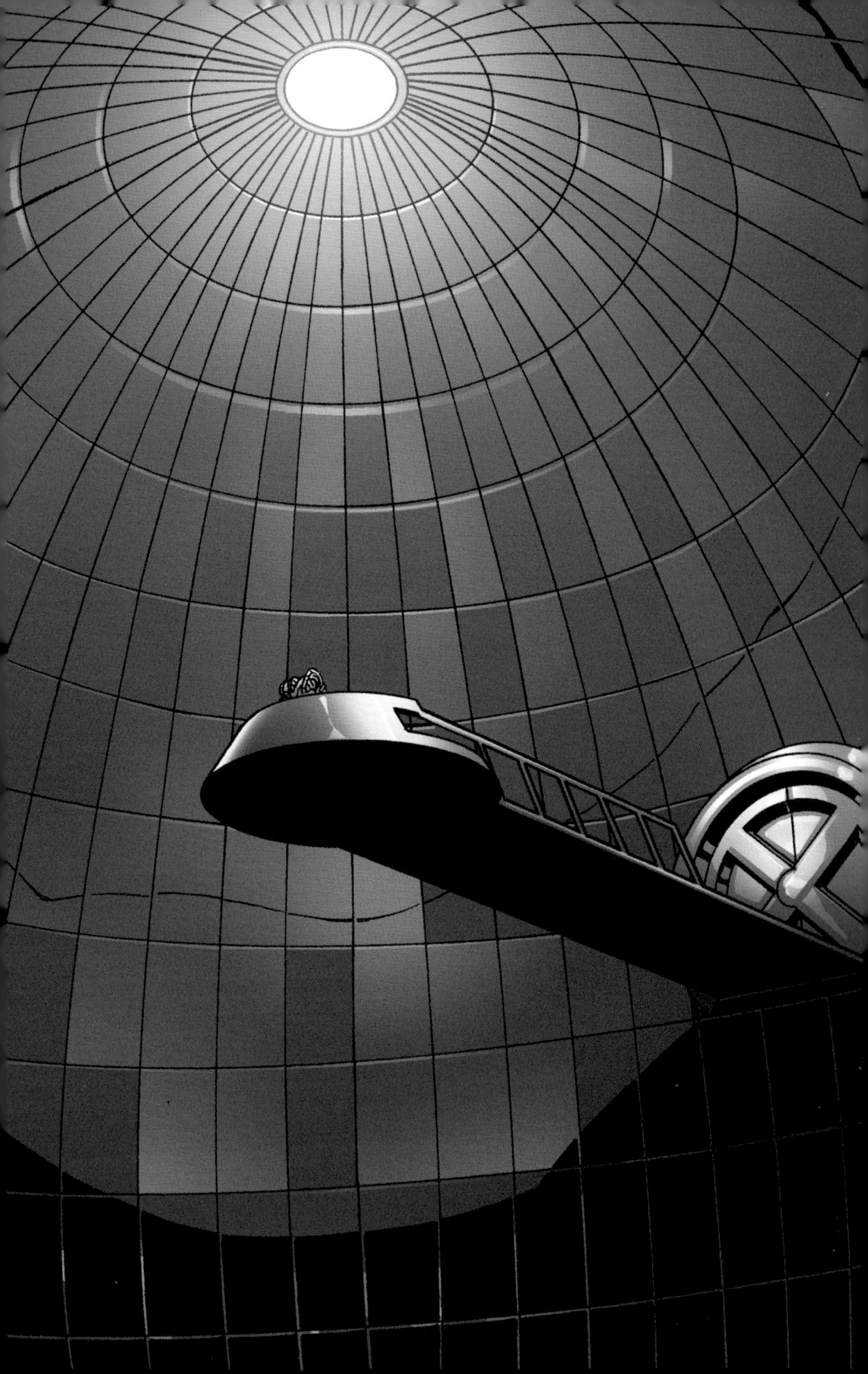

Xavier returned to the United States and founded a school for gifted children. The academy had a secret purpose of providing a safe haven for mutants where they could learn to use their abilities and function normally in the outside world. With the help of Cerebro, a machine of his own invention that allowed him to locate mutants psionically and measure their powers, Xavier was able to find and recruit members for his X-Men team. In addition, Charles sought to foster good mutant-human relations by providing a positive example of mutants with his superhero team, the X-Men. Standing against him was Magneto with a band of mutants he called the Brotherhood of Evil Mutants.

Recently, Xavier has teamed up with Magneto to rebuild the island of Genosha, a haven for mutants, which his evil sister, Cassandra Nova had tried to wipe out during her reign of terror. Nova was defeated by the combined might of the X-Men.

SECRETS

- Professor X regained the use of his legs several times over the years, only to be felled by some other disaster or health crisis that once again put him back in his wheelchair.

- Xavier met and fell in love with the alien Princess Lilandra from the Shi'ar Empire and took time off from the X-Men to live on her world.

- Professor X served as the unknowing and unwitting host of the evil psychic force known as Onslaught. It took the combined efforts of the Fantastic Four, the Avengers, and the Hulk to defeat the mental monster.

STATUS Active

Left: *Cerebro*

Princess Lilandra with guards

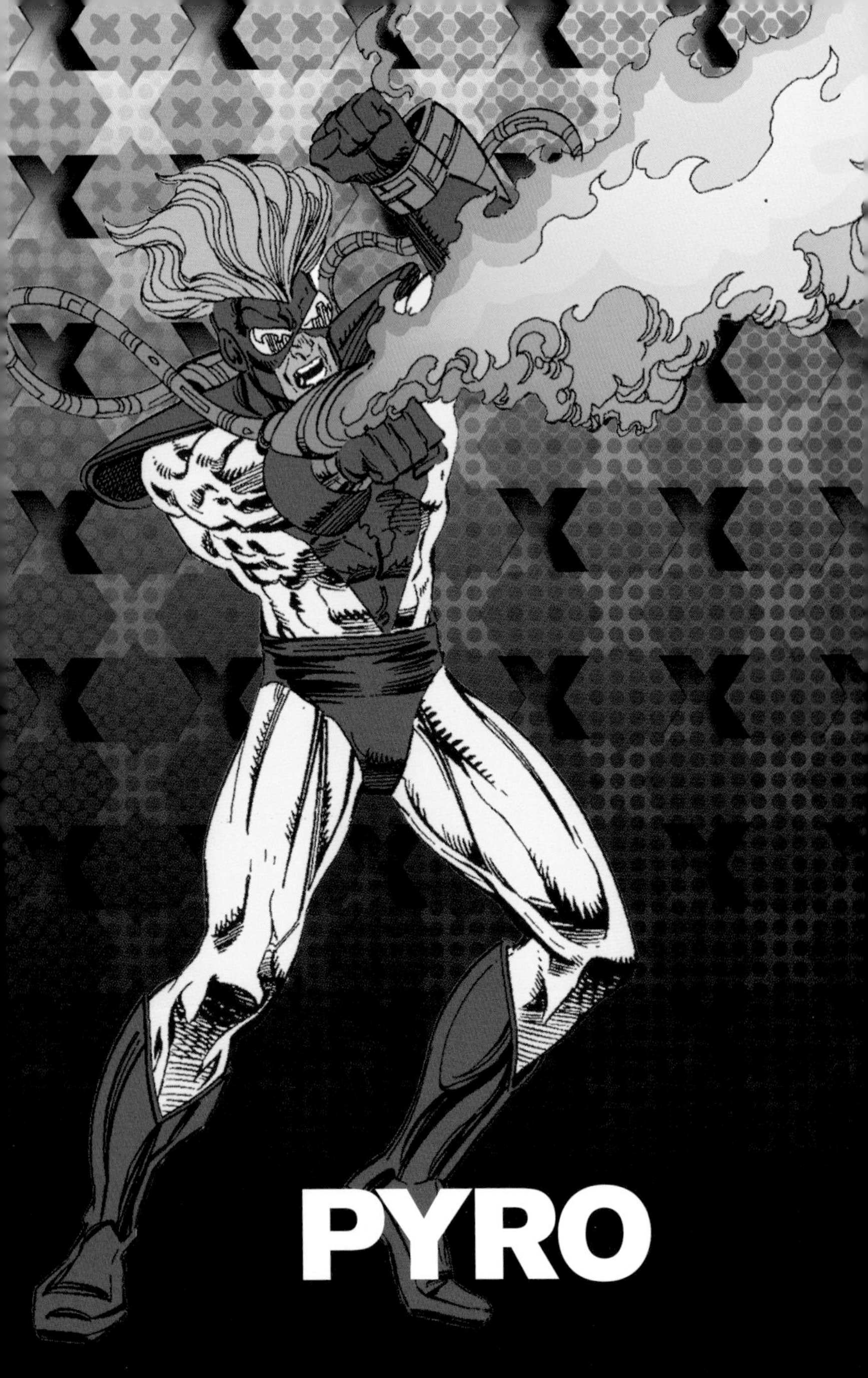
PYRO

POWERS

Psionically shapes fire by enlarging it or shrinking it to the size, intensity, and heat he desires; cannot actually create fire (normally uses a cigarette lighter or some sort of flamethrower to start fire), but can mold it; cannot be harmed by any fire he controls; can form animals out of flame and give them a shape; one of his fiery lions could actually tear something apart with its claws.

SECURITY BRIEF

St. John Allerdyce was born in Sydney, Australia. His flame power emerged when he was a teenager, but he could see no way to profit from its use so he didn't pay much attention to it.

Allerdyce worked in Southeast Asia (including Vietnam) for a number of years as a newspaper journalist and writer. He then met Mystique. She discovered he had mutant powers and recruited him for her version of the Brotherhood of Evil Mutants. Later, when Mystique formed the Freedom Force working for the United States government, Pyro joined that team as well.

When the Freedom Force disbanded, Pyro once again joined the Brotherhood of Evil Mutants, now led by Toad. That group was defeated by the mutant team, X-Force. Soon afterwards, Allerdyce discovered he had contracted the Legacy Virus, a disease that only affected mutants. In an unusual twist of fate, Pyro died saving an anti-mutant Senator's life.

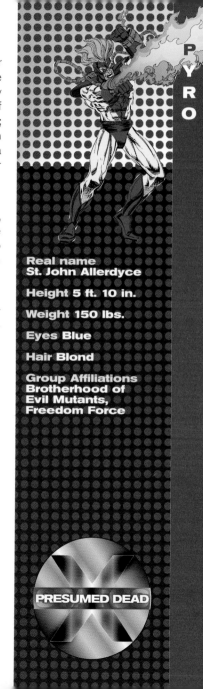

P Y R O

Real name
St. John Allerdyce

Height 5 ft. 10 in.

Weight 150 lbs.

Eyes Blue

Hair Blond

Group Affiliations
Brotherhood of
Evil Mutants,
Freedom Force

PRESUMED DEAD

SECRETS

- Senator Robert Kelly was a firm believer that mutants were a menace to society and should be forced to register with the government. When Pyro sacrificed his life saving the Senator by killing the mutant assassin Post, Kelly had a change of heart and realized that mutants deserved the same protections as any other citizen. But Pyro's sacrifice was in vain, as the Senator was shot and killed soon afterwards by an anti-mutant terrorist.

- Allerdyce wrote novels based on his experiences in southeast Asia, as well as a series of Gothic romances. Though the critics hated his work, audiences loved it.

- Pyro could not normally be shot, as his flames would melt bullets before they hit him. When he contracted the Legacy Virus, Pyro's flame power grew erratic; he was once hit by a bullet and sent to the hospital.

- Pyro was treated for a bullet wound in the hospital by mutant Dr. Cecilia Reyes. Her force shield protected her from Pyro's unmanageable fire power. An unregistered mutant she was later dismissed from the hospital.

STATUS Presumed Dead

Senator Robert Kelly

*Right: **Pyro fighting with Wolverine***

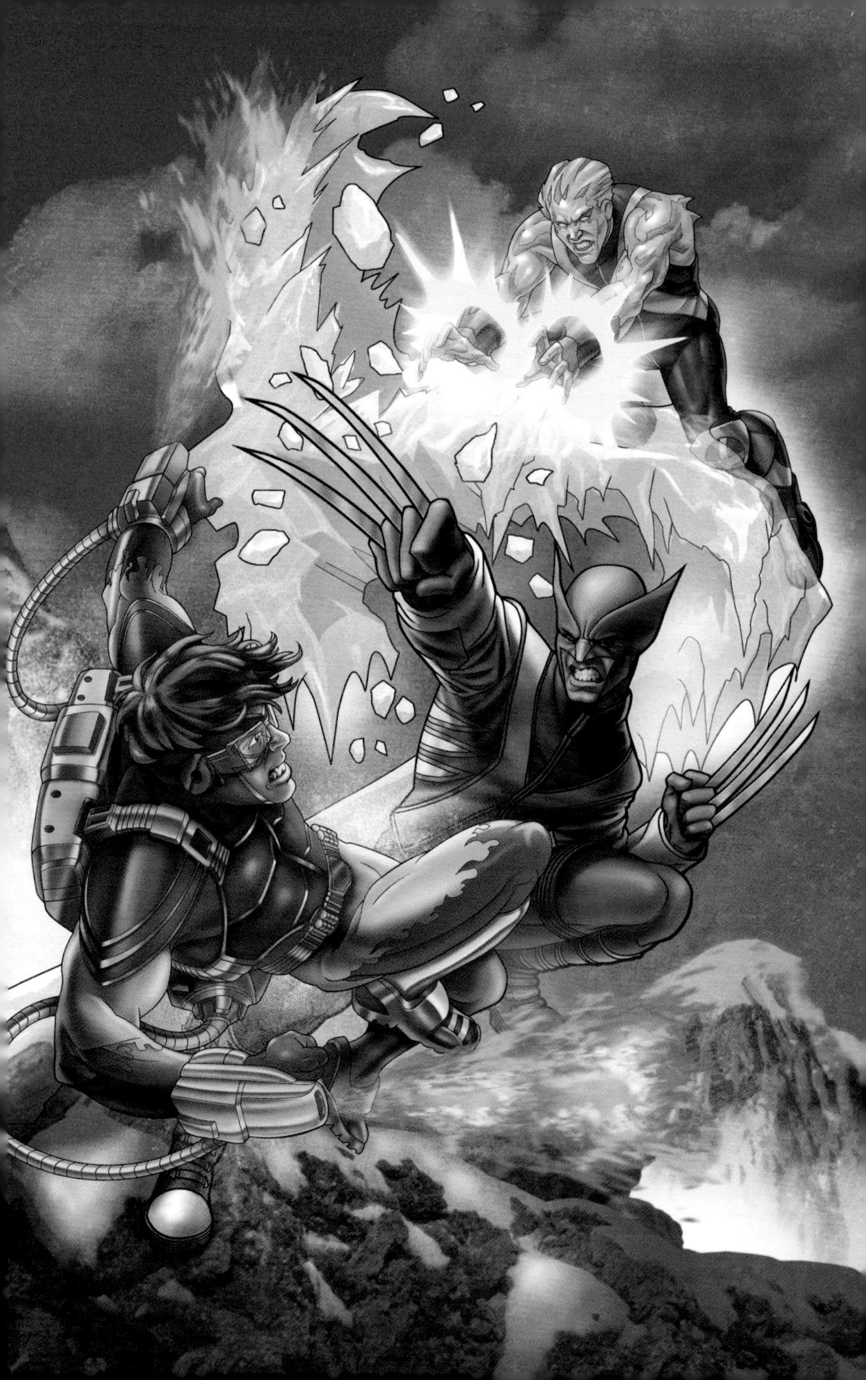

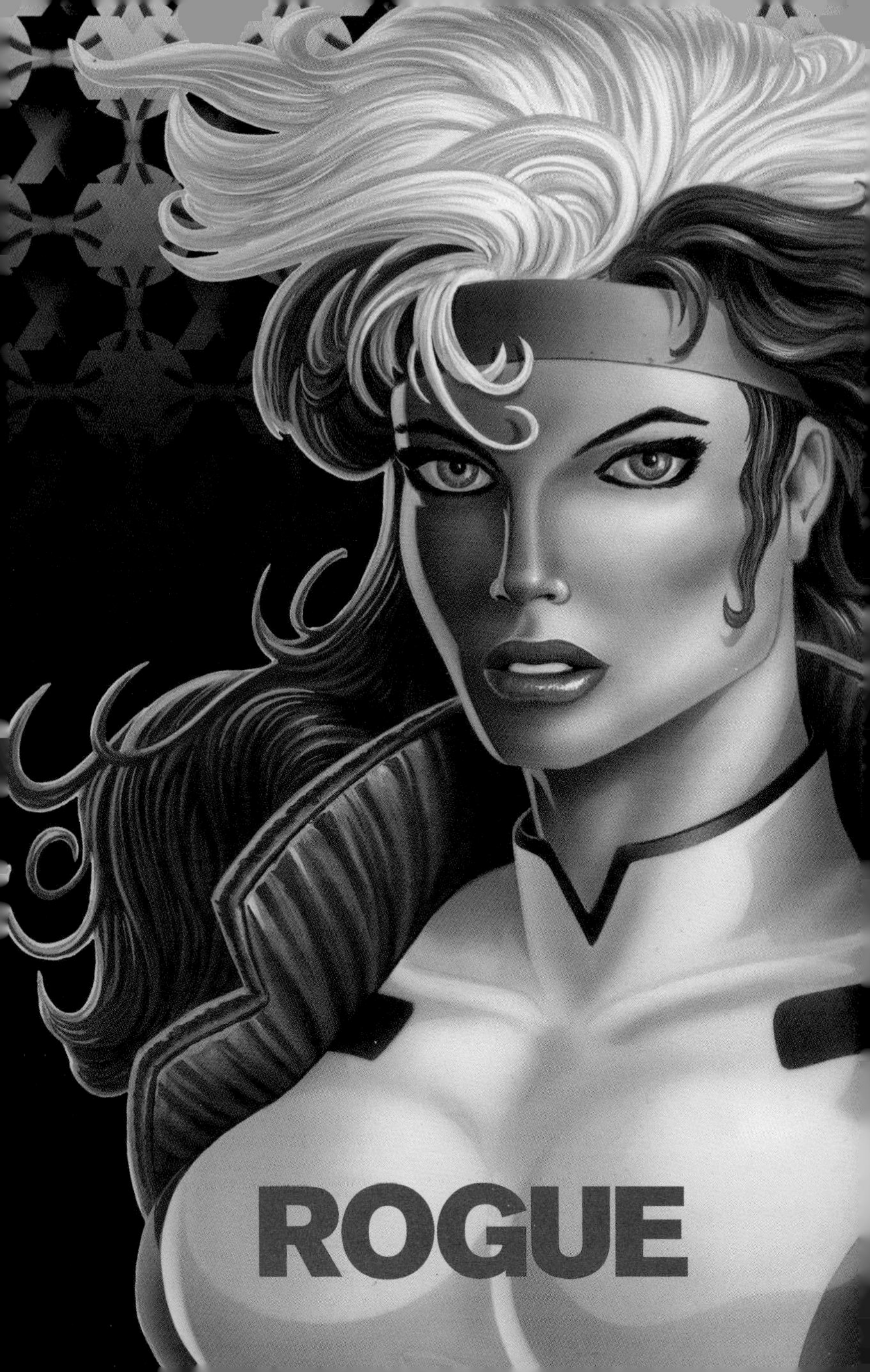
ROGUE

POWERS

Possesses mutant power to temporarily absorb the thoughts, memories, and actions of other beings (both human and mutant) upon making skin-to-skin contact; prolonged contact resulting in a possible permanent transfer of powers; could fly; was endowed with limited super strength, invulnerability, and mysterious seventh sense.

SECURITY BRIEF

Little is known about Rogue's earliest life. She lived as a child with her family in Caldecott, Mississippi, and then ran away from home because of her very strict aunt. As a pre-teen, Rogue dated a neighborhood boy, Cody Robbins. Rogue's powers first appeared when Cody Robbins tried to kiss her and the skin-to-skin contact ripped his memories, knowledge, and personality from his body, putting him into a coma from which he never recovered.

When the townspeople learned that Rogue was a mutant, some of the wilder residents hunted her down with intent to kill. She was saved by the unexpected interference by the mutant known as Cable, who was involved in a dangerous assignment at the time and couldn't take her with him. Instead, he left Rogue alone in the bayous, where she was found by the mutants, Mystique and Destiny.

Mystique raised Rogue for the next ten years and recruited her into the Brotherhood of Evil Mutants. Rogue fought on their side for a few years, battling the Avengers, the X-Men, and Dazzler. It was during this period, she had a long battle with Carol Danvers, Ms. Marvel, and absorbed all of that superwoman's incredible powers.

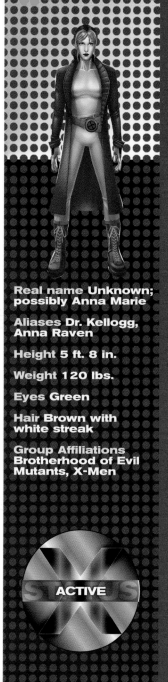

**R
O
G
U
E**

Real name Unknown; possibly Anna Marie

Aliases Dr. Kellogg, Anna Raven

Height 5 ft. 8 in.

Weight 120 lbs.

Eyes Green

Hair Brown with white streak

Group Affiliations Brotherhood of Evil Mutants, X-Men

ACTIVE

Rogue and Gambit

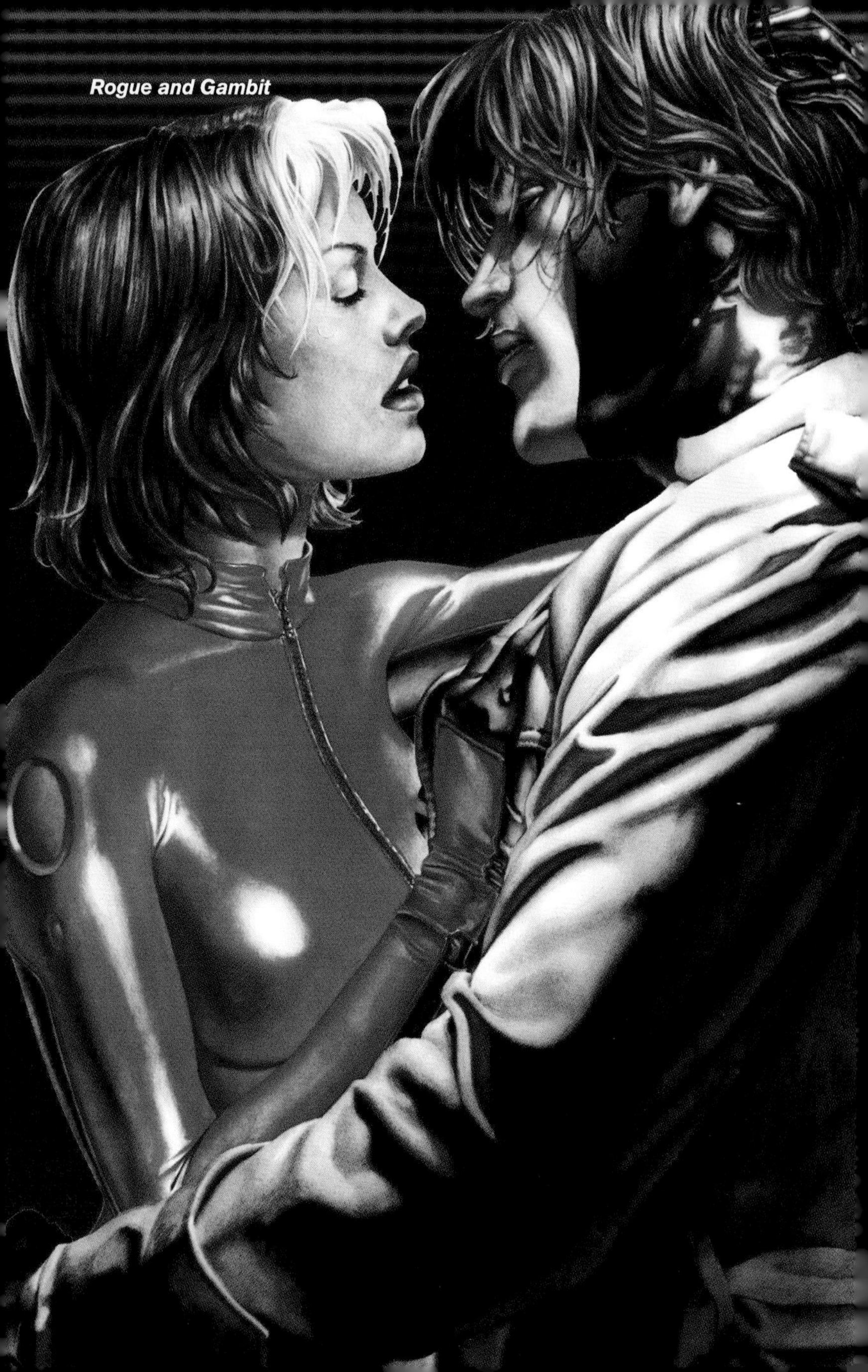

Absorbing all the memories of people she had overwhelmed was slowly driving Rogue crazy. Mystique offered no help so Rogue turned to Professor X. He helped her learn to adjust to her life and Rogue became a member of the X-Men, although she was initially treated with suspicion and dislike. She has had a romantic attachment to Gambit, albeit a difficult one, since no other mutant can touch Rogue without fear of losing his or her powers.

Recently, Rogue lost her Ms. Marvel powers during a battle with the superhuman, Vargas. Later, Rogue gained the powers of the mutant Sunfire as he was dying.

SECRETS

- Nightcrawler is Mystique's son. Thus, Rogue and Nightcrawler consider themselves siblings.

- When Rogue absorbed Carol Danvers's powers, she also developed a buried alternate personality of Danvers, which later threatened to overwhelm her thoughts.

- Sometimes, when Rogue absorbs another person's personality, she also duplicates some of that person's features.

- Rogue's absorbing power works on some aliens as well as humans.

STATUS Active

Sunfire

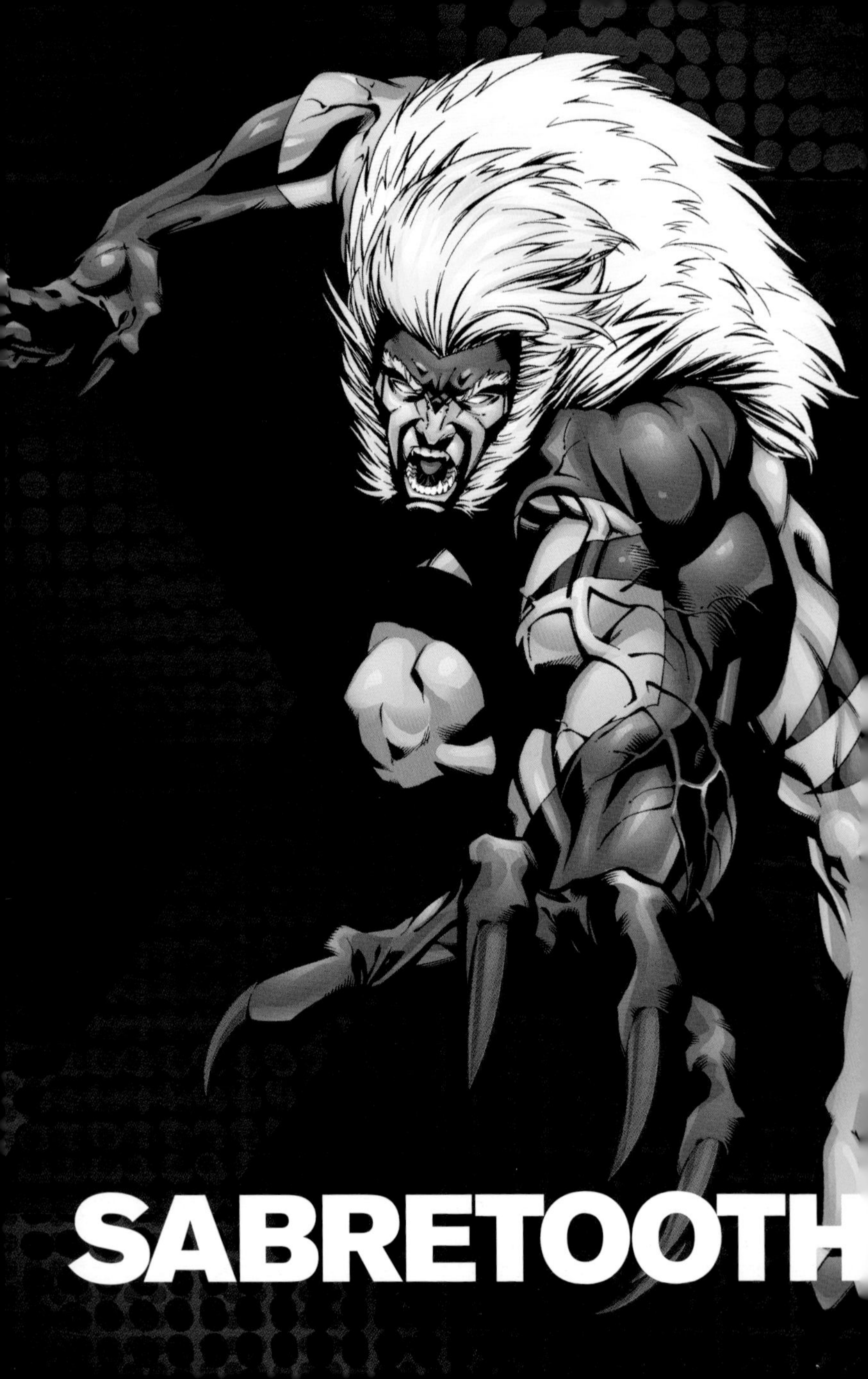
SABRETOOTH

POWERS

Has the power to regenerate and heal his body at speeds hundreds of times faster than ordinary humans; easily recovers from injuries that would kill most people; can regenerate important sensory organs such as eyes as well as large sections of missing flesh; healing factor renders him invulnerable to most poisons and diseases, restores his stamina (allowing him to fight at peak skill for days), and retards his aging factor; constant cellular regeneration of his body gives him extremely enhanced senses, including perfect night vision even at hundreds of yards and the ability to track someone entirely by scent.

SECURITY BRIEF

Sabretooth, a mutant mercenary, is a graduate of the secret Weapon X training program and not all facts remembered after such assignments are real. Thus, he is not sure of his origins, his loyalties, or even that his real name is Victor Creed. All he knows is that he is a near indestructible mutant who enjoys killing. For years, he thought he was Wolverine's father, but DNA testing proved that this wasn't the case.

When he was a young man, Sabretooth was known to have sired a son, Graydon Creed, with another mutant, Mystique. Graydon was born a normal person, and founded an anti-mutant organization. Later, he ran for president. He was assassinated by his own mother.

For a long time, Sabretooth worked for Mr. Sinister, as one of Sinister's group, the Marauders. It was during these days that Sabretooth helped launch the Mutant Massacre.

After being captured by the X-Men, Sabretooth began being treated by Professor X for his killer mania. The X-Men tried to help

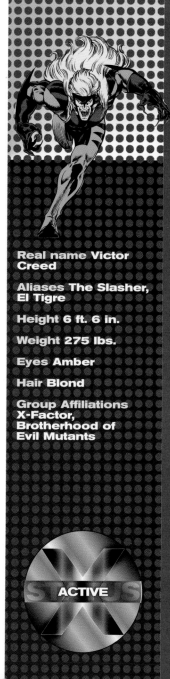

**S
A
B
R
E
T
O
O
T
H**

Real name Victor Creed

Aliases The Slasher, El Tigre

Height 6 ft. 6 in.

Weight 275 lbs.

Eyes Amber

Hair Blond

Group Affiliations X-Factor, Brotherhood of Evil Mutants

ACTIVE

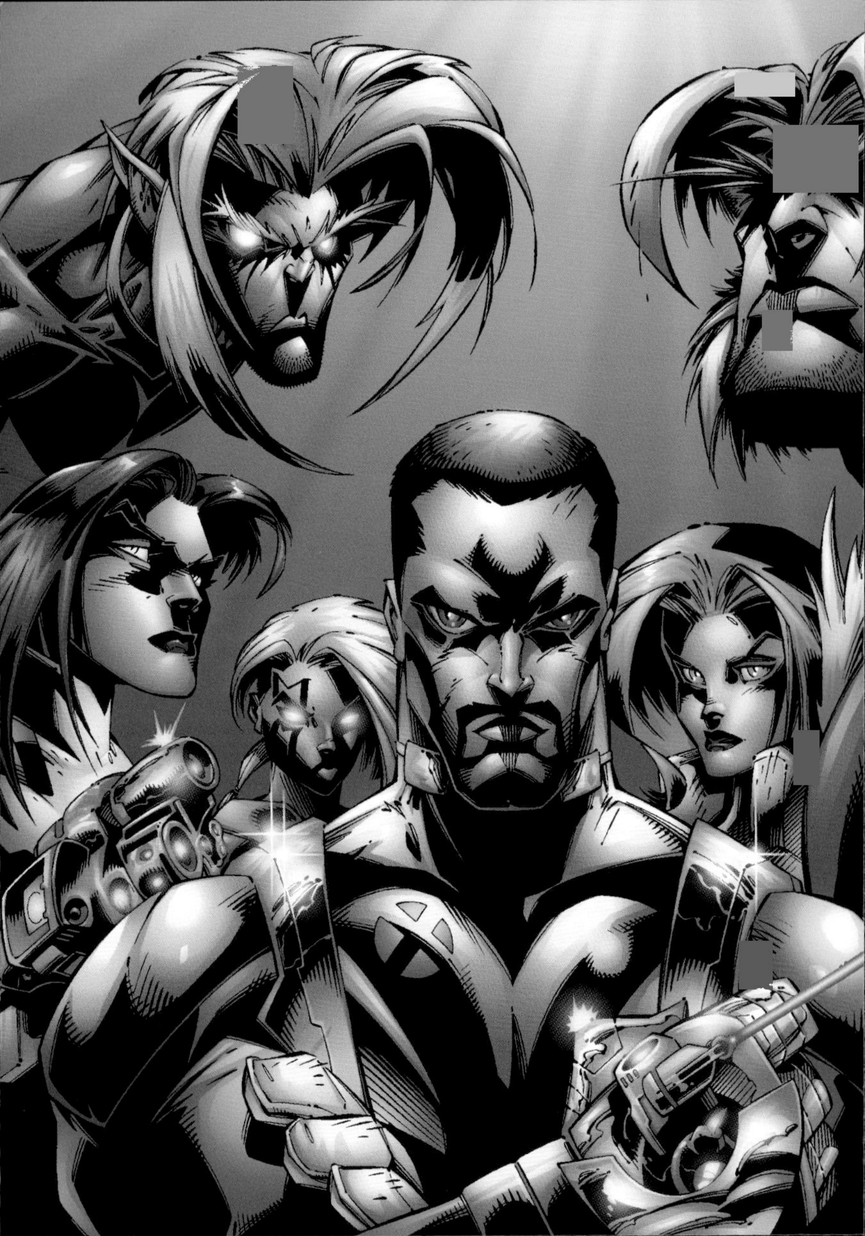

Sabretooth but his mania for killing remained uncontrollable. After several battles with the group, Sabretooth was later recruited into X-Factor.

As part of X-Factor, Sabretooth worked for the government, hunting mutants. After a short time he escaped and returned to mercenary work. He then joined Mystique's version of the Brotherhood of Evil Mutants. Later, he was forced into a new version of the Weapon X program, but he escaped. At present, he is working as a freelance killer, serving whomever is willing to pay his fee.

SECRETS

- The C.I.A. agents who worked with Victor Creed in the 1960s evidently gave him the code-name, Sabretooth.

- Sabretooth is an excellent fighter. He was trained by the C.I.A., Weapon X, the Foreigner, and HYDRA organizations. He is also an expert hunter and tracker, and has worked with the Exiles.

- Sabretooth's appearance suggests that he has a primitive brain. He does not. Sabretooth routinely hacks into government databases to steal classified information, and has escaped the highest ranked security prisons.

STATUS Active

Left: *Sabretooth with X-Factor*

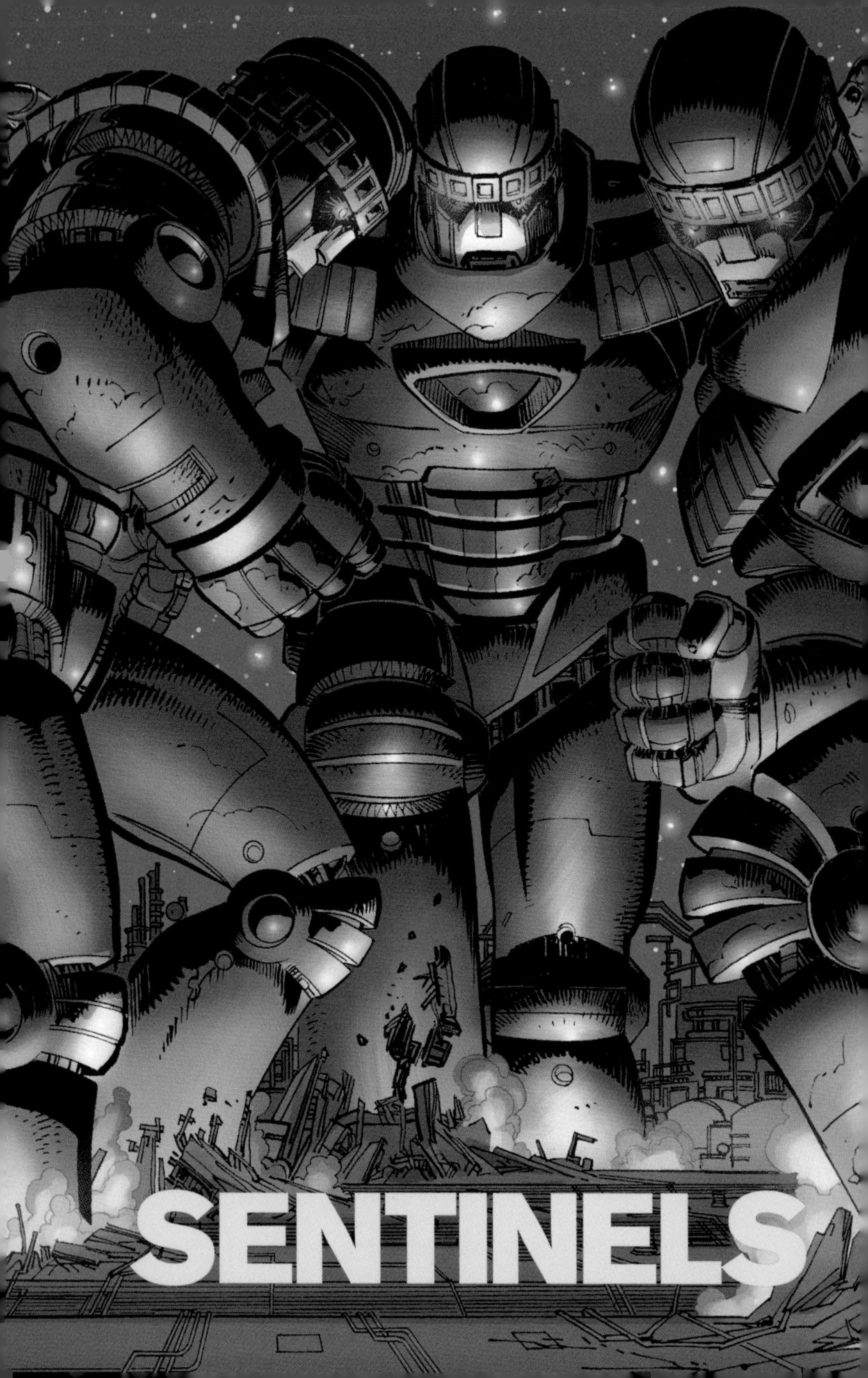
SENTINELS

POWERS

Can fly, shoot energy blasts from different parts of their bodies, and detect mutants at long range; some can change form and re-assemble after being attacked; possess vast physical strength; bodies are highly resistant to damage; variants have the ability to learn from the attacks they face and create defenses against them.

SECURITY BRIEF

The Sentinel robots were created by Dr. Boliver Trask, who developed them out of fear that mutants would replace humankind if they were not destroyed. In a television debate between Dr. Trask and Professor X, Trask espoused this belief, then activated the secret army of Sentinels he had created. However, Trask had given Master Mold the ability to reason. The giant Sentinel determined that the one way to protect mankind from mutants was to rule humanity. Xavier and Trask were abducted and taken to Master Mold by Sentinels, but the two men were rescued by the X-Men. Trask finally realized that the Sentinels were a worse enemy to mankind than mutants. He sabotaged the main Sentinel base, destroying Master Mold and all of the Sentinels in an explosion that took his own life as well.

Trask's son, Larry, took up where his father left off and continued to develop Sentinels. Larry built a new batch of Sentinels, and was killed by them.

Since that time, Dark Beast reprogrammed a number of Sentinels owned by the government to fight superheroes during Onslaught's reign of terror. Recently, Cassandra Nova, the dead-alive sister of Professor Xavier, used the latest models of Sentinels to attack the mutant inhabitants of the island of Genosha.

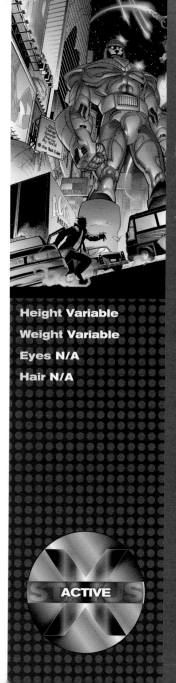

S E N T I N E L S

Height Variable

Weight Variable

Eyes N/A

Hair N/A

ACTIVE

Sentinels are more than the metal and circuits that make them robots. They are the physical embodiment of humanity's fear of change, and those different from itself.

SECRETS

- Sentinels cannot be destroyed.

- Most Sentinels have limited self-awareness and learning circuitry that allows them to adapt.

- Larry Trask, son of the creator of the Sentinels, was unaware that he was a mutant and protected by a medallion he wore that prevented Sentinel equipment from detecting his condition. He was killed by the new generation of Sentinels he helped perfect.

- In an alternate future created by Mystique's assassination of Robert Kelly, a mutant-hating United States Senator, Sentinels were empowered to wipe out mutants mercilessly and killed most of the X-Men as well as many other beings with superhuman powers.

STATUS Active

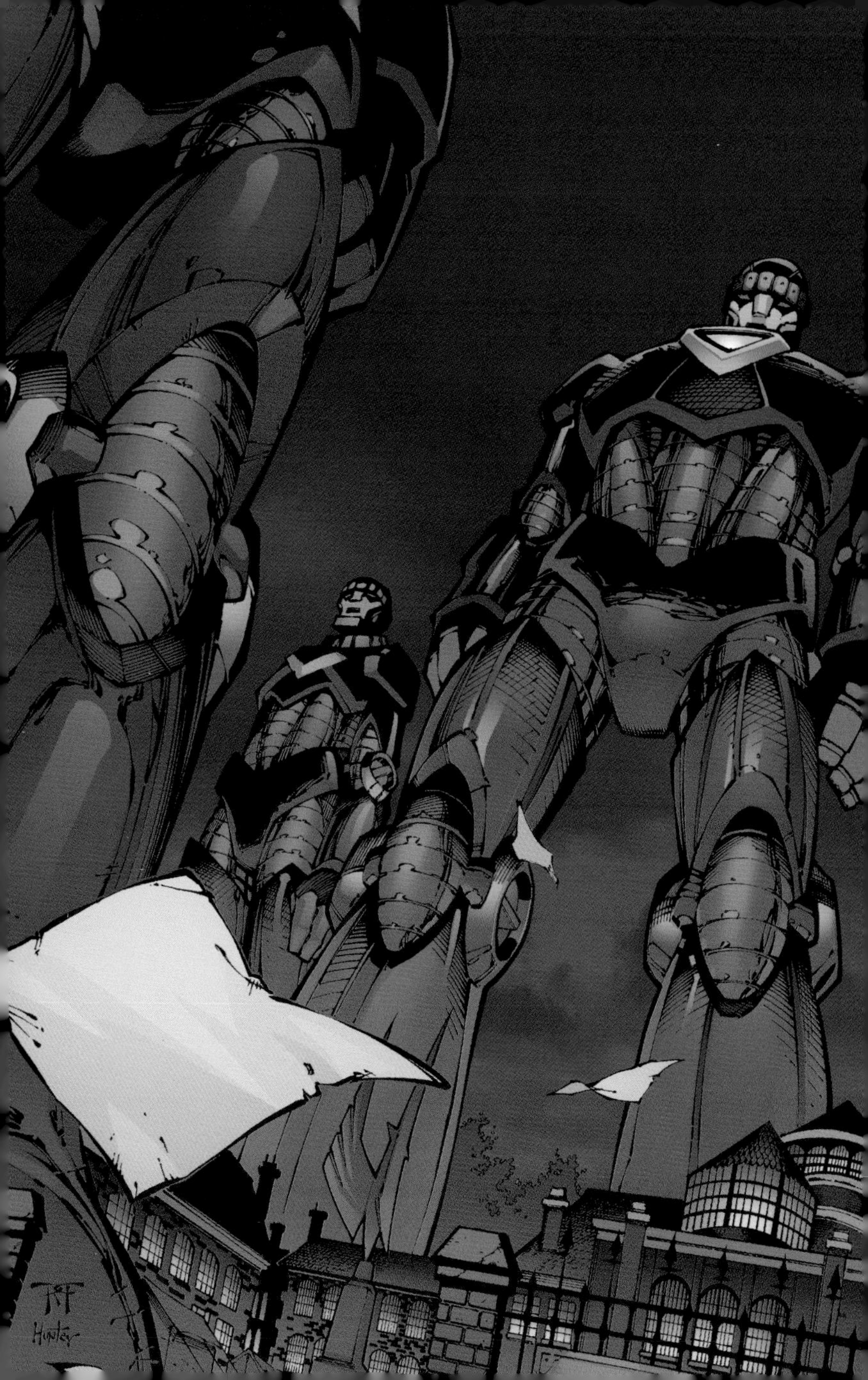
Hunter

SHADOW KING

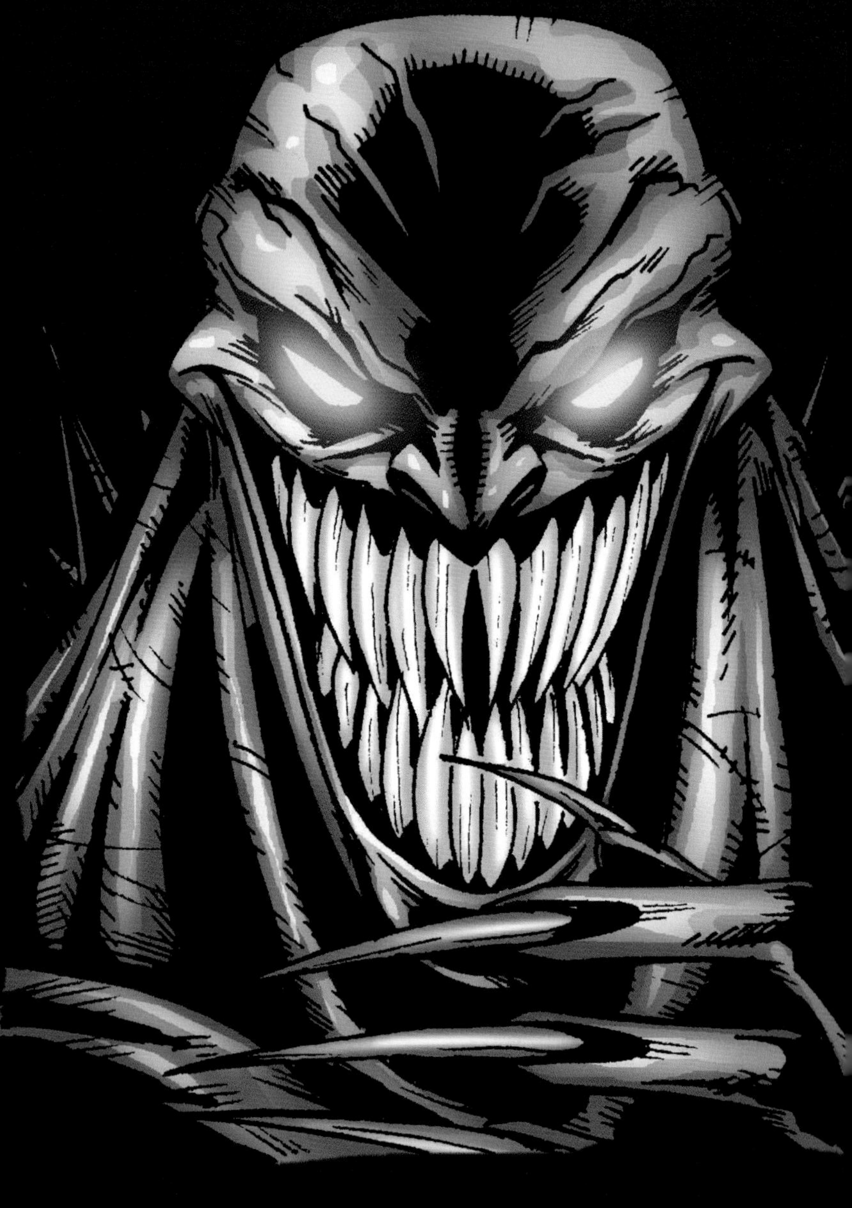

SHADOW KING

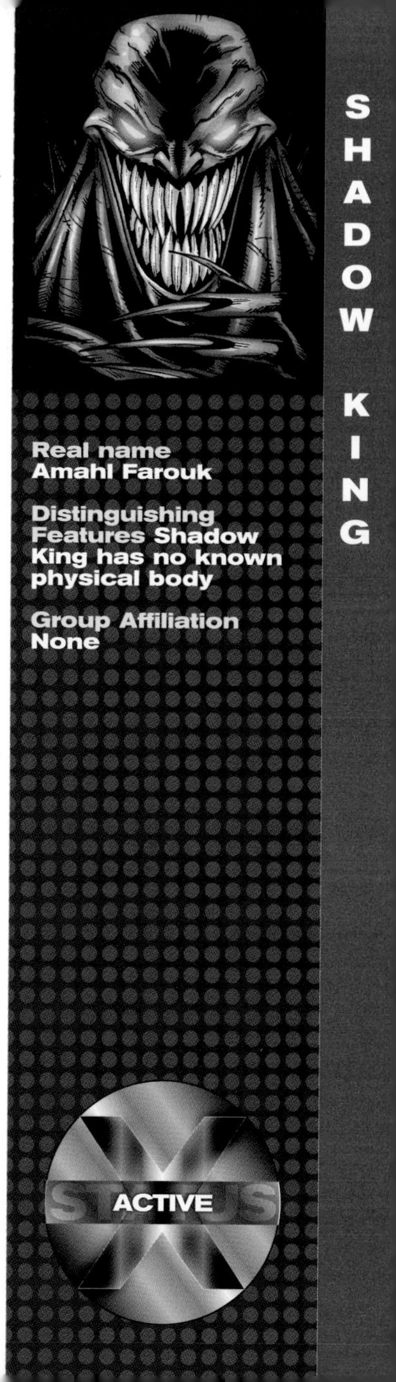

Real name
Amahl Farouk

Distinguishing Features Shadow King has no known physical body

Group Affiliation
None

STATUS: ACTIVE

POWERS

One of the most powerful mutant telepaths in the world; has strong mental powers linked to the astral plane; can take possession of the minds of other people; can fight visitors to the astral plane.

SECURITY BRIEF

Little is known about Amahl Farouk before his initial contact with Charles Xavier in Cairo nearly a half-century ago. Xavier, still a young man, was touring the world and while in Egypt came across a gifted child, Storm, with incredible psionic gifts. The Shadow King had also stumbled across Storm and wanted her for his crime empire. Xavier and the Shadow King fought on the astral plane, with Xavier winning. The Shadow King's physical body was destroyed—however, his mind survived.

Several years later, the Shadow King gained control over the mutants who lived on Muir Island, the home of Dr. Moira MacTaggert. The combined efforts of the X-Men and mutants who belonged to X-Factor were necessary to thwart the Shadow King's plans. Since the Shadow King existed entirely on the astral plane, he could be defeated only, not killed.

In Africa the Shadow King took over the native tribe who once revered Storm as a goddess. With their help, he trapped the X-Men, one of whom, Psylocke, evaded his mental traps and fought him on the astral plane. The Shadow King was defeated yet again.

Recently, Psylocke was killed and the Shadow King attacked the X-Men again. His main target was Rogue, but Rogue, who had absorbed Psylocke's powers, was able to use them and defeat the Shadow King.

Psylocke

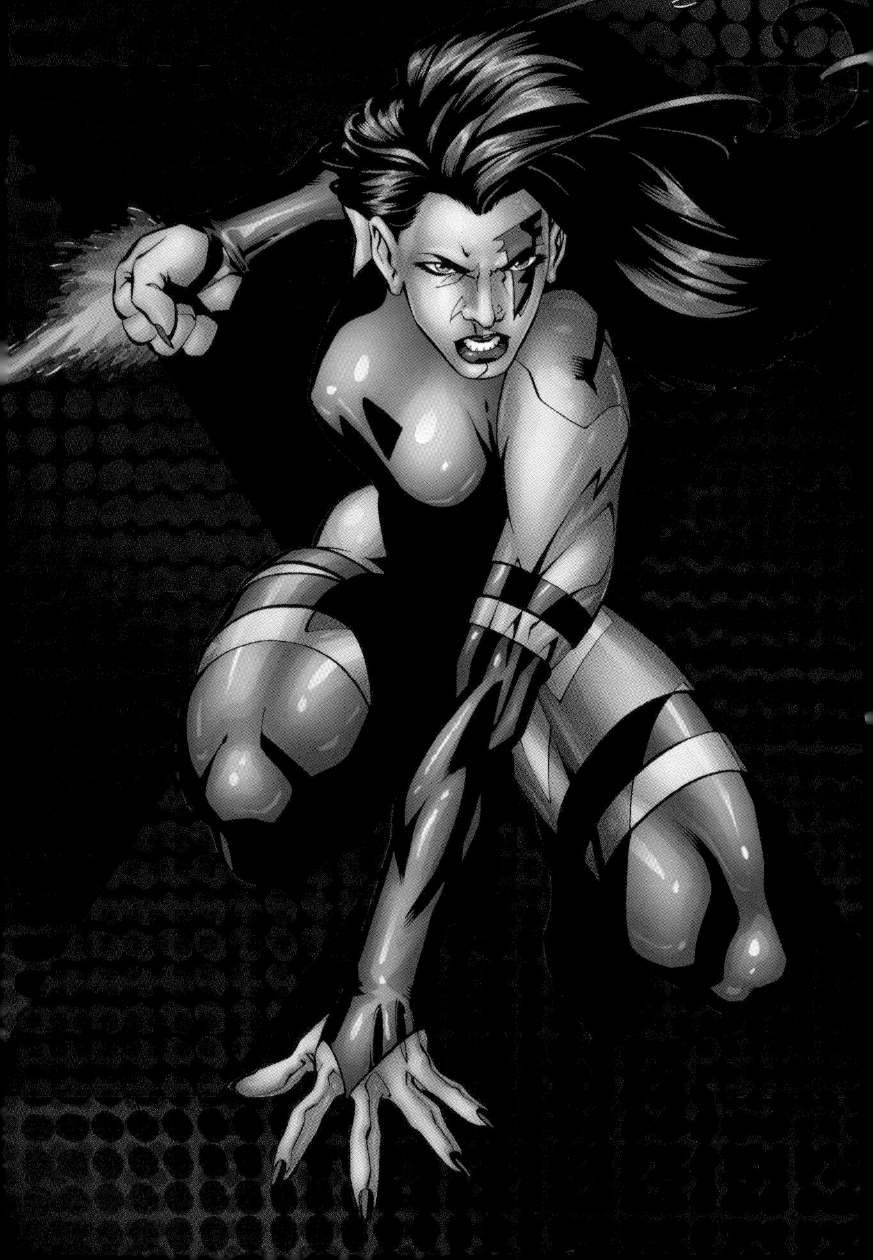

SECRETS

- The Shadow King once possessed Karma, a member of the New Mutants, and used her to build a crime network stretching from Los Angeles to Cairo.

- Magik, another of the New Mutants, pretended to make a deal with the Shadow King so she could free her teammates from his mental domination. They then all attacked him, freeing Karma from his mental chains.

- The Shadow King's battle with Psylocke caused a psychic backlash that affected people throughout the world.

- At one point, Psylocke gave up her telepathic powers to keep the Shadow King imprisoned on the astral plane.

STATUS Active

Karma

The Shadow King admiring Psylocke

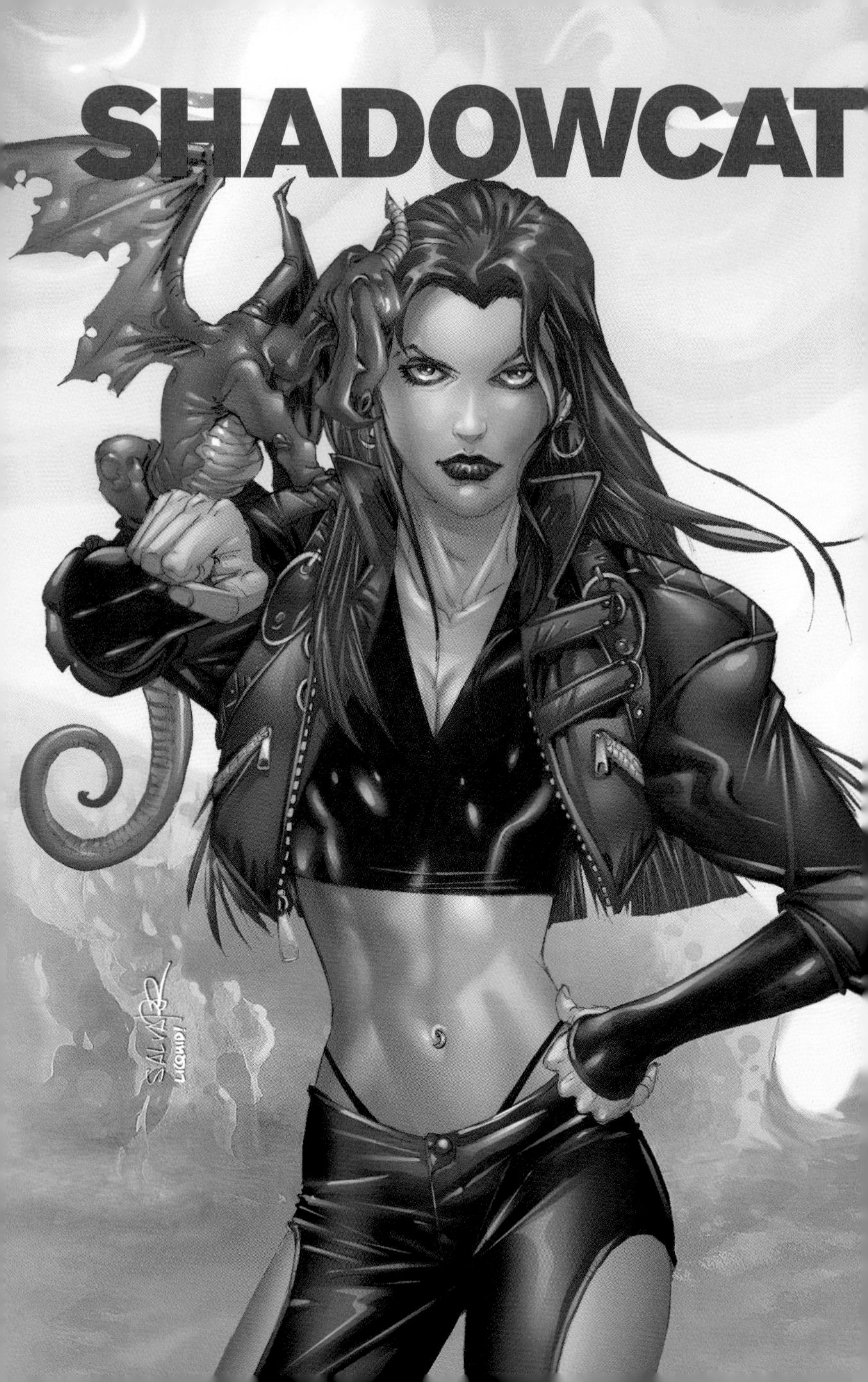
SHADOWCAT

POWERS

Has the power to "phase" body through solid objects by shifting atoms of her tissues through intra-atomic spaces; can phase other objects (e.g., clothing) and individuals accompanying her; can phase through organic and inorganic matter, including another living body, without causing injury to self; disrupts active electrical systems in all objects phased through; phases through objects at same ground speed achieved before penetration; unable to breathe while phasing, so can phase only for duration of breath and/or available oxygen supply; can synchronize ground speed with Earth's rotation about its axis to phase faster than 400 feet per second; can walk on air while phasing; reflexively able to assume phase state instantaneously when endangered; virtually intangible while phasing, although not invulnerable to psionic attacks, mystical powers, or certain applied energies.

SECURITY BRIEF

Katherine "Kitty" Pryde is the granddaughter of a Holocaust survivor. Kitty developed her mutant power of "phasing" when she was only thirteen years old. Soon after discovering her mutation, she was approached by Professor X of the X-Men and Emma Frost, the White Queen of the Hellfire Club, each of whom was anxious for her to join their organizations. Not liking Frost, Kitty chose to attend Professor X's academy. When the White Queen kidnapped the Professor and the X-Men, Kitty was instrumental in their rescue. She thus became the youngest member of the team, taking the code name, "Sprite." Later, she changed her code name to "Ariel."

While fighting an alien race called the Brood, Kitty was saved from death by a small alien dragon-like beast, which she adopted as her pet

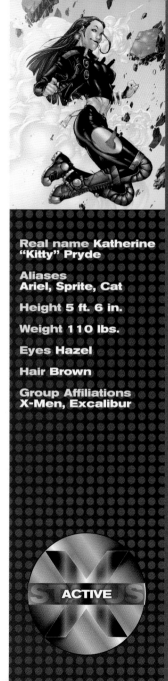

S H A D O W C A T

Real name Katherine "Kitty" Pryde

Aliases Ariel, Sprite, Cat

Height 5 ft. 6 in.

Weight 110 lbs.

Eyes Hazel

Hair Brown

Group Affiliations X-Men, Excalibur

ACTIVE

Katherine "Kitty" Pryde

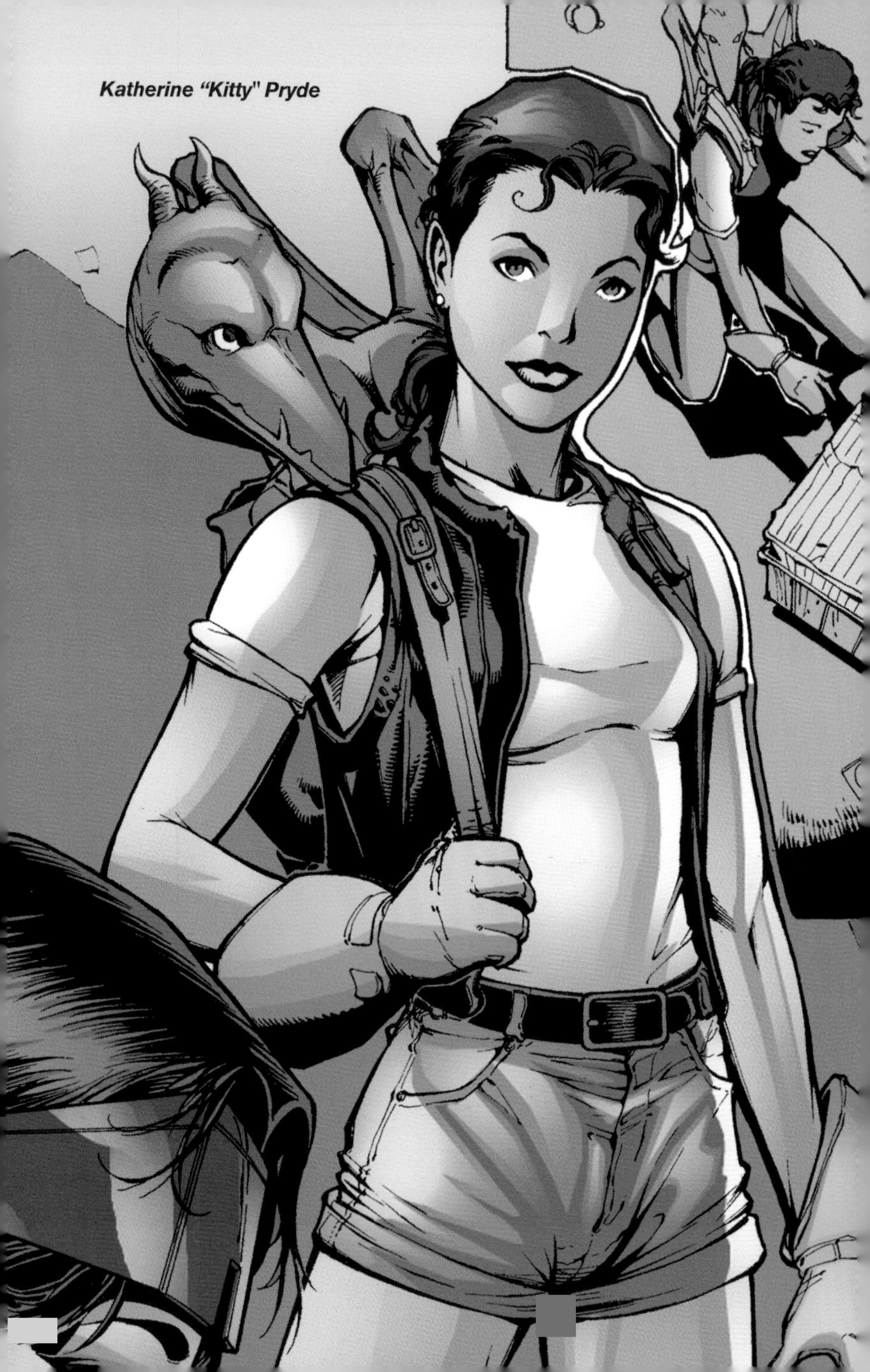

and named Lockheed. After returning from space, Kitty became romantically involved with Colossus, but the relationship didn't last. Kitty, however, did become close friends with Colossus's sister, Illyana.

Several years later, Kitty was possessed by the spirit of the demon ninja, Ogun, who filled her mind with martial arts training and sent her to kill Wolverine. Working together, Kitty and Wolverine eventually defeated Ogun. Afterwards, Kitty changed her code name to Shadowcat.

While recuperating at Professor X's mansion from a wound suffered during the Mutant Massacre, Shadowcat learned that the other X-Men had supposedly been killed in Dallas. Finding herself unaffiliated, she joined the British mutant group, Excalibur. After numerous assignments with them, she returned to the United States when the group disbanded and the X-Men revealed that they were still alive.

Shadowcat left the X-Men again when Colossus died while putting an end to the Legacy Virus. Trying to lead a normal life, she enrolled in the Robert A. Heinlein School for Engineering and Astrophysics in Chicago. Recently, she returned to the X-Men and discovered that Colossus was not really dead.

SECRETS

- Shadowcat once served as a temporary agent of the international law enforcement agency S.H.I.E.L.D.

- During the Mutant Massacre, Shadowcat was hit by Harpoon's energy spear and was stuck in a phased state that left her body slowly disintegrating. She was cured through the combined efforts of Mr. Fantastic (of the Fantastic Four) and Dr. Doom.

- For a short time, Shadowcat controlled the magic Soul Sword, which she inherited from her friend, Illyana.

- Shadowcat is a master of computer technology. She is also a trained gymnast and a professional dancer.

STATUS Active

Lockheed

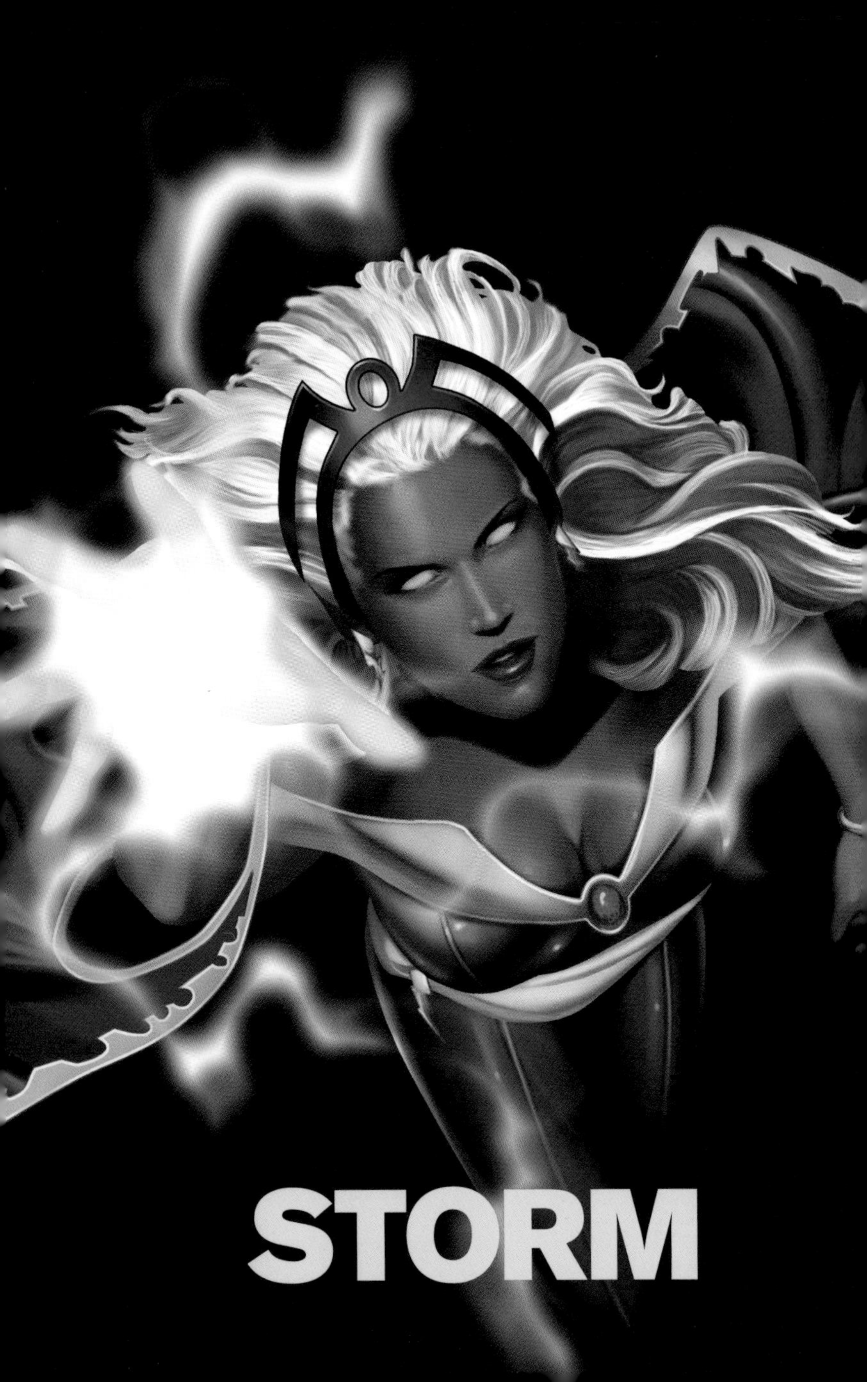
STORM

POWER

Has the mutant power to control elements of the weather, including lightning, rain, snow, and wind within an area approximately one-mile wide; when using weather, her eyes turn white; can generate lightning bolts and fly on the winds; can use the wind to lift heavy objects and throw them; can manipulate wind to deflect bullets; expert martial arts fighter; adept at picking locks and breaking and entering.

SECURITY BRIEF

Ororo Munroe was born in New York City, the daughter of N'Dare, an African princess, and an African-American photographer, David Munroe. Shortly after Ororo's birth, her parents moved to Cairo. When she was still a child, a plane crashed into their house, killing her mother and father and trapping Ororo inside the devastated structure. The nightmarish events resulted in Ororo developing claustrophobia later in life.

Left an orphan on the streets of Cairo, Ororo became a thief working for the bandit, Achmed el-Gibar. It was during this time that Ororo had a brief encounter with Profesor X and his rival telepath, Shadow King. She escaped both.

Soon after her twelfth birthday, Ororo was compelled to travel south. Her two-thousand-mile journey south took her more than a year to complete, during which time she discovered her powers to control the weather.

Ororo's trek ended in the Serengeti, the ancient home of her mother's people. Here she became known as the "Goddess of Life," as she used her powers to help the natives. It was here that Professor X found her and asked Ororo to become a member of his second team of X-Men.

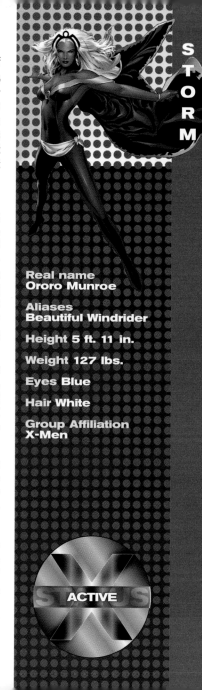

S T O R M

Real name
Ororo Munroe

Aliases
Beautiful Windrider

Height 5 ft. 11 in.

Weight 127 lbs.

Eyes Blue

Hair White

Group Affiliation
X-Men

ACTIVE

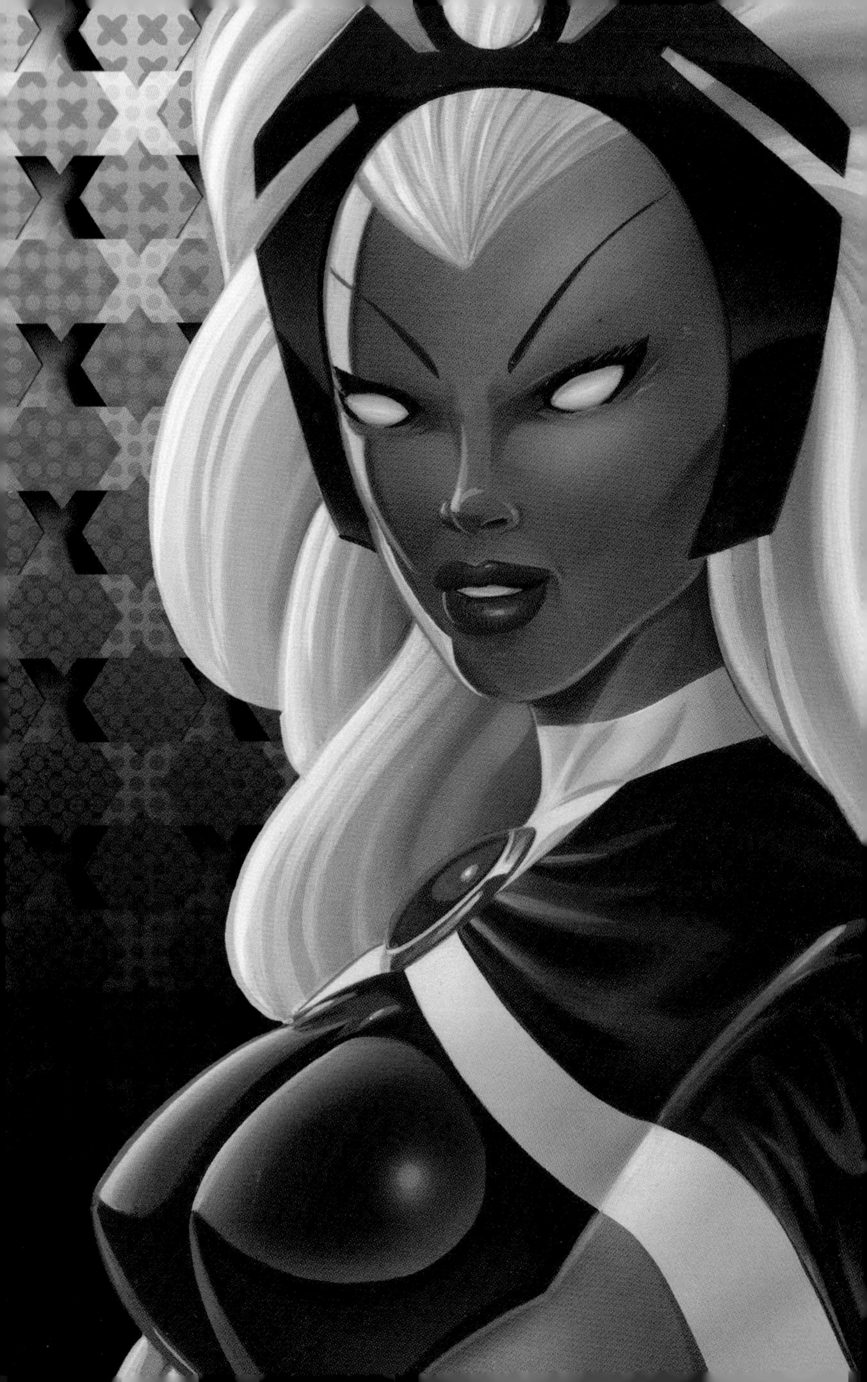

Ororo, known now as Storm, proved to be an excellent leader and powerful addition to the new team. When Shadowcat joined the group, Storm served as her mentor. Storm is one of the most powerful mutants in the world. She has been involved romantically with Forge.

When it was discovered that the mutant Destiny had written a series of diaries, the Books of Truth, describing the fu-ture, Storm led a team of X-Men searching for them. Afterwards, Storm, unhappy with Professor X's leadership of the X-teams, assumed control of the X-Treme Sanction Executive, a special team of mutant police.

At present, Storm lives in Africa.

SECRETS

- When she was on her trek homeward, Storm saved Prince T'Challa, the teenage prince of Wakanda from a band of mercenaries. They planned to use him in a blackmail scheme aimed at his father. The two teens fell in love but Storm was compelled to complete her journey and T'Challa had to return to his home country. As adults, they're still friends.

- The mutant called The Nanny turned Storm into a child. Losing her memory, Storm once again became a thief. During that time, she met Gambit. When her mind was restored, she recruited him for the X-Men.

- Storm once fought Callisto, for leadership of the group of mutants known as the Morlocks. Both women agreed not to use their mutant powers in the fight. Storm won the battle by stabbing Callisto in the heart. Another Morlock healed Callisto and later she became one of Storm's closest friends.

STATUS Active

Callisto

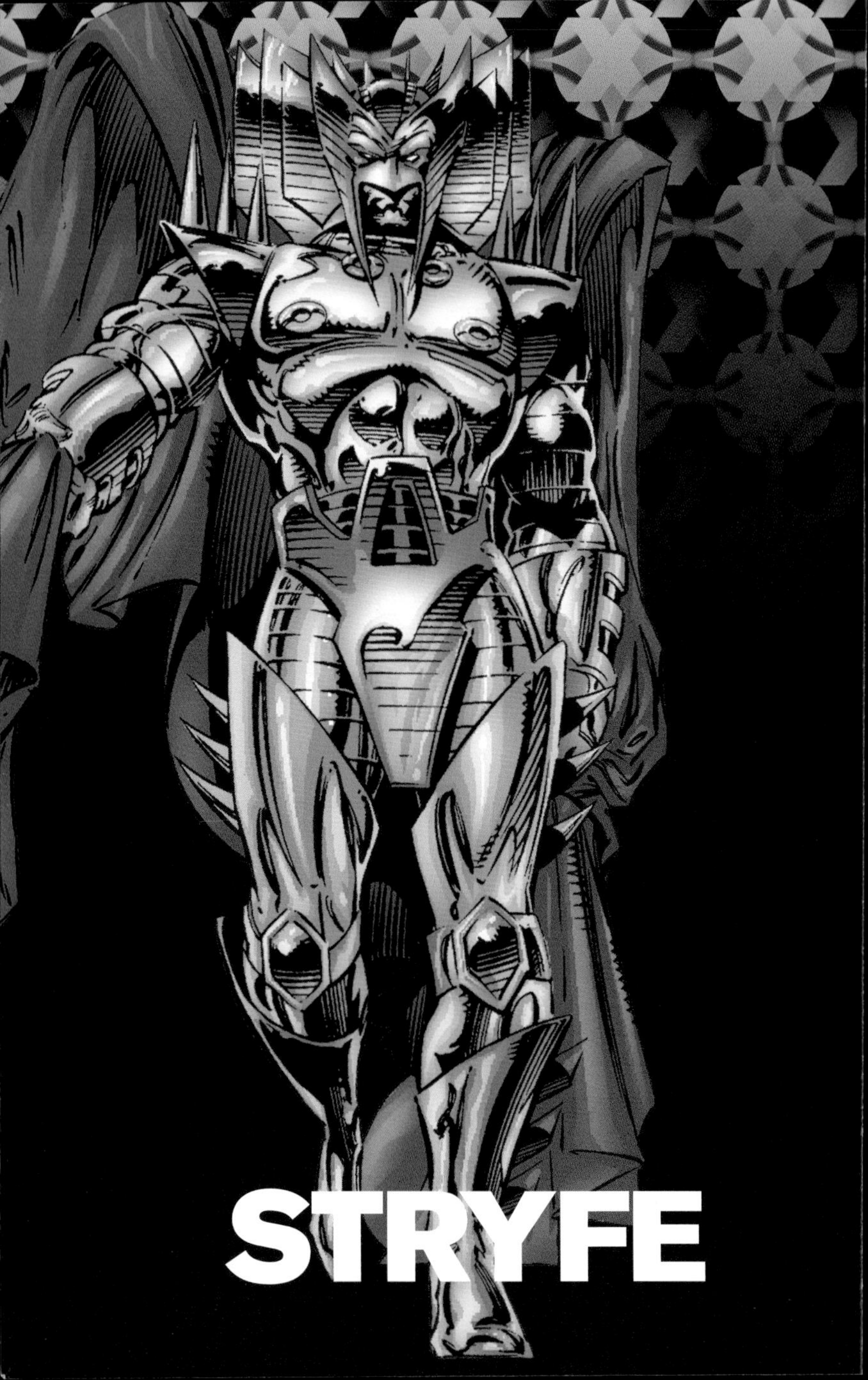

STRYFE

POWERS

Telepath and telekinetic of near unlimited power; clone of the mutant, Cable, but free of the techno-organic virus that weakens Cable; undisciplined in use of mutant powers.

SECURITY BRIEF

Nathan Christopher Charles Summers is the child of Cyclops and Jean Grey. Apocalypse, sensing that the child would someday grow up to be one of his most dangerous enemies, kidnapped Nathan as an infant and infected him with the techno-organic virus, a fast-spreading disease that ultimately would change him into a machine. Scott Summers and Jean Grey rescued Nathan from Apocalypse's base on the Moon, but Nathan seemed doomed until a visitor from the far future, who called herself Askani, told Scott and Jean that she could save the baby, but only if she took him into the future, never to return. They agreed.

Askani brought the baby twenty centuries into the future. Her clan members cloned the baby just in case he did not survive. Nathan's clone was not affected by the disease.

When the forces of Apocalypse, who ruled the far future, attacked the Askani haven, they captured Nathan's clone. Apocalypse decided to raise the baby as his own and named the child Stryfe. Apocalypse's body was wearing out from centuries of decadent living and he planned to transfer his mind and essence into Stryfe's body when the boy was older.

When he reached his teenage years, however, Nathan, now known as Cable, prevented Apocalypse's transfer into Stryfe. Feeling threatened by Cable, Stryfe traveled back two thousand years to contemporary times. Pretending to be Cable, Stryfe attacked Professor X. Later, he formed a dangerous mutant underground

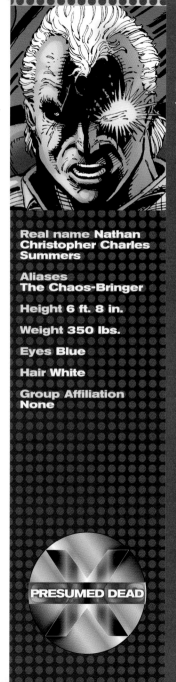

**S
T
R
Y
F
E**

Real name Nathan Christopher Charles Summers

Aliases The Chaos-Bringer

Height 6 ft. 8 in.

Weight 350 lbs.

Eyes Blue

Hair White

Group Affiliation None

PRESUMED DEAD

known as the Mutant Liberation Front. Then, in his most heinous act, Stryfe gave Mr. Sinister a canister containing the Legacy Virus, a near incurable disease that only affected mutants.

Cable returned to the present as well, in pursuit of Stryfe, and the two identical warriors fought numerous times. Stryfe finally died while fighting an alien virus that threatened all life on Earth.

SECRETS

- For much of his life, Stryfe believed he was the son of Scott Summers

and Madelyne Pryor and that Cable was the clone. He once kidnapped Scott and Jean Grey in revenge for how poorly he had been raised.

- Strfye and Cable battled on the Moon until Cable opened a rift in space-time into which they both fell. Only Cable escaped alive. However, Stryfe's consciousness remained in Cable's mind and almost took over his body.

STATUS Presumed Dead

Cable vs. Stryfe

Right: **X-Men fighting Stryfe**

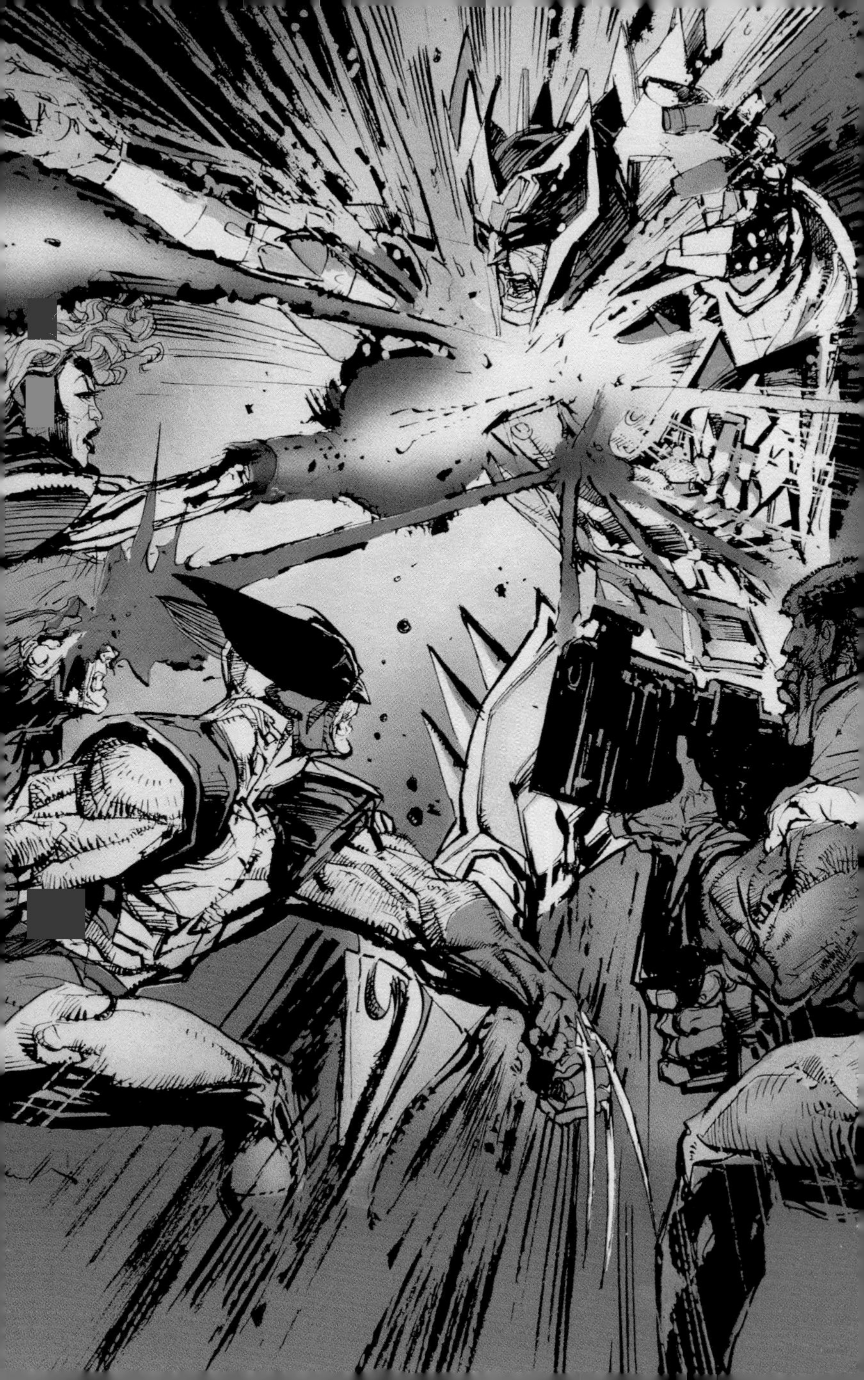

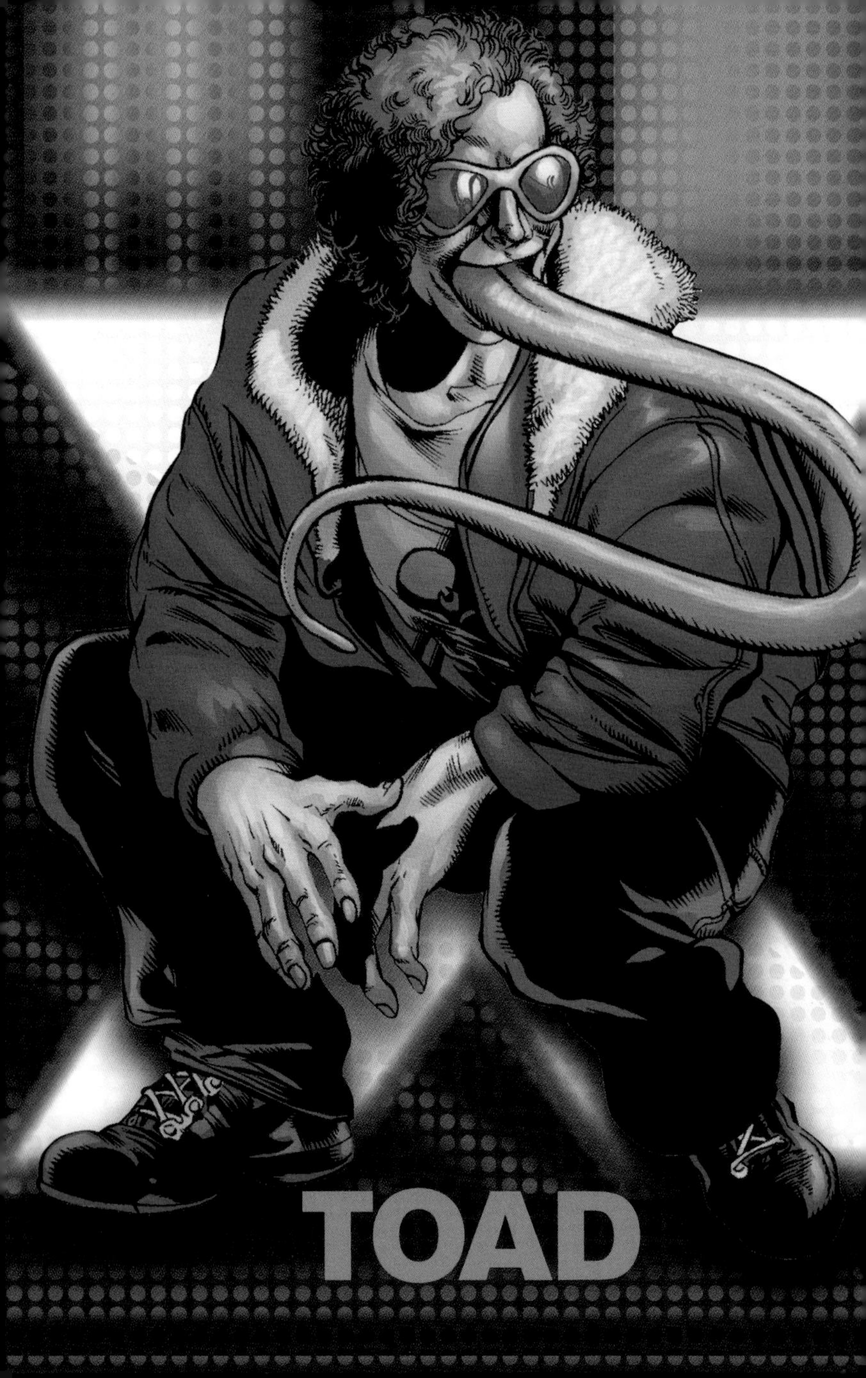
TOAD

POWERS

Although possessing only normal intelligence, has enhanced physical strength, particularly in his legs, which allows him to make super-human leaps; has incredible agility; can lift one ton with his arms and raise three tons off the ground with his legs; can reach out with his tongue and grab people or objects; spits a highly toxic chemical from his mouth.

SECURITY BRIEF

Mortimer Toynbee was left as a baby by his parents at an orphanage in England. An ugly child with a strange physique, he was scorned by the other children and grew up an outcast. He sought acceptance by becoming a member of Magneto's Brotherhood of Evil Mutants. Toad was briefly obsessed with another member of the group, the Scarlet Witch. Over the years, Toad has shown remarkable skill at staying hidden from danger. Having worked as an assistant for Magneto and several other criminal masterminds, Toad knows a great deal about modern technology. While he's not an inventor, he does know how to make things work.

SECRETS

- Toad's skin gives off highly toxic chemicals, which give him a terrible odor. When the alien being known as the Stranger kidnapped Magneto from Earth, he took along Toad by accident.

- Toad learned super science on the Stranger's home planet.

- For a short period of time, Toad served as leader of the Brotherhood.

STATUS Active

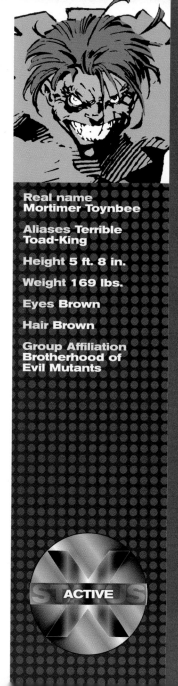

T
O
A
D

Real name Mortimer Toynbee

Aliases Terrible Toad-King

Height 5 ft. 8 in.

Weight 169 lbs.

Eyes Brown

Hair Brown

Group Affiliation Brotherhood of Evil Mutants

ACTIVE

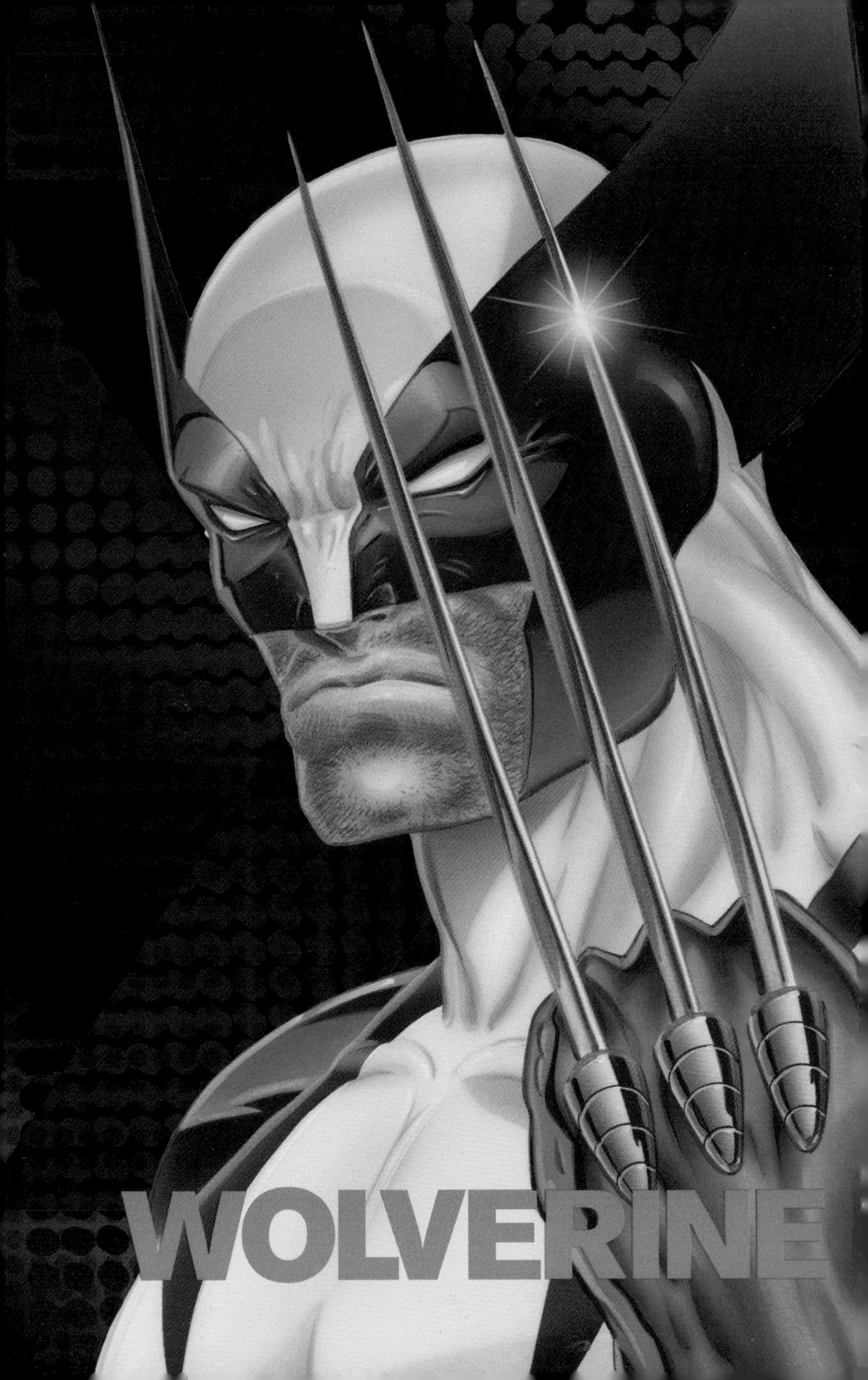
WOLVERINE

POWERS

Possesses incredible healing and regenerative powers—heals at a speed hundreds of times faster than any human; can regenerate organs; immune to disease and poison; immunity slows his aging process (looks no more than 30, but is over a 100 years old); healing factor may protect him from terrible memories by blanking out horrible experiences; has heightened senses of a predatory animal; can hear and see far objects much easier than any human and can track a person by scent; has three retractable claws inside each forearm which he can release between the knuckles of his hands; claws made from bone, and like his entire skeleton, are coated with the unbreakable metal compound, adamantium; cutting ability of claws is limited only by the driving force of his body, not the cutting edge of the claws.

SECURITY BRIEF

James Howlett was the son of wealthy Canadians, John and Elizabeth Howlett, who lived in 19th-century Alberta. James was in poor health so his parents paid a girl, Rose, to take care of him. A third teen, Dog, spent a lot of time around the mansion. Dog was the son of the estate groundkeeper, Thomas Logan (James's actual father).

One day, Dog killed James's pet. In retaliation, John fired the elder Logan. Thomas tried to get Elizabeth to leave with him. When John entered the room, Thomas killed him. The death of his father set off James's mutant powers. His claws emerged, and he killed Thomas and badly scarred Dog.

James disappeared, but resurfaced as a laborer for a mining company in British Columbia. He was a strong, tough worker who used the name, Logan, but was called Wolverine by his friends.

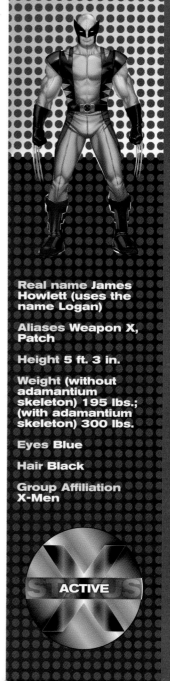

WOLVERINE

Real name James Howlett (uses the name Logan)

Aliases Weapon X, Patch

Height 5 ft. 3 in.

Weight (without adamantium skeleton) 195 lbs.; (with adamantium skeleton) 300 lbs.

Eyes Blue

Hair Black

Group Affiliation X-Men

ACTIVE

Three years later, Dog tracked him down. The two fought and when Rose attempted to intervene and stop Dog's death, she was accidentally speared by Wolverine's claws. Wolverine disappeared for many years.

Much later, Wolverine served as a test subject for the secret Weapon X Project where the indestructible metal, adamantium, was bonded to his bones. In the 1980s, he worked as a Canadian secret agent, fighting super menaces on the U.S./Canadian border. In one battle, he defeated both the Incredible Hulk and the Wendigo.

Professor X recruited Wolverine to join his new team of X-Men. At first Wolverine did not get along well with Cyclops but after a few months the two men reached a truce. Wolverine became close friends with Nightcrawler. He also acted as a mentor for the young mutant Jubilee, who many team members considered his unofficial sidekick.

At present, Wolverine is involved with all the X-Men teams and he also works with the mutant law agency, the X-Treme Sanction Executive.

SECRETS

- Due to his extended life span, Wolverine has spent many years sharpening his combat skills. He is a master of unarmed combat and is perhaps the deadliest hand-to-hand fighter in the world.

- Wolverine was once engaged to Lady Mariko Yashida, the daughter of a Japanese crime boss.

- Wolverine fought with Nick Fury, Captain America, and the Black Widow against the Nazis during World War II.

STATUS Active

Wendigo